Inauthentic

Inauthentic

THE ANXIETY OVER CULTURE AND IDENTITY

VINCENT J. CHENG

Rutgers University Press

New Brunswick, New Jersey, and London

Library of Congress Cataloging-in-Publication Data

Cheng, Vincent John, 1951–
    Inauthentic : the anxiety over culture and identity / Vincent J. Cheng
        p. cm.
Includes bibliographical references (p.) and index.
    ISBN 0–8135–3400–3 (hardcover : alk. paper)—ISBN 0–8135–3401–1
(pbk. : alk. paper)
    1. Ethnicity—United States. 2. Group Identity—United States. 3. Authenticity
(Philosophy) 4. Minorities—United States—Psychology. 5. Racially mixed people—
United States—Psychology. 6. Biculturalism—United States. 7. United States—Ethnic
relations. 8. United States—Race relations. I. Title.
    E184.A1C4457 2004
    305.8' 00973—dc22

                                                                    2003018874

A British Cataloging-in-Publication record for this book is available from the British
Library.

A version of chapter 2 was first published as "Of Canons, Colonies, and Critics: The
Ethics and Politics of Postcolonial Joyce Studies" in *Cultural Critique* 35 (winter 1996–
1997) and is reprinted by permission of University of Minnesota Press. Portions of
chapter 3 were first published as "Authenticity and Identity: Catching the Irish Spirit" in
Semicolonial Joyce, edited by Derek Attridge and Marjorie Howes (Cambridge
University Press, 2000), and as "'Terrible Queer Creatures': Joyce, Cosmopolitanism,
and the Inauthentic Irishman" in *James Joyce and the Fabrication of an Irish Identity*,
edited by Michael Patrick Gillespie (European Joyce Studies 11, Editions Rodopi, 2001);
reprinted by permission.

Manufactured in the United States of America

CONTENTS

ACKNOWLEDGMENTS

I would like, first of all, to thank all the friends and colleagues who read various chapter drafts-in-progress and whose thoughtful insights and suggestions were immensely helpful. These include Richard Yarborough, Abdul JanMohamed, Derek Attridge, Marjorie Howes, Teresa McKenna, Tania Modleski, Robert Newman, Ben Shreiber, David Schulman, Dan Greenwood, Viet Nguyen, Crystal Parikh — and, most especially, Maeera Shreiber, Rachel Adler, Margot Norris, and King-Kok Cheung.

I am grateful to the Tanner Humanities Center at the University of Utah for giving me the fellowship that allowed me to complete this book.

At Rutgers University Press, Leslie Mitchner has been wonderful and supportive; I also thank Pamela Fischer, Alison Hack, and Molly Baab for their excellent work.

I want to thank Ciming Mei for taking the Hanukkah menorah which my wife's mother had given us on the occasion of our adopted Taiwanese baby boy's conversion to Judaism — a menorah made out of mahjong tiles! — and turning it into a marvelously appropriate book-cover design, with red-white-and-blue candles and thoroughly inauthentic lettering in a font called Wonton (used in Chinese restaurants).

Finally, this is a book that deals with topics and issues that both infuse and arise from my own life, my personal experiences. I wish especially to thank those who have shared that personal life most closely — and who have thus influenced and shaped my evolving understandings of both a personal identity and a collective, evolving authenticity: my mother and my late father, my sisters, Teresa and Chiquita, and especially my wife, Maeera, and my son, Gabi. What I am I owe to you.

Inauthentic

CHAPTER 1

Introduction

THE ANXIETY OF IDENTITY

⌐·

Identity, always identity, over and above knowing and thinking
about others.

—Edward Said, "Empire of Sand"

These days everyone was insisting on their identity, coming out
as a man, woman, gay, black, Jew—brandishing whichever features they could claim, as if without a tag they wouldn't be human.

—Hanif Kureishi, *The Black Album*

$\mathcal{T}$he world has been witnessing a sur-
prising resurgence in European nations of a nativist, extremist nationalism,
often directed at foreigners, immigrants, and Jews—from the rise to prominence of Jean-Marie Le Pen in France's presidential elections, to the continued
influence of right-wing leader Joerg Haider and his anti-immigrant Freedom
Party in Austria, to the growing power, in two of Europe's traditionally most
tolerant nations, of right-wing leaders: Pim Fortuyn in the Netherlands and,
in Denmark, Mogens Glistrup, founder of the extremist Progress Party, who
wants to expel all Muslims. Says Simon Serfaty of the Center for Strategic
and International Studies in Washington, D.C., about this European phenomenon: "There are multiple forces that challenge these nations and their citizens: too many immigrants, the European Union, the intrusion of American
culture. People see it as a kind of invisible invasion." As a result, he notes in
an interview with the Associated Press, "there's a deep, widespread and genuine concern over issues of personal and national identity" (*Salt Lake Tribune*
4/24/02: A16).

A similarly, and related, deep and widespread concern over issues of
identity—in the midst of global culture and hybridity—is manifesting itself
in the United States. As Chinese American writer Gish Jen notes: "We wonder who we are—what does it mean to be Irish-American, Cuban-American,

Armenian-American?—and are amazed to discover that others wonder, too. Indeed, nothing seems more typically American than to obsess about identity. Can so many people truly be so greatly confused? We feel very much part of the contemporary gestalt." In the presence of such a gestalt of confusion and anxiety, she notes, we search for the recognizably genuine—and then "how awed we feel in the presence of tradition, of authenticity" (*New York Times Magazine* 5/7/00: 28). Indeed, a *New York Times* story (5/12/02: 12) titled "Nordic Culture Thrives as Young Seek Out Roots" provides a clear encapsulation of this search for authenticity. Quoting Norwegian natives who have emigrated to the United States and who now find contemporary Norway to be succumbing to global inauthenticity ("Everything in Norway has become too Americanized," say Greta and Oddvar Medhaug; "they all speak English"), the author of the article notes that "the Medhaugs may have trouble finding authenticity in the old country, but back in the United States, home to more than twelve million people who claimed Scandinavian ancestry in the 2000 Census, things have seldom been more robust." Historically, over eight hundred thousand Norwegians left Norway for the United States, and today there are as many Norwegian Americans (4.5 million) as there are citizens of Norway; only Ireland witnessed a greater exodus to the United States in terms of percentage of its total population. Citing the exploding popularity of Nordic-language and folklore classes, the story notes that this resurgence is fueled by third- and fourth-generation Scandinavian Americans choosing to embrace a culture that their grandparents "may have tried to play down in an effort to fit into this country"—for it is the young who particularly "want some connection to their Nordic past." As one such young Norwegian American, Knute Berger, is quoted as saying, "There's a shared sense of nostalgia for this culture that we took for granted." Sirpa Duoos, the Finnish American co-host of a weekly public radio show ("The Scandinavian Hour"), mourns the loss of such authenticity even in the home country: "The saddest thing is that I think Finland and the other Nordic countries are losing their identity at home. We seem to value that heritage more than they do." In this attempt to hang on to—and to freeze—an "authentic" culture and identity which they do not want to see change or evolve into something seemingly less "authentic," thousands of Scandinavian Americans are signing up for classes in the individual native languages, in Scandinavian folklore, even in Viking nautical skills—and turning out for cultural pride parades (such as the Norwegian Constitution Day parades on May 17, *Syttende Mai*). These are examples of what I call the contemporary "heritage industry." Having lost a sense of their own cultural identity in an increasingly globalized world, such seekers are embarked on a search of the "true" Norwegian—or Finnish, Swedish, Danish, and so on—spirit.

*I*t is a premise of this book that modern and contemporary cultures—especially First World cultures—are increasingly marked by an anxiety over authentic cultural identity. Basically, I ask this question: Why do we still cling to notions of authenticity and authentic identities—in an increasingly globalized, hybridized world that has deconstructed and exploded notions of authentic essences and absolute differences? Who is "authentic" and who is "other" in a given culture? Who can speak for the other? What do we mean by authenticity? These are critical issues that our contemporary world, brought both closer together and further apart by globalism and neocolonialism, struggles with in many registers. This study probes these issues in a number of different registers, through a series of chapters investigating several particularly revealing case studies on the pursuit of authenticity and identity. Each chapter explores, in different registers, the ways and patterns by which we construct "authenticities" (the terms *authentic* and *authenticity* should always be read, in this study, as framed by scare quotes) to replace these seemingly vacated identities.

As a scholar of modern literature and culture—specializing in Irish studies, postcolonial studies, and racial and minority discourses—these are issues that I have long been considering, especially in the wake of my latest book, *Joyce, Race, and Empire*. In a sense, I feel that I have been preparing all my life for a study on authenticity and identity. Unlike people who grow up with a clear sense of their national or cultural identities, I have struggled with such concepts and issues my whole life: my personal background is that of an internationalist childhood, spent peripatetically wandering from country to country, a Chinese boy raised by Roman Catholic priests and nuns (mostly Polish missionaries) in Mexico and Brazil. As a native Chinese speaker born in Taiwan to two Chinese diplomats from the Chinese provinces of Canton (Guangdong) and Hupei, I grew up living in many different countries and racially varied cultures in Asia, Latin America, North America, and Africa—especially in Mexico, Brazil, the United States, Canada, and Swaziland. Thus, the pursuit of a stable and authentic identity—whether national, racial, cultural, personal, or otherwise—was for me a very complicated, perhaps doomed, proposition from early on. This project, thus, is strongly informed by (indeed, haunted by) both my scholarly and my personal interests.

In personal terms, for example: even being "Chinese" was not only a birthright (we spoke Mandarin at home, celebrated Chinese cultural traditions, ate Chinese food) but was itself a highly problematic notion. It was a racial distinction of absolute difference/otherness by which some chose to mark me and thus render me invisible within their particular social hierarchies and constellations; it repeatedly marked me as a "foreigner" even though I was able to adapt myself to each specific culture and language enough to pass as a native speaker, and even though I at times felt myself to be as "Mexican" or "American" (or whatever) as I felt "Chinese"; it rendered me nonetheless indelibly and authentically "Chinese" in the eyes of many, in spite of the fact that I had left Taiwan at the age of four and had lived as long or longer in each "foreign" country than I had in "China" (yet could never be thought of as authentically Mexican, American, or whatever). Furthermore, the notion of an essential and authentic "Chinese" identity had already, early in my life, been deconstructed for me by the very fact that, since early childhood, our family dinner table conversations were obsessively charged with political discussions concerning the "real China," within a binary Taipei/Beijing dialectic that was mutually exclusive and antagonistic: Wasn't the Nationalist government in Taipei the "authentic" Chinese government? Could the Communist regime in Beijing really speak for China? Surely *both* of them could not be simultaneously called "China"? But did the native Taiwanese islanders and aborigines have any claim to being also "real" Chinese? And so on. And now that I have been an American citizen for many years, married to a white Jewish American woman, father of an adopted son from Taiwan who is being raised Jewish, it seems to me more and more that we are almost all inauthentic contradictions: Is my real/authentic identity now "American"? Is it Chinese? Is it "Asian American"—whatever that means? And what is my son? Indeed, what are any of us—in the postmodern, global community?

The existence of one's "nation" as a natural trait that we are born into— like one's "race" or gender—is for most of us an unquestioned fact so taken for granted that we seldom wonder what it is that we mean by our "nation" and our inherent belief in a national identity. But as Benedict Anderson has so persuasively argued, each nation is an "imagined community" whose members share confidence in a sense of an authentic national identity and homogeneous community. This is, he argues, a necessarily reified and imagined identity and community in view of the great heterogeneity and difference that actually exists within any national population. Anderson's general point about national identities is equally true of the cultural, racial, and ethnic identities we similarly construct as imagined communities with authentic and definable essences. Indeed, we each know Anderson's general point to be true at a personal, experiential level (even if we share the communal fantasy at a discursive level): for the fact is that I, for example—as a Chinese male who grew up in various countries overseas but who am now a naturalized American—find myself perhaps having much more in common with, say, certain individual Canadian women or individual Dutch nationals or individual African Americans or individual gay males—than with most other heterosexual Chinese American males. Nevertheless, so strong is our neoreligious impulse and yearning toward an authentic identity that we continue to believe that words like *African American, Irish Catholic, Serbian* or *Bosnian, Chinese, Jewish* have real, inherent, and definable meanings with the aura of authenticity. Why—in our post-twentieth-century world of global communication and international commerce—should this be still so (and be so in such an insistent, sometimes violent, manner)?

This study, then, will investigate the nature of the authentic and our investment in what folklorist Regina Bendix calls the "A-word," taking up a number of "authentic identities" as particular case studies. Discussions about national and ethnic identities by even the most scrupulous scholars and politicians repeatedly circle around the notion of authenticity. Whether it is the struggle by Irish or Indian nationalists to define a national identity for their emerging postcolonial nations or the call for a national German *leitkultur* by the right wing in contemporary Germany in an attempt to beat back the cultural effects of foreign immigration and the supposed contamination of German cultural purity, national and cultural authenticity functions as a quasi-religious locus of transcendence, in much the same way that the concept of "nation" itself operates, as Anderson has so skillfully demonstrated.

The pressure to define a unique and authentic national character and identity, one that is distinct from all others (preferably having originary and premodern roots, an always already-manifest destiny), may indeed be growing even more urgent with the globalization of our own postmodern era—the world of global markets, global media, and neocolonial economies—where cultural and natural distinctness and distinctions are fading, and cultures all grow increasingly to resemble, not distinct and separate uniquenesses, but predictable simulacra of millennial inauthenticity, complete with CNN and a McDonald's in every village. As Bendix suggests, "Behind the assiduous documentation and defense of the authentic lies an unarticulated anxiety of losing the subject" (10). This central point will be the major critical thread of argumentation connecting the book's various chapters—that is, the ways in which our world tries to deal with the anxiety about losing cultural authenticity, subjectivity, and distinctiveness.

It is along these lines, perhaps, that we might speculate on the cultural forces behind the continuing reification of authenticity and ethnic identitarianism in the world today—at a time when one might be tempted to imagine the need for such militant identity politics to be less necessary, with distinct cultures gradually melding into a transnational global culture: rather than needing now to depend less on cultural differences and identities, previously distinct cultures suffer an anxiety about the perceived loss of identity and subjectivity, thus requiring the continuing construction and maintenance of fantasmatic identities and authenticities so as to continue to be able to assert difference and superiority (rather than global sameness and what Irish scholar Seamus Deane calls the "harmony of indifference" [*Heroic* 15])—whether in the forms of World Cup soccer competitions, sectarian politics, or ethnic warfares. Indeed, one might suspect that one of the repressed logics behind the reluctance of the Irish Republican Army (IRA) or of Hamas to come to the bargaining table is that once the independence and freedom they have so long been seeking actually come to pass and they join the global community, the stridently nativist and "authentic" identity that has given them their very raison d'être for so long would then cease to exist and so they themselves would cease to exist or be "real" in any meaningful way.

The subject of "authenticity and identity" is, of course, extremely broad, with an endless number of relevant focuses and topics (and thus potential chapters). In the chapters that follow, I offer up a series of specific, interdisciplinary case studies on these issues—each of which, it will be clear, grows out of my longstanding interests and thinking about such issues in both my scholarly career (as a scholar specializing in Irish studies, postcolonial studies, and race studies, and for years the director of an Asian American studies program) and my personal life (as a Chinese native and naturalized U.S. citizen, as the husband of an active Jew who is also a scholar in Jewish studies, as the parent of an adopted Taiwanese child).

Chapter 2 discusses the dynamics of authenticity within the U.S. university system and the nature of authentic and inauthentic voices in the academy. This is the one chapter in the book focusing specifically on issues of authenticity in academia, especially in literary studies. Using various academic developments (including the "postcolonializing" of Irish studies and Irish authors like Joyce), the chapter investigates the relationship between the literary canon, cultural market forces, and academic appropriation of "authentic" native ethnic and postcolonial voices. Whereas I use my own particular fields of academic specialization (postcolonial and Irish studies, especially Joyce studies) to initiate this discussion, the issues are broadly applicable to vexing problems in academic and multicultural writing and teaching—as well as to parallel questions outside the academy—such as: Can or should white folks write from the positions of native peoples? What happens when white Americans apply for teaching positions in (or teach) African American studies, postcolonial studies, or ethnic studies? What are the ethics of such transactions and appropriations?

Chapter 3 has two parts, on the debates and controversies surrounding Irishness and Irish identity, occasionally using Joyce's works as reference points. The first part introduces the notion of authenticity as I am using it and then investigates the mechanics and rhetoric of authenticity by asking what Irishness is and, by analogy, what any authentic identity is. The second part discusses the debate, for the past century and even today (with continuing political implications), between the arguments for a global, hybrid, and cosmopolitan Irish culture and those for a local, nativist, and essential Irishness (parallel debates exist, of course, in numerous national cultures). Along the way, I speculate on what I call "Irish chic," on why Irishness—so long a much maligned and pejorative ethnic identity—has become so fashionable in Europe and the United States today.

Chapter 4 investigates the complexities and contradictions in a world in which adoption has come out of the closet to be accepted as respectable and even admirable (after all, we now give tax breaks to adoptive parents)— and the resultant proliferation in First World countries of mixed-race, mixed-nation children adopted from Third World countries. What sense, if any, of authentic identity can be available to such children (like my own)? And how do we deal with their "difference"?

Chapter 5 investigates the shifting meanings of the notions of Jewishness and Jewish identity—terms which keep sliding unevenly between the registers and paradigms of religion, ethnicity, race, culture, and nation. In the resultant and heightened anxiety over who and what is authentically Jewish, twentieth-century and contemporary Jewish history (including the Holocaust and the Palestinian intifadas) have become important touchstones in shaping the identity awareness and identity construction of diasporic Jews.

Chapter 6 discusses the complexities of ethnic identity—and the increasing popularity of mixed-race or cross-ethnic affiliations—in contemporary

U.S. culture, focusing particularly on the bizarre but important identity we have created and named "Asian American" and the interesting prospects and possibilities such a brand-new identity category may allow for. The book then ends with a brief Coda (Chapter 7), speculating on some of the implications and conclusions of this study.

*A*s should be clear, this is an interdisciplinary project with a large scope and broad cultural significance, addressing some of the most vexing problems of culture, identity, and globalism in our world today. I hope that this study will be of interest to a cross-disciplinary readership within but also beyond the academy—to scholars and readers interested in modern culture, cultural studies, race studies, postcolonial studies, U.S. ethnic studies, Irish studies, and modern literature. I have tried to make these chapters accessible to such a broad (rather than specialist) readership. In a way, this study feels like a logical culmination of many of my interests, both scholarly and personal, allowing me to try to come to grips with key issues and questions that have dogged both my own life and my scholarly pursuits—issues and questions which also reflect major challenges and cruxes in our contemporary world. These are issues that I will no doubt continue to grapple with and try to understand further, and increasingly.

CHAPTER 2

Who Can Speak as Other?

AUTHENTICITY, POSTCOLONIALITY, AND THE ACADEMY

The Postcolonial Joyce

Let me begin this discussion about authenticity and canonicity in the literary academy with James Joyce—for in the canon of modern English literature, there is perhaps no more "canonical" a figure than Joyce. Such literary and academic canonization has produced a massive Joyce scholarly industry, with a significant and voluminous display of published scholarship, textbooks, college courses, doctoral dissertations, faculty appointments, and scholarly symposia. Joyce's canonical status has been to a large degree achieved over the past six decades through the academy's estimation of Joyce as a revolutionary prose innovator within a high modernist context. But critical studies of Joyce have begun a radical reevaluation, compellingly re-presenting Joyce instead as an anticanonical, anti-imperialist, and even nationalist writer—via the lenses of contemporary postcolonial theory and cultural criticism. To the "canonical Joyce" we have responded with the "postcolonial Joyce."

One longstanding effect of this canonization—of the elevation of a native, Irish Catholic, colonial writer like Joyce into the pantheon of the European modernist greats—was rather insidious: it shifted attention away from the manifest political content and ideological discourse of Joyce's works by emphasizing his unarguably potent role and influence in stylistic revolution. "The net effect is to neutralize the ideological potency of Joyce's texts, to defang the bite of Joyce's politics" (Cheng, *Joyce* 3)—allowing us for decades to maintain a convenient blind spot when it comes to the political, wishing—like Gabriel Conroy in Joyce's *Dubliners* story "The Dead"—to believe that literature was above, and separate from, politics.

In contrast to this "canonical Joyce," a number of Joyce studies have tried to recover Joyce's texts as politically engaged. In my own *Joyce, Race, and Empire*, I argued, via detailed analyses of Joyce's works, that "Joyce wrote insistently from the perspective of a colonial subject of an oppressive empire" (i), anticolonial and nationalist in sympathies but resistant to certain forms of Irish nationalism—while housing within his works a dialogic and "symptomatic representation of the various ideological positions on these issues in turn-of-century Ireland" (9). Enda Duffy, in *The Subaltern Ulysses*, has gone as far as to call *Ulysses* "the starred text of an Irish national literature[,] . . . nothing less . . . than *the* book of Irish postcolonial independence" (2–3), a "guerrilla text" that has "all the time been covertly operating as a postcolonial novel" (5). In *James Joyce and Nationalism*, Emer Nolan also claims that "*Ulysses* powerfully suggests Joyce's hostility to British colonial rule in Ireland" (57). Both Duffy and Nolan counter the previously "presumed certainty of [Joyce's] unsympathetic representation of Irish separatist nationalism" (Nolan xi) by arguing that "Joycean modernism and Irish nationalism can be understood as significantly analogous discourses" (Nolan xii)—in effect by positing Joyce, as it were, as a pro-nationalist writer.

David Lloyd, writing in *Anomalous States: Irish Writing and the Postcolonial Moment*, also reads Joyce's texts as politically progressive and liberating; but, interestingly, he—unlike Duffy and Nolan—sees them as *anti*nationalist texts, based on a critique of Irish cultural nationalism as a repressive and homogenizing regime which, through its obsession with Celticism as an authentic national identity, sublates diversity and difference. Lloyd explores what he calls "the anti-representational tendency in Irish literature" (as in *Ulysses*) and "the hybrid quality of popular forms" which manage to "exceed the monologic desire of cultural nationalism" (89). In this line of argumentation, critics like Lloyd and Luke Gibbons (and to some extent myself) are following a postcolonial as well as poststructuralist deconstruction of authenticity and identity as discursively constructed, fragmented, and ultimately hybrid.

In thus positing an "antinationalist" Joyce, Lloyd's stance is in essence not unlike Colin MacCabe's earlier argument in *James Joyce and the Revolution of the Word*, though they come to similar conclusions by very different routes. MacCabe—like Seamus Deane, Terry Eagleton, Fredric Jameson, and others—argues that stylistic and linguistic resistance to narrativity and narrative conventions (the "revolution of the word") is itself a political act in that it refuses constrictive colonial and nationalist agendas via a writerly desire that exceeds the limitations of both conventional narrative representation and nationalism, thus exploding the myth of a unified personal and national identity. *Finnegans Wake*, for example, with its decentered free play of signification, is for MacCabe "the primer for a failed revolution" (*"Finnegans"* 5).

A more recent example of such a linguistic rationale for arguing Joyce's subversiveness is found in Eagleton's *Heathcliff and the Great Hunger*: "But the free play of the signifier which results from Joyce's literary scavenging has as its referent (Ireland) a place where such freedom is largely absent. Hence the 'free state' of his fiction" (257). *Finnegans Wake*, Eagleton argues, by "estranging the English language in the eyes of its [English] proprietors, struck a blow on behalf of all [Joyce's] gagged and humiliated ancestors" and "returned the compliment to the colonizers" (269). Eagleton goes on even to suggest that *"Finnegans Wake* can blend diverse cultures as indifferently as it does because they have all been magically levelled, released by the signifier from the power relations which hold between them in everyday life. Its author's sceptical distance from the political is in this sense one source of its subversive force" (270). In other words, in still another (and surprising) twist on the "canonical Joyce," Eagleton returns to the notion of an apolitical Joyce, but only to argue that such a stance (and dis-stance) allowed Joyce to make a subversive and political statement via his subversive styles and language.

As we can see from this brief survey, postcolonial perspectives and postcolonial critics of Joyce are themselves hardly homogeneous. What they do all share is a view of Joyce's work as politically engaged and potentially subversive, a subaltern voice attempting to respond to colonial conditions and oppression. As Deane notes: "Subversion is part of the Joycean enterprise. . . . There is nothing of political or social significance which Joyce does not undermine and restructure" ("Joyce the Irishman" 44). Collectively, we have constructed what I would call the "political" or even "postcolonial" Joyce as a response to the "canonical Joyce" of earlier decades.[1]

Can these two Joyces, or general conceptions of Joyce, be somehow squared? Do these more recent critics manage successfully to uncanonize Joyce, allowing for the emergence of a new, subaltern, colonial voice speaking against the discourse of empire? Or does the undeniable history of canonization and institutionalization—which have created the Joyce scholarly industry—in effect negate, neutralize, and mute any potentially empowering alterity of voice in the Joycean text? And, in the process, are we displacing other subaltern, colonial, and native voices? These are the issues I explore in the present chapter.

Who Is Postcolonial?

Central to these issues is the question of whether Joyce in particular and Irish literature in general are even appropriate subjects for "postcolonial" study. More broadly: Are the Irish postcolonial? Even though it is clear that Irish history is one victimized by systemic and longstanding imperial violence and colonial domination, these questions are still rather vexed and problematic for both the Irish and the Anglo-American academic scenes today.

In one sense, the answer is obvious: yes, of course the Irish are authentically postcolonial, and Irish culture is of course an appropriate subject for postcolonial studies; it would be an insult borne out of ignorance to maintain that Ireland's geographical as well as racial proximity to England made it any less a victim of imperialism. Within academia, however, the questions are not so simple. To begin with, there is still—within the academic institutions in Ireland, England, and the United States—considerable resistance to (and controversy over) the politicization and postcolonializing of canonical Irish figures like Joyce (and even Yeats) —often the result of a nostalgic desire to maintain a clear and comfortable demarcation between literature and politics.[2] But this sort of resistance was perhaps to be expected.

More startling is the fact that although colonial/postcolonial studies has become a vibrant and potent force within the Anglo-American academy, even postcolonial and minority scholars themselves sometimes have mixed feelings about the place of Irishness. As a nonwhite scholar who had been given a fellowship to write a book about Joyce and imperialism, I was criticized by some of the other fellows in our minority-discourse fellowship program (at the University of California's Humanities Research Institute, 1991–92) for wasting my energies on a canonical "dead white male." Similarly, Marilyn Reizbaum, writing about Scottish and Irish women's writing, laments the fact that when postcolonial feminist scholars like Gayatri Spivak catalogue postcolonial feminist texts, "women writers in (postcolonial) cultures that may be seen as dominant (white, Christian), despite the way in which those cultures have been marginalized by hegemonic ideologies, have not been included for consideration in these terms" (166). Or, for example, Elleke Boehmer's study of *Colonial and Postcolonial Literature* excludes Ireland from the category of "postcolonial" because "its history has been so closely and so long linked to that of Britain" (4). By such a measure, India should be excluded too! In other words, brown Indians can be postcolonial, but not white Irish: this is, in effect, a self-imposed essentialism (by scholars of subaltern or minority studies), mirroring the imperial discourse's racist categories of absolute difference. The Irish, long "racialized" by English imperial discourse as "white negroes" (see Cheng, *Joyce* ch. 2) and as "not white/not quite" (to use Homi Bhabha's phrase), are thus caught in a double bind: essentialized as racially other by the English imperial self but denied the fraternity of victimhood by nonwhite colonials (Indians, Africans, and so on)— in short, caught in a postcolonial no man's land, carrying no identity card within the identity politics of authentic postcolonial discourse.[3]

The motives behind such an exclusion of Irishness have, I suspect, a lot to do with the institutionalization of canonical Irish authors, in which Oscar Wilde, George Bernard Shaw, Yeats, Joyce, and Samuel Beckett are already very much part of a modernist literary canon. Andrew Lakritz recounts that the members of his postcolonial reading group decided that Franz Kafka was not appropriate for their discussions (despite his "minor" status for Deleuze and Guattari) because Kafka is "major literature for the academy" and "his works are advertisements for his canonical image" (3). As with the double bind of Irishness as a postcolonial status, so also here Kafka's texts suffer a "double bind—a writer who is marginalized in his culture and writes a powerful critique of that culture but who later becomes championed as a major cultural voice by the academy" (Lakritz 3); this certainly also describes Joyce's relationship to both Irish and English culture. The question becomes, then, whether a Kafka or a Joyce can qualify to speak for the voice of "minority" concerns and minor literatures—and if not, who *can* speak?

Part of the problem then is a history of reception and institutionalization: as Lakritz points out, "The paradox seems to be that, while these texts in their own way seek imaginative routes to social change, the structures of authority through which they are channeled and distributed [including universities, college curricula, and academic conferences] are the very structures against which such social change would have to compete. Such authority to speak itself, according to this hypothesis, would have to be dismantled for the social order to achieve the kind of equalitarian state [such authors] imagine and seem to desire with some real intensity" (6). Furthermore, the practical reality is that academic treatises on Irishness (or on other "minor" cultures) very frequently follow an anthropological paradigm, in which Irish culture is represented/interpreted by a non-Irish person to a non-Irish audience. Anthropology, writes Vietnamese filmmaker Trinh T. Minh-ha, is "mainly a conversation of 'us' with 'us' about 'them,' of the white man with the white man about the primitive-nature man[,] . . . in which 'them' is silenced. 'Them' always stands on the other side of the hill, naked and speechless. . . . 'Them' is only admitted among 'us,' the discussing subjects, when accompanied or introduced by [one of] 'us'" (98). This practice underscores one of the vexing problems resulting from the entrance of Joyce studies (and of Irish studies in general) into the postcolonial field: So *who* gets to speak for authentic Irishness and for Irish postcoloniality?

Who Can Speak?

Who can speak on such matters? Who gets to speak for the Irish as postcolonials? Can a non-Irish person (like myself) do so? Are there more (and less) "authentic" voices for Irishness as a colonial or postcolonial condition? As Eagleton warns in the preface to *Heathcliff and the Great Hunger*, "For an Irish writer to intervene these days in debates over Irish culture and history is always a risky business; for a semi-outsider [like Eagleton] it is well-nigh suicidal" (xi). After all, even native Irish scholars—as has happened with Lloyd, Gibbons, Nolan, and Duffy, in various ways—can be attacked for supposedly losing or betraying their understanding of Irishness amid their theorizations of Irish postcoloniality. Such critiques—of both Irish and non-Irish scholars—presuppose a hard and essential authenticity that can be identified as "Irish." Nolan points out that authenticity remains an important theme in the work of certain Irish scholars (such as Richard Kearney and Declan Kiberd), "whereas the theorists to which they are occasionally indebted attack the very idea of a self to which one might be true or false" (17). Furthermore, as I have pointed out, "Irish natives are themselves hardly homogeneous in character or essence," and a postcolonial study "written by one Irish person is likely to differ very significantly from those written by other Irish natives"; to argue that only an Irish person is qualified to speak about Irishness and Irish topics is, I would suggest, in essence "a position little different, in its unexamined implications, from the insidious argument that only English people should be allowed to teach Shakespeare or that I, being Asian, should have become an engineer (rather than a professor of 'English')" (Cheng, *Joyce* 11–12). If, however, anyone can potentially speak about Irishness, do we not risk robbing the colonial subaltern (once again) of his/her own voice?

To begin with, most of these critics themselves, influenced by contemporary cultural and poststructuralist theories, endorse the deconstruction of supposedly authentic or originary identities—a position which repeatedly clashes against nationalist urges to construct an identifiable national identity and authenticity. Furthermore, these critics believe that Joyce's texts themselves argue against such reifications of a national or cultural authenticity.

Nolan, for example, suggests that "'Irishness' is heterogeneous for Joyce, but it also represents a kind of originary heterogeneity: its definitive characteristic is its quality of eluding definition" (148). I myself argue, and have tried to show, that Joyce's works "become increasingly informed by his sensitivity towards the nature of the hybridity, ambivalences, and interpenetrations" involved in cultural and discursive formations (Cheng, *Joyce* 56). Most insistent on this point is Lloyd, who points out that *Ulysses* "circulates not only thematically but also stylistically around adulteration [as opposed to purity] as the constitutive anxiety of nationalism" and that an episode like "Cyclops" "dramatizes adulteration as the condition of colonial Ireland at virtually every level" (*Anomalous* 106). *Ulysses*, Lloyd argues, refuses to fulfill the narrative demands consistent with the socializing functions of national identity formation, and its radicality comes from its insistence "on a deliberate stylization of dependence and *inauthenticity*, a stylization of the hybrid status of the colonized subject as of the colonized culture, their internal adulteration and the strictly parodic [and hybrid] modes that they produce in every sphere" (110; my emphasis).

If "Irishness" is itself an unstable and questionable concept, presumably then there is no such thing as an authentic voice for Irish postcoloniality and the Irish condition. But the real problem isn't only, it seems to me, with authenticity as a theoretically unsupportable concept, as it is also with the real-world implications of "speaking *for*" others, of robbing the colonial subaltern once again of a voice. I have in mind particularly two, not unrelated, manifestations of this problem as it plays out in academia, and so I will address them collectively as one: (1) the problems of English and U.S. (French, German, and so on) academics "speaking for" postcoloniality and Irishness (or Indian-ness, etc.); and (2) the particular and new problem of Joyce studies becoming representative, and thus "speaking for," other native colonial or postcolonial discourses.

If we are willing to challenge the notion of an essential authenticity, then are we willing to condone such problematic examples of "speaking for" as the following: a book about the African experience called *African Atto* (1973) was written by someone named Mohammed X, a pseudonym, it turns out, for Ku Klux Klan leader David Duke; another Klan member, Asa Earl Carter, wrote under an alias *The Education of Little Tree*, the "true story" of a Native American child's return to his roots; and, more recently, an award-winning novel by an American "Latino" author named "Danny Santiago" was, it turns out, actually written by a White Anglo-Saxon Protestant male at Yale University (see Callaghan 197).[4] As Dympna Callaghan argues about disturbing cases like these, "The appropriation of subordinate identities by privileged whites demonstrates that endeavors to compensate for the exclusion of racial 'minorities' from the means of literary production can become the very means for continuing this exclusion" (197).

But let me bring up two much more complex case studies, not so easily dismissed, for us to consider. First, a gifted white Canadian writer named Anne Cameron writes several well-received first-person narratives about the lives of Native Canadian women. At the International Feminist Book Fair held in Montreal in 1988, Cameron is asked by a group of Native Canadian writers to "move over," as they put it, claiming that her work is disempowering for indigenous authors like themselves; Cameron agrees to do so. While Cameron's own motives were never in question, the argument was that her writing was harmful because it would be Cameron rather than native writers themselves who will be listened to and read as the authoritative voice of the Native Canadian experience—once again recycling the anthropological paradigm. As Linda Martín Alcoff points out, "Persons from dominant groups who speak for others are often treated as authenticating presences that confer legitimacy and credibility on the demands of subjugated speakers; such speaking for others does nothing to disrupt the discursive hierarchies that operate in public spaces" (99).

From this one might conclude that it is better not to speak for others at all, not to intervene so as not to act appropriatively (like the Englishman Haines in Joyce's *Ulysses*). However, such a retreat from "representation" and "speaking for" is frequently politically detrimental or even suicidal. First of all, the likelihood is that Cameron (whether or not her works are accurate and authentic) may have in fact helped open up *greater* interest in Native Canadian writings—a process that would help create a real forum and market for native voices. Second, as Alcoff points out, "There are numerous examples of the practice of speaking for others that have been politically efficacious in advancing the needs of those spoken for, from Rigoberta Menchú to Edward Said and Steven Biko [we might add Anglo-Irish examples like Charles Stewart Parnell and Yeats]. . . . In some cases certain political effects can be garnered in no other way" (107). After all, should the source of an intervention matter as much as the effect or impact it has? As Gayatri Spivak repeatedly points out, "The invention of the telephone by a European upper-class male in no way preempts its being put to the use of an anti-imperialist revolution" (quoted in Alcoff 115). Alcoff concludes that "in order to evaluate attempts to speak for others in particular instances, we need to analyze the *probable or actual effects of the words on the discursive and material context*" (113); in other words, we must ask where the "speaking for" goes and what it does and whether it enables or disables the empowerment of those spoken for.

In the case of Cameron, I ventured that it might actually help enable an otherwise nonexistent market for Native Canadian writings. I would be less optimistic in the second, dramatic case I discuss here, which was popularly known as "The Vicar and Virago Affair": "In Britain in 1988, the British Broadcasting Company (BBC) expressed interest in the work of a new writer, Rahila Khan, a feminist from the Indian subcontinent whose work purported to describe the life and experiences of young Asian women in Margaret Thatcher's Britain" (Callaghan 195). The BBC broadcasts of Khan's work were followed by an agreement with Virago Press, the prominent feminist publishing house, to publish a collection of Khan's stories, so as to include work of a feminist writer from the Third World. When it later leaked out that Rahila Khan was really a white, male, middle-class vicar from Brighton named Toby Forward, a national furor ensued; the controversy became known as the Vicar and Virago Affair. Forward claimed that authenticity and personal experience should not be required to validate creative writing; as he said, "The unspoken assumption behind most of this was that all imaginative literature, all fiction, is autobiographical. Later I was to be accused of pretending to occupy a position I didn't hold, to speak with a voice that wasn't mine. I had thought that was the purpose of art" (quoted in Callaghan 196); after all, it's "fiction." According to African American critic Henry Louis Gates Jr., "Like it or not, all writers are 'cultural impersonators'" (quoted in Callaghan 196), and an argument for authenticity in fact ends up segregating people by drawing boundaries of essentialist categories of ethnicity, race, and gender. Neither of these writers—Cameron and Forward—were "authentic" native writing subjects; yet since a definable authenticity may be a nostalgic fiction, each of them wrote texts that were arguably authentic enough to both native and nonnative readers. So is the only difference between Cameron and Forward that the former was more honest about her own identity? Does such authenticity—privileging the author's authenticity over the text—even matter (in our age of the "death of the author")? In response to such a privileging of authorial authenticity, Gates "offers the compelling example of slave narratives, which, even when inauthentic, could be used for the abolitionist cause, and when genuine nonetheless participated in the same literary conventions as fictional narratives" (Callaghan 206).

But I would, *pace* Gates, go back to Alcoff's criterion: that "we need to analyze the *probable or actual effects of the words on the discursive and material context*" (113), that we need to keep in mind both the motives and the real-world impact. In the case of the Vicar and Virago, it became clear that both the vicar and Virago Press were interested in tapping into an already viable and significant new market/interest in diversity and ethnic writing; as Forward put it, "We had found a gap in the market and we set about filling it." Such deliberate and market-driven impersonation *would* seem more likely to challenge the viability of native voices and writings. And this brings up the issue of real-world market forces, which a purist claim for merely doing "imaginative writing" occludes. I would like now to apply some of these same questions, borne out of these two examples of fiction, to the academic milieu and issues under discussion.

Canons and Markets

In parallel fashion, what happens to postcolonial studies when canonical authors, like Joyce, get recoded as colonial or native voices? Does postcolonial study then get diluted and lose some of its impact? Does it get appropriated and thus taken over by "dominant" voices within academia, in effect get defanged of its subversive bite? Is the result of such appropriation a bleaching out of difference, in which *everyone* can claim the position of colonized subaltern (like the claim that "whiteness is ethnic too")—thus rendering difference laughable, in a new twist on what Deane calls "the harmony of indifference" (*Heroic* 15)? In the process the canonical author, in this case Joyce, now newly postcolonialized, nevertheless still retains his canonicity. So is it fair for Joyce studies to have its cake and eat it too?

Let me begin with some of the problems of becoming canonical in the first place. Native Irish scholars and readers might well resent English and U.S. scholars' attempts to fashion a hegemonic reading of a native son like Joyce, a project that would marginalize their own voices within such an enterprise; as Nolan points out, the "persistent Irish unease with Joyce" registers, in part, "the existence of an important site of resistance to the canonical or institutionalized James Joyce" (xiv). Indeed, this is a process that we might call the "mainstreaming" of an Irish (or Indian, Nigerian, etc.) cultural difference; Nolan points out further that "it is not difficult to appreciate how attractive Joyce must appear to an *English* critic who wishes to appropriate a body of Irish literature for the 'mainstream' tradition" (105; my emphasis). Joyce has similarly been appropriated by Western feminist scholars (like Julia Kristeva and Hélène Cixous) to speak for a subaltern feminism; Spivak's response to Kristeva's comments about Joyce is that "there is something even faintly comical about Joyce rising above sexual identities and bequeathing the proper mind-set to the women's movement" (quoted in Nolan 202). Or, as Eagleton points out, "When a previously dominant group begins to speak the language of cultural unity or diversity, it is understandable if their subordinates detect in this rhetoric a way of perpetuating their privileges in displaced form. When men begin to speak of how much, after all, they and women share in common, feminists are properly on the alert" (*Heathcliff* 271).[5] Women should thus be rightly suspicious of a male Joyce as a spokesman for feminine *jouissance*; and Irish natives should be equally suspicious of English and U.S. representations of Irish texts.

But I would want to ask the same question of our anticanonical attempt to postcolonialize Joyce, to recontextualize these texts in their colonial history and culture, and thus presumably to restore a sense of cultural specificity and difference. Aren't we, after all, really doing much the same thing as "an English critic who wishes to appropriate a body of Irish literature for the 'mainstream' tradition" or as white men who begin to speak the languages of cultural unity, diversity, and feminism—by appropriating a white canonical author like Joyce to represent the colonial and postcolonial conditions? After all, "Joyce" as a scholarly institution already has an entrenched position in the academy; to construct a "postcolonial Joyce" does not in any way displace or erase the canonical, high modernist Joyce, but merely expands the academic terrain Joyce covers. By thus expanding "Joyce" into the field of postcolonial studies, are we not replicating an imperialist paradigm by letting an already-dominant canonical author take up some of the scarce academic space allotted to native, ethnic, and postcolonial writings in the academic canon—and thus once again silencing or displacing writers from other native traditions, representing those others with our own already-dominant voices? Isn't this another version of Karl Marx's "they cannot represent themselves, they must be represented"? For me, this is a very important and troubling implication of the two-fisted engine of first canonization and now postcolonialization of Joyce studies.

One might argue, as Lloyd does, that canonization after all is itself already a process of radical deculturalization: "It may seem improbable, for example, that three such canonical writers as Yeats, Joyce, and Beckett could be read in relation to minority cultures in the United States or even to writers of more recently decolonizing states. This is, however, to forget that canonization is itself a process of appropriation, abstracting works from their dialogical relation to traditions which the canon cannot accommodate" (*Anomalous* 8). To then reread Yeats, Joyce, and Beckett in minority or colonial contexts would, it would follow, be a salutary attempt to restore some dialogical relation to cultural traditions and historical/political context. However, as Karen Lawrence has reminded us: "The desire for a place in the canon for previously marginalized texts may lead to a greater pluralism that nevertheless does not fundamentally alter our thinking about canonicity" (7–8).

Furthermore, to reread and re-envision a canonical text in its specific, historicized, colonial context may be itself a losing battle; as Derek Attridge points out about J. M. Coetzee's work, "If Coetzee's novels do gain admittance to the canon, then, it will become increasingly difficult to read them *against* the canon, since their uniqueness will be dissolved by the ideologically determined voice that the canon grants" (231). This has indeed been the case with Joyce studies, in which a canonized Joyce was read for decades according to the periodized and canonical criteria of high modernism, effectively bracketing anticanonical readings of a uniquely Irish and colonial difference; however, "if [such native writings] do not gain admittance [to the canon]," Attridge goes on to note, "it will become increasingly difficult to read them at all, since the only voice available to them is the voice granted by one canon or another" (231). There is a double bind here for colonial/postcolonial writing: canonicity confers a voice to those previously silenced, but effectively also muffles and distorts the power (and authenticity) of that voice in the very process. As Lakritz points out, the popularity in the United States of an African American woman's novel like Zora Neale Hurston's *Their Eyes Were Watching God* is a double-edged sword, for the price paid by the novel for becoming a part of the canon is that it will be harder to see in its proper cultural context: "Hurston's book is an event with an impact that is daunting—a best-seller for the publisher, an industry of academic critics, the object of symposia, workshops, classrooms, research projects funded by both the government and private organizations. For now, it is central, no longer sitting on the margins" (24).

Again, we run into the paradox that the very structures of authority through which these texts and voices seeking social change must be channeled in order to even have an audience are the very structures and institutions they are trying to overcome: such voice-granting authority would itself need to be dismantled for the actual intended effects of subaltern voices to be accurately heard. And what is true of texts is also true of critics. Thus critics like Spivak are, as Lakritz notes, "trying to negotiate the very complicated positionality of the postcolonial critic who, on the one hand, declares herself to be on the side of social justice . . . but who, on the other hand, speaks from a position of the elite, the class against which the subaltern is defined" (7); what we need to recognize is that (in Lakritz's words) "because I am an elite I have the luxury of feeling empathy for the oppressed. The very authority I have permits such identification, which undoubtedly threatens *and* maintains that authority at the same time" (12; my emphasis).

Consequently, we must be particularly alert to and conscious of the dynamics of canonicity, particularly to the blind spots it encourages. As Lloyd reminds us, any radical cultural studies investigating and articulating cultural formations "will have to engage explicitly with the critique of the state for which those formations are its unrecognizable" (*Anomalous* 10)—that is, its particular blind spot, occluded and repressed. In the case of Irish nationalism, that occlusion is, Lloyd argues, that Irish nationalists sometimes construct "an identity which sublates difference in self-conscious unity" (46), thus reproducing the very narrative of universal development which is at the core of imperialism's self-legitimation. I would like to ask if this isn't also what happens in postcolonial criticism of authors such as Joyce?

Surely Joyce *should* be read within the context of colonial history, from a postcolonial perspective; I am not so naive as to suggest that it were better for us to do *nothing*. But then, what is next? Milton as postcolonial writer? (Studies of Shakespeare—or Calderón—and empire are already unremarkably common in the Western academy.) Such moves might presage the sort of appropriation involved in the logic that "we are all ethnic" or that "white is ethnic too," encouraged by the current Western climate of a politics of identity and victimhood, in which individuals (within the academy and without) are rushing proudly to prove their slight bit of Native American heritage or celebrating their Italian American roots or joining Robert Bly's men's movement (in which mostly white, middle-aged males try to compete with feminist sisterhood by banging drums in Native American "sweat lodges" so as to open up their hearts and pores to each other).[6] Within the academy this has taken the form of everyone claiming some subaltern identity from which to speak. At the Modern Language Association Convention in Chicago in December 1995, one of the largest plenary sessions was a forum on "Ethnicity and Writing/Reading," in which four speakers—two white women, one Jewish male, and Bhabha—engaged in a virtual celebration of how they were each ethnic and postcolonial (a position I would dub "postcolonial lite").[7]

More troubling in our particular context may be the possibility that by privileging major "minor" writers (like Joyce and Kafka, whose cultural situations are arguably marginal and "minor"), we may be helping to make neglected minority writers even more minor (Renza 35–36). It is we in the Western academy, after all, who have access to the structures and institutions of speech and representation, and so we are more likely to be listened to as authenticating presences, conferring legitimacy for subaltern voices; but such a process does not by itself disturb or disrupt the hierarchies of public discourse, in which the neglected subaltern voice is still silent.

Let me make clear that I am *not* saying that I believe Joyce displaces "true" colonial or postcolonial voices, because from the vantage of the Irish context Joyce *is* a "true" and authentic colonial author and *not* a metropolitan writer—and it is certainly important and necessary for us to read him as such. But what I *do* wonder about is whether the Western academy is able to engage in postcolonial studies *now*, at this moment in its discursive history, only because it has become now safe to do so—at a time when such issues no longer need be repressed by a discursive blind spot and colonialism seems to be an institution of the past. And is it safer to do so with Joyce than with, say, writers who cannot be appropriated so easily into the traditional canon? Indeed, is Joyce already too tainted and compromised a canonical product to be an effective representative of colonial perspectives? I can understand Peter Hitchcock's reservations, on reading my study *Joyce, Race, and Empire*, that although establishing Joyce's "postcolonial" politics is a laudable accomplishment, "I'm just worried that if Joyce is readily available as the ardent anti-imperialist his rather large shadow might obscure a different way of telling" (letter to me of 31 January 1996).

Similarly, examples of responses to the interest in both academia and the commercial literary marketplace in subaltern voices—such as the inauthentic ethnic writings of David Duke, Asa Earl Carter, "Danny Santiago," and "Rahila Khan"—all suggest that Callaghan may be right when she remarks that such appropriation of subaltern identities proves that "endeavors to compensate for the exclusion of racial 'minorities' from the means of literary production can become the very means for continuing this exclusion" (197). Even without being outright and blatantly dishonest (as in the above examples), even with genuinely liberal and sympathetic motives (as most of us have), we as academics need to be cautious of what Caren Kaplan calls "a form of theoretical tourism on the part of the first world critic, where the margin becomes a linguistic or critical vacation, a new poetics of the exotic" (361)—intellectual slumming, as it were, however well meant. Such "theoretical tourism," like much actual tourism, merely replicates the dynamics and paradigms of colonialism.

As Edward Said has argued, "The history of fields like comparative literature, English studies, cultural analysis, and anthropology can be seen as affiliated with the empire and, in a manner of speaking, even contributing to its methods for maintaining Western ascendancy over non-Western natives" ("Secular" 28); it is thus particularly crucial to be conscious of, and to try to ward off, the inherent risk to our oppositional efforts of becoming institutionalized, of turning resistance and marginality into dogma and absolutism. Nor should we pretend to speak in what Said calls "a timeless vacuum, so forgiving and permissive as to deliver the interpretation directly into a universalism free from attachment, inhibition, and interest" (34).

The dogmas of imperialism are a matter not only of political history but of very current global capitalism and market forces, including the ample and varied one we call multiculturalism, in which we are very much implicated. As Forward (the vicar) puts it, "We had found a gap in the market and we set about filling it." The spatial metaphor of a gap already suggests a limited amount of space; so whatever fills it is crowding something else out. Such are the marketplace realities of both multinational capitalism and canon formation. In a conversation with Sneja Gunew, Spivak notes that "when the cardcarrying listeners, the hegemonic people, the dominant people, talk about listening to someone 'speaking as' something, I think *there* one encounters a problem. . . . They cover over the fact of the ignorance that they are allowed to possess, into a kind of homogenization" ("Questions" 60). The result, as Gunew points out, is that "they choose what parts they want to hear, and they choose what they then do with this material . . . within the context of multiculturalism" and consequently, whether in terms of funding or dissemination of published works, certain people are elevated as representative of all "others," and "you don't hear about the rest, because 'we [now] have covered that' and those few token figures function as a very secure alibi" (quoted in Sawhney 209).[8] In terms of academia, one might note that Spivak herself functions as one of those privileged voices that allow us to feel that by reading *her* we have "covered" South Asian postcoloniality and need not salve our intellectual consciences further by somehow rooting out copies of *Subaltern Studies* or untranslated Urdu novels to put in our bibliographies or syllabi; in terms of canon formation, one might note how easy it has become to put Chinua Achebe or Hurston or Salman Rushdie on a reading list as the representative African or African American or South Asian. One still never has to venture beyond a slightly amended canon, and *Things Fall Apart* is quickly converted into "Things Harden into Rigidity"—in which individual subjectivity is codified into representative objectivity, and the canonical dilemma of "coverage" is again resolved by tokenism. As Sabina Sawhney notes, "Thus, the subjectivity of the other is erased in order to countenance its construction as an object, as an *effect* of knowledge for the subject" (210).

Implicit in my arguments here, you will have observed by now, is the assumption that the relationships between contemporary dominant and subaltern forces in the literary and academic marketplaces operate in such a way that ethnic identity and cultural marginality become, at times, commodified objects demanded by market forces growing out of a (generally salutary and certainly necessary) growing awareness of difference and diversity in the multi- or cross-cultural world. This is hardly an original or remarkable observation. But episodes like the Vicar and Virago Affair, once their liberal outer shells have been punctured, remind us of the ways in which the "other" is frequently adopted (even by feminist presses like Virago or by Rahila Khan's readers like ourselves) as a way to commend ourselves for being on the side of the marginal, opening up for the dominant culture a feel-good window of liberal benevolence. Do politically progressive and postcolonial studies of Joyce offer the same comfortable, "feel-good" satisfactions and reassurances?

Conclusion

Let me put the question another way: In having overcome the modernist/aestheticist blind spot which sublated politics and separated it from literature, what blind spots are we today conveniently perpetuating so as to allow us to finally "see" and read Joyce's postcolonial and even nationalist valences? What does it mean that it is okay to do political and postcolonial readings of Joyce today, whereas such cultural theorizing would have been unthinkable in earlier decades? What is the "unrecognizable" which our own cultural theories need to try to recognize? On a particularly gloomy day, I might be tempted to say this: that the moment a topic is taken up enthusiastically by the academy, it is already "safe" and neutralized, defanged, no longer threatening. Indeed, "postcoloniality" and postcolonial studies allow a "feel-good" (I'm okay, you're okay) comfort without actually having to displace any troubling hierarchies; they allow us to take the moral high ground without risk. (I should carefully qualify here that I write from the position of a scholar in the United States, for whom the possibility of theoretical tourism or intellectual slumming carries no serious personal risk since I have a secure, dominant, and institutionalized position from which to take on such ventures and to which I can return at will; a native scholar or writer from Ireland, India,

Nigeria, etc., often has no such safety net.) The actual-but-occluded risk, the "unrecognizable" if you will, may involve having to deal with the real issues and real-world consequences of our theorizing, to which we remain happily blind.

Let me approach this by asking two questions that might occur to me on that very gloomy day: *Why* are the practitioners of postcolonial studies predominantly situated in, or products of, the U.S. academy, and why has this field taken such fertile root there with scholars and students (some of whom previously had thought of "Colonial" only as a style of furniture or as the proud name of their neighborhood motel)? Why does the study of "colony" find more fertile ground among U.S. scholars than in, say, the English or, even more, the Irish or Indian academies—where its presence is still volatile and controversial? Once posed, the questions bring up immediately obvious answers. First, by investigating the colonial histories of English, French, Belgian, German, and other empires, a U.S. literary culture can decry such despotic cruelties as the legacies of European imperialism while occluding its own troubled history of colonialism and neocolonialism. Second, the "post" in the postcolonial suggests an unthreatening "past," implying that these are issues that an American can safely take sides on now because they carry no risk to one's *present* culture—either temporal or geographical (rather, they are the miserable legacies of those brutish Brits or Krauts). The U.S. academy can energetically investigate the deplorable history of English imperialism by fashioning its own twist on what Roy Foster calls "therapeutic Anglophobia" ("Anglo-Irish" 99). Like Meredith's "sentimentalist," we would enjoy—without incurring the immense debtorship for a thing done (*Ulysses* 9.550–551).[9]

That debtorship (and unrecognized blind spot) has to do, not surprisingly, with the Western academy's own implication in Western colonialism. During the weeks I was writing this chapter, I heard an excellent paper by Jennifer Margulis on child labor in Pakistan, India, and Nepal—in which, as a graduate student exploring postcolonial issues, she noted that such a topic "does not form the subject of the narrative of Departments of English or Comparative Literature." Margulis goes on to note that "while a discourse about past African and American slavery, analyses of slave narratives, and, especially, theories of postcolonial literature have emerged in recent years, the stories of bonded laborers in [contemporary] Southeast Asia remain untold"; while we can comfortably exist by investigating *past* slavery, we conveniently relegate the existence of slavery to the past. It needs to stay unrecognized, since our very own existence and daily comforts depend on just such multinational exploitations: we benefit greatly from child labor in Third World nations. Are we willing to throw away our Nikes and our Persian carpets because they come from multinational conglomerates that hire thousands of slave laborers to make them? In spite of the academy's fast-growing interest in and the popularity of Third World narratives and in the voices of the other, we do not very often pry open those Pandora's boxes which contain truly uncomfortable knowledge or which seriously challenge and disrupt the foundational hierarchies which we are attempting to dismantle in our theorizing.

Finally, let me return to Joyce for a moment by asking parallel questions: Why, of all the many Irish writers whose work is steeped, like the dyer's hand, in the deep hues of a miserable colonial legacy, has *Joyce* been so much the focus of the academy's efforts at postcolonial studies of Irish texts? Is the "postcolonial Joyce" itself in danger of being functioned by the academy as a native informant (or token) for its institutionalized (and pre-scribed) ethnographic discourse of colonial otherness? Why don't we (in the Anglo-American academy) read very many other, less well-known Irish writers (Maria Edgeworth, Gerald Griffin, William Carleton, James Clarence Mangan, Sheridan Le Fanu, and others) from such a theoretical and political vantage point? (The Field Day Group's work or that of the Subaltern Studies Group in India, for example, has hardly had a major impact yet in U.S. academic circles.) It is impossible, I think, not to conclude that at least some *part* of the answers is this: that we can now "postcolonialize" a reified construct named "Joyce" in part precisely *because* he is already canonical and thus already defanged and rendered safe, sanitary, unthreatening; no matter what we do, Joyce is already part of the canonical tradition, and we can explore him to our heart's content, feeling duly postcolonial and multicultural—without actually needing to venture outside the familiar, canonical pale, without actually having to read "native," noncanonical authors/others. We can have authenticity without risk. In this sense, the postcolonial "Joyce" *does* displace other voices—while contemporary postcolonial Joyce studies provides us the luxury, as scholars of modernism in the Western academy, to have it both ways, allowing us to speak for and on behalf of the subaltern other, while at the same time never needing to be seriously threatened from behind our ivy-covered office windows.

I have no simple solutions. I am certainly *not* saying that we should all stop doing postcolonial or even political criticism of Joyce, for that would be an even more absurd disservice to the cultural/historical specificities of an Irish literary discourse. But I would argue that we cannot allow *Joyce* to stand in either for other colonial/postcolonial texts by less well-known, native authors (from Nigeria, Pakistan, Jamaica, and so on) or even for other less well-known Irish writers, who must also jostle for some space in that "gap" designated as "Irish literature" on our reading lists, bibliographies, syllabi, and bookshelves—so hugely dominated already by the formidable shadows of Yeats and Joyce. Joyce *is* deservedly postcolonial, and we *should* approach him as such; but we must also be vigilant not to allow ourselves to transform him into a representative commodity, as the vicar did with "Rahila Khan," something that can, like an ethnic token or a native talisman, take the place of other native voices. Rather, we should try to use a postcolonial Joyce as a means to pry open, to shift, the criteria and perspectives for canonical inclusion—to make some room also for other but *different* (and not previously canonized) texts from other cultures, as part of a process that can help illuminate a constant (if uncomfortable) awareness that imperialism and colonialism are still a fact of life in which we are very much implicated, rather than a comfortable tonic in the midst of the culture wars. We should strive, to quote Gyan Prakash, "to return to the history of colonialism without rehearsing the naturalization of colonialism as History" (6). Otherwise the search for genuine or authentic native voices will serve only to provide us with a feel-good liberal and multicultural glow—while in actuality merely recycling tokenism and nostalgia.

CHAPTER 3

Inventing Irishness

AUTHENTICITY AND IDENTITY

⤚•

Catching the Irish Spirit

In the opening pages of James Joyce's *Ulysses*, the Englishman Haines, visiting Ireland in order to study its native culture and folk customs, tries speaking Gaelic—as a linguistic marker of genuine Irish identity—to the old milkwoman, a presumably authentic Irish figure. What is it, after all, that defines Irishness? The speaking of Gaelic? Old age and peasant status? But the old milkwoman doesn't understand, and Mulligan comments wryly that "he's English . . . and he thinks we ought to speak Irish in Ireland" (*Ulysses* [hereafter *U*] 1.431–432). According to Haines's view, then, the milkwoman does not pass muster, is not sufficiently and authentically Irish.

But who or what *is* "Irish"? What defines Irishness? Is it Irish blood (a tautological concept in itself)? Is it residence in Ireland (but then how about all the "wild geese" and emigrants)? What are the essentials or essences needed to qualify as "Irish"? And who gets to say what qualifies as genuinely Irish? The issue of defining "Irishness" was a central one in Joyce's own time (1882–1941), which witnessed the attempts by a nationalist movement to forge a national identity—and is still a visceral and urgent issue in Ireland today, with the continuing debates about the positions of North and South, Catholic and Protestant, republican and unionist, citizen and emigrant, the place of Irish Americans, and so on. Is perhaps the best we can do Leopold Bloom's vague and hapless vacillation that "a nation is the same people living in the same place. . . . Or also in different places" (*U* 12.1417–1431)?—a position which, one might add, seems less hapless and rather more viable since the May 22, 1998, referendum—the Good Friday agreement—on Northern Ireland.

$\mathcal{R}$ecently I received in the mail an advertisement for an Irish American publication, the *Irish Voice Newspaper*: "CATCH THE IRISH SPIRIT!" the ad urged me in big bold lettering. Catch the Irish spirit: well, at one level—at the level of popular culture—the United States has indeed, of late, been catching the Irish spirit. Witness the popularity and omnipresence of Irish culture in U.S. cultural life today: popular films (everything from *Michael Collins* and *The Crying Game* to *The Secret of Roan Inish, A Circle of Friends, The Boxer, Waking Ned Devine,* and so on); popular music and dance (Enya, Clannad, U2, Cranberries, Sinead O'Connor, the Riverdance craze, and so on); even literature, with the growing popularity of numerous Irish poets and novelists, capped in 1997 by the surprising *Angela's Ashes* phenomenon. Even *TV Guide* and *Newsweek* both pointed out that a notable trend in TV programming is the number of new shows featuring Irish folks.[1] One might well speculate why this is so: What are the reasons for this phenomenon in contemporary U.S. culture, what I call "Irish chic"; what is the "cultural work" being performed? Whatever the reasons, in the United States today, Irishness is clearly "in"—in striking contrast to the pejorative cultural valence of "Irishness" throughout most of U.S. history. And if you subscribe to the *Irish Voice Newspaper*, presumably you, too, can catch the Irish spirit.

But the seemingly straightforward formulation—"Catch the Irish Spirit"—masks some not-so-straightforward implications. First of all, what *is* "the Irish spirit"? Is there any such thing? Can we even know what it is? And, second, how does one *catch* it? Can it even be caught—and presumably transferred or adopted? Or can it only be inherited and innate, "native" and "natural" only to those who are already authentically Irish—and thus a quality or essence *not* subject to acquisition or subscription or belated membership?

I daresay that we each carry with us certain personal assumptions about the Irish spirit, such as: Gaelic inflections and influences; the rural and peasant West; the Connemara hills; folk traditions; pub culture and a communal life of bibulous, even drunken, joviality; music, dance, and the arts; the gift of gab; an emotional and temperamental, sometimes sentimental, mind-set; a brooding and poetic imagination; a quality of mists, fairies, spirits, and an ineffable mystique or otherworldliness. All of these and more are perhaps part of the cultural baggage we take with us on our travels to Ireland, looking for the real, the authentic, the hidden Ireland; armed with Fodor's and Michelin's the way English tourists (like Haines) were armed, a century ago, with travel guides like Mrs. S. C. Hall's *Ireland: Its Scenery, Character, etc.*

(1841–1843) and *Tales of Irish Life and Character* (1910) or Clifton Johnson's *The Isle of the Shamrock* (1901), we arrive on the emerald shores intent on catching the real Ireland, the true "Irish spirit."

As a tourist coming from the center of empire, Haines in *Ulysses* reflects one discourse—that of the colonizer—that fashions Irish character and identity as one of "otherness"—in that process of racialized "othering" so familiar now to scholars of colonial and imperial discourses. The Irish were depicted as ineradicably other from the English, defined through their difference, their very alter-ity. Haines's opinion—"he thinks we ought to speak Irish in Ireland"—thus smacks of the same hegemonic cultural needs as the desire of white U.S. culture to construct the authentic Native American, to view the American Indian (or Irish) other as quaint, primitive, "wild Irish"— as dead stereotype of an absolute difference. Controlling the dissemination of popular images, the conquering culture was able to fashion a hegemonic discourse about the conquered people as distinctively and ineluctably other, a discourse frequently used to justify and even encourage brutal domination and violence against the conquered culture.

For a nationalist movement then, the issue of wresting back the power to define oneself and one's own national identity is understandably of paramount importance. But there is a perilous dilemma in such a national project of self-definition: in order to combat the pejorative labels of an imperialist English discourse of Irishness, in response to the anxiety of a loss of subjectivity and self-representation, and in order to prove that the Irish are indeed a very particular people distinct and different from all other peoples, it is an almost irresistible urge to define oneself (one's national identity) in terms of one's specific distinctiveness—that is, and once again, in terms of one's specific "otherness" (even sometimes one's otherworldliness, what Cheryl Herr has called the Irish "elsewhere"). That is to say, ironically, that both projects— that of a racialist imperial discourse and that of a nationalist self-definition— are, although emanating from very different political positions, both engaged in defining Irishness as distinctively other and different; in this way, the two projects sometimes merge in a parallel attempt to find or define an authentic "otherness" known variously as the Irish self, the Irish mystique, the Irish soul, the Irish spirit, the Irish mind. As Declan Kiberd writes, "If [nationalist intellectuals] were to create an *authentic movement*. . . . If they were to invent Ireland, they must first invent the Irish" (*Inventing* 100, 136; my emphasis). This leads to the striking but inescapable paradox at the heart of the project of national self-definition: the *invention* of an authentic self.

cA s Kiberd's reference to "an authentic movement" exemplifies, discussions about national identities by even the most scrupulous scholars repeatedly circle around what folklorist Regina Bendix calls the "A-word": After all, what is an "authentic movement"—as opposed to, say, an "inauthentic" one? As Bendix argues, in her groundbreaking study of folkloric and ethnographic theory titled *In Search of Authenticity*:

> European nationalism was part of the effort to cast off monarchical government and establish democratic institutions. Yet the notion of national uniqueness harbors a conservative ethos of the past. Because of the insistence on national purity or authenticity inherent in the idea of a unique nation, the notion of authenticity ultimately undermines the liberating and humanitarian tendencies from which it grew. The universalist aspirations implicit in casting out the old order are contradicted by the particularist emphasis that each nation constructs to distinguish itself from all other nations. In emphasizing the authentic, the revolutionary can turn reactionary, a process all too vividly played out in global political movements of the late twentieth century. (8)

Bendix suggests that it was the notion of authenticity (and "the rhetoric of authenticity") which legitimated folklore and ethnography as scientific disciplines in post-Enlightenment Western culture (5). This notion of, and desire for, a national uniqueness embodies, for many national mythologies, the Romantic legacies of the sublime and the transcendent: "Original, genuine, natural, naive, noble and innocent, lively, sensuous, stirring—the string of adjectives could be continued" (15)—all adjectives which have also been frequently used to describe authentic Irish folk culture. In short, national authenticity functions as a transcendent, neoreligious quality, much as the concept of "nation" itself (according to Benedict Anderson).

The pressure to define a unique and authentic national character and identity, one that is distinct from all others (and preferably originary and premodern, an always already-manifest destiny), may indeed be growing even more urgent with the globalization of our own postmodern era—the world of global markets, global media, and neocolonial economies—where cultural and natural distinctness and distinctions are fading, and cultures all grow increasingly to resemble, not distinct and separate uniquenesses, but predictable simulacra of millennial inauthenticity, complete with CNN and a

McDonald's in every village. "Behind the assiduous documentation and defense of the authentic lies an unarticulated anxiety of losing the subject" (Bendix 10).

It is here, perhaps, that we may glimpse a hint of the cultural forces behind the continuing reification of authenticity and ethnic identitarianism in the world today—at a time when one might be tempted to imagine the need for such militant identity politics to be less necessary, with distinct cultures gradually melding into a transnational global culture: rather than needing now to depend less on cultural differences and identities, previously distinct cultures suffer an anxiety about the perceived loss of identity and subjectivity, thus requiring the continuing construction and maintenance of fantasmatic identities and authenticities so as to continue to be able to assert difference and superiority (rather than global sameness and what Seamus Deane calls the "harmony of indifference" [*Heroic* 15])—whether in the forms of World Cup soccer competitions, sectarian politics, or ethnic warfares.

In the particular case of Irish chic in U.S. culture, what is still identifiable (at least to a popular audience) as a distinct and authentic ethnic/cultural identity—Irishness—can thus function within that culture as a still-legitimate way to deal with ethnicity, and even class and race, without actually having to stray from the familiar (i.e., whiteness): indeed, this seems to be how Irishness functioned in the monster-hit movie *Titanic*, in which Irish/Gaelic music (at least of the Enya-influenced New Age variety) would well up whenever darker ethnicities and lower-class people were being represented, eliding all specificities and difference into a generic otherness-as-Irishness; when the heroine wants to leave her stuffy upper-crust company up there in First Class, she goes down below to Third Class and whoops it up by pulling up her skirts and doing an Irish jig. In the United States today, Irishness may be both popular and comfortable precisely because it remains an identifiable (and presumably authentic) ethnicity that is nonetheless unthreatening and familiar; in both academia and in popular culture, one can have the ideological justification of doing ethnic studies or "performing ethnicity" simply by doing Irish studies—while actually still working within the familiar and with whiteness, and without having to actually venture into the more threatening theaters of racial and Third World otherness.[2]

In order to convince ourselves of our uniqueness and authenticity in a world of increasingly global sameness, we have created a booming "market of identifiable authenticities" (Bendix 3)—especially in the combined and closely related markets known as folklore studies, museum collecting, cultural anthropology, and tourism. Thus, the authentic Aran sweater or the thatched-roof cottage become markers or talismans for the authentic Irish experience: that exuberant search for what the great eighteenth-century theologian and folklorist Johann Gottfried von Herder called the "soul of the people" is a seductive but troubling and complex quest to "pinpoint the ineffable": "Folklore," as Bendix points out, "has long served as a vehicle in the search for the authentic, satisfying a longing for an escape from modernity. The ideal folk community, envisioned as pure and free from civilization's evils, was a metaphor for everything that was not modern." Taking advantage of this ideal, "the most powerful modern political movement, nationalism, builds on the essentialist notions inherent in authenticity, and folklore in the guise of native cultural discovery and rediscovery has continually served nationalist movements since the Romantic era" (7).

However, there is an intrinsic, structural paradox to this quest to locate the authentic, to "catch" the soul or spirit of an authentic Irishness. Over fifty years ago Walter Benjamin delineated the dilemma of authenticity in the age of mechanical reproduction: "Precisely because authenticity cannot be reproduced," Benjamin writes, "the arrival of certain techniques of reproduction . . . has provided the means to differentiate *levels of authenticity*" (52, n. 3; my emphasis). Previous to the age of mechanical reproduction, Benjamin argues, art existed in the world of *cult*, seducing us through its aura—which depends precisely on inaccessibility and remoteness. In an age of mechanical reproduction, aura becomes tarnished by reproduction, and as a result "secularization affords authenticity the place previously held by cult value" (53, n. 8; see Bendix 6). Our own contemporary world of color Xeroxes, lip-synching contests, and Elvis look-alikes has perfected the art of the copy (is it Ella or is it Memorex?), making a mockery of the notion of an "original" or an "authentic" copy; if imitation is the highest form of flattery, nowadays such flattery also robs the original of its exclusive aura. In a world where we can no longer clearly distinguish between Ella and Memorex, between a photocopy and an original document (even faxed signatures are now accepted as legal documents), between a Rembrandt and a skillful forgery—the authentic item hovers somewhere between a transcendent talisman with sacred powers and a shabby trinket from the Araby bazaar.

This process of degradation—from authenticity to its material reproduction or textual representation—involves a further paradox. Once a cultural commodity has been identified as authentic, its market value rises, as does the demand for it. Unlike, say, Rembrandts or Cezannes, folkloric items *can* be endlessly replicated: any member of the group (say, residents of the West of Ireland) can start making them and declaring them to be authentic cultural goods—thus again devaluing each separate item as well as the very notion of the genuine and the authentic.

These paradoxes end up forcing the range of the authentic (and the very essence of authenticity) further and further into the past: as Bendix points out, "declaring a particular form of expressive culture as dead or dying limits the [possible] number of authentic items, but it promotes the search for not yet discovered and hence authentic folklore" (9). Or, in Jean Baudrillard's terms, "in order for ethnology to live, its object must die, by dying, the object takes its revenge for being 'discovered' and with its death defies the science that wants to grasp it" (7). The search for the authentic, then, is an intrinsically hopeless quest to "catch" and pin down something already defined as ungraspable.

This quest for authenticity, in a nationalist politics, frequently takes the familiar form of a national nostalgia for origins, a yearning for a premodern and uncontaminated past that somehow authorizes and defines the authenticity and essence of the cultural present. Bendix notes that, in the history of folklore studies, ever since the time of Herder and the Sturm und Drang Romantics, "the verbal art of the peasantry became [the primary] means for humanity at large to get in touch with authenticity"—especially in the activities of "pilgrimage, and its commodified form, travel," as "loci of transcendence" (17). The latter is certainly true of the familiar rite of passage of Irish Americans "returning" across the big pond to "rediscover" the authentic homeland—as it is equally true of Haines's Passage to Ireland (in *Ulysses*) in search of authentic Irish folklore.

Playing native informant to Haines's imperial ethnography, Buck Mulligan understands the paradoxes of commodification and the ethnographic mentality, as he entertains the Englishman with a bawdy story about "old mother Grogan": "—That's folk, he said very earnestly, for your book, Haines. Five lines of text and ten pages of notes about the folk and the fishgods of Dundrum. Printed by the weird sisters in the year of the big wind" (*U* 1.365–367). Mulligan's own self-consciously nonsensical parody of Irish "folk" lore reflects his understanding of exactly what the ethnographic discourse is looking for (and its structural indistinguishability from reproducible parody): having trotted out some morose local color and verbal wit in the person of Stephen Dedalus, he now tells colorful stories about "fishgods" in "the year of the big wind" ("Can you recall, brother, is mother Grogan's tea and water pot spoken of in the Mabinogion?"), and then unveils his most promising local specimen, the old milkwoman.

The entire scene with the milkwoman is a wonderful parody of the ethnographic encounter with a tribal culture, with Mulligan acting as interpreter/ informant. "—The islanders, Mulligan said to Haines casually, speak frequently of the collector of prepuces" (*U* 1.393–394). Mulligan's self-consciously parodic orchestration and manipulation of the scene manages actually to engage Haines's ethnographic interest in both Stephen's Irish wit and in the milkwoman as an essentialized specimen of Irish folksiness. What Mulligan knows Haines is looking for are the comfortably static images of an essentialized stage Irishness, such as colorful verbal wit (Stephen) and primitive, folksy backwardness (old milkwoman). Such images are not only marketable commodities but in their more insidious implications "could be used to justify any aspect of the colonial enterprise" (Webb 5). "Primitive" peoples have been repeatedly functioned within what ethnohistorian William Simmons calls "anthropological fictions," "the purist notions that native cultures resist history, or that they disappear in its presence" (7)—in what ethnohistorian James Axtell describes sarcastically (in discussing Native American history) as "the short 'pathetic' story of the 'inevitable' triumph of a 'booming' white 'civilization' over a 'fragile' 'primitive' culture" (7); all of these attempts to freeze a static backwardness onto a native culture collude to construct a European/imperial sovereignty of self in what James Clifford calls "master narratives of cultural disappearance" (214).[3]

In this way Haines's quest parallels the project of what Kiberd calls "narrow-gauge nationalists" in Joyce's time: both attempted to define an Irish uniqueness and authenticity as a static otherness already frozen in the past. As David Lloyd points out, the nationalist agenda constructed an identity that "writes out" some of the actual realities of its contemporary present (such as the contemporary feminist and labor movements) in order to facilitate the construction of a dead but authenticating past—which is to suggest that an authentic folk culture is so only if it in fact no longer exists and thus can be reified and sentimentalized. As Lloyd goes on to write, "A celticist nationalism engages in a revalorization of social or cultural traits whose material conditions of possibility it in fact seeks to eradicate" ("Counterparts" 132); in short, Gaelic-ness is of greatest use to Celtic nationalists when it can be construed as dying, archaic, and premodern—and thus of sentimental and nostalgic value in constructing and authenticating an invented national identity. As a result, both the English imperial discourse of Irish otherness and the narrow-gauge nationalist construction of a distinct and unique Gaelic otherness collude in the process that Renato Rosaldo has succinctly coined "imperialist nostalgia."

Kiberd describes this process thus: "Part of the modernization process was the emergence of nation-states, which often arose out of the collapse of the old ways of life and so were badly in need of legitimation: this was afforded by the deliberate invention of traditions, which allowed leaders to ransack the past for a serviceable narrative. In this way, by recourse to a few chosen symbols and simple ideas, random peoples could be transformed into Italians or Irish, and explain themselves by a highly-edited version of their history" (*Inventing* 140). For such a mythologizing/authenticating function, Gaelic culture was almost perfectly, indeed frighteningly, tailor-made: after all, it was already a dying culture (brutally eradicated by both the English and the famine) whose records of its own traditions and culture had been systematically destroyed for centuries by the English; in this cultural vacuum the "invention of traditions" could take place relatively unhindered. "Gaelic Ireland," Kiberd writes, "had retained few institutions or records after 1601 to act as a brake on these tendencies: all that remained were the notations of poets and the memories of the people. [Consequently,] these played a far greater part in [Douglas] Hyde's remodelled Ireland than they did in many of the other emerging European countries" (140)—where the invention of authentic traditions at least still had to face *some* ongoing reality checks.

What resulted is a construction of Irish national identity around the idealization of a rural and primitive West: "Like other forms of pastoral," Kiberd notes, "this complex of ideas was a wholly urban creation, produced by such artists as W. B. Yeats and George Russell and by such political thinkers as Eamon de Valera and Michael Collins. They were, to a man, the urbanized descendants of country people, and they helped to create the myth of a rural nation" ("Periphery" 5). And the emerging Irish Catholic middle class embraced this sentimentalized national mythology about rural Ireland as the authentic Ireland.

One critical problem with such a discursive logic is that the concept of authenticity implies and mandates the existence of its opposite, the inauthentic, the fake, the nonauthorized: it is here that the violence of discourse (in Jacques Derrida's sense) takes place—and where Joyce parted company with a Gaelic nationalism weaned, as he put it, on "the old pap of racial hatred" (quoted in Ellmann 237). By valorizing some things as authentic or essential one necessarily brands other things—a feminine oral tradition, say, or Protestants, Italians, and Jews—as inessential, illegitimate, un-Irish. Kiberd has remarked that "the ludicrous category *un-Irish* was among [the] weird achievements" of the narrow-gauge nationalists (*Inventing* 337). Various forms of sport, literature, dance, etc.—as well as ethnic or racial heritages (Jewish, Italian, Anglo-Irish, black)—thus risked being denounced as "un-

Irish." Yet what does it really mean to be an "inauthentic" Irish person, or an "un-Irish" Irish citizen? It *is* a positively bizarre category, that of the in-authentic Irishman (a category Oscar Wilde embraced with relish). It is one thing to have urban guilt—as with Gabriel Conroy's *seoninism* (in Joyce's *Dubliners* story "The Dead")—over not being sufficiently in touch with the rural West. But it is another thing when the folkloric rhetoric of authenticity is used by ethnic nationalisms to discriminate against an Irish Jew born in Ireland or—as we have seen too often in this century—used to justify acts of "ethnic cleansing." As Bendix (20–21) argues:

> A very thin line separates the desire for individual authenticity and the calling to convince others of the correctness of a particular ren-dering or localization of the authentic. The most powerful and last-ing example of this double legacy in folklore's disciplinary history is the (ethno)nationalist project. Textualized expressive culture such as songs and tales can, with the aid of the rhetoric of authenticity, be transformed from an experience of individual transcendence to a symbol of the inevitability of national unity. . . . [Such a rhetoric] could legitimate its collectivized corollary of cultural authenticity and serve in the unambiguous exclusion and annihilation of all who could not or would not belong.

If the English imperial discourse had sought a primitive Celtic other as the foil to Englishness, the Gaelic Revival now searched for many of the same elements in "the true Celtic other within." "The Gaelic *Ur*-ground," as anthropologist Lawrence Taylor calls it, "was to be sought on such outposts as the Arans, west of Galway, or the Blaskets, off the southwest Kerry coast"; it was there that both anthropologists and the public came to look for "'au-thentic' voices . . . of a pure western, primitive wisdom" (216).

In fashioning such an authentic Irish spirit, the Revivalists needed to be selective and inventive, purging some of the folk legends of their more sordid, vulgar, or obscene elements, under the urging of such historians as Samuel Ferguson and Standish O'Grady. As T. W. Rolleston wrote in 1887, "We *want* the Irish spirit, certainly, in Irish literature[,] . . . but we want its gold, not its dross" (19; quoted in Gibson, "History" 58). O'Grady intended for these idealized legends to be a safe haven to which "the intellect of man" could turn "for rest and recuperation" when "tired by contact with the vul-garity of actual things" (I.22). This sentimentalized whitewashing of sordid and vulgar realities was certainly at odds with Joyce's attempt to make the

Irish take a good look at themselves in his nicely polished looking glass. (Though, to be sure, there were also other Revivalists—D. P. Moran, for instance—who, like Joyce, objected to this very selective, laundered version of Irish history and literature.)

But it was embraced by much of the movement, with the Revivalists and the nationalists collaborating in purveying the idealized image of "a generic, ahistorical peasantry" (Kiberd, "Periphery" 11) in the Blasket or Aran islanders—while ignoring the fact that their world was one actually riven with class snobberies and other dissensions. On this issue even the usually pragmatic Michael Collins wore rose-tinted lenses: "Impoverished as the people are . . . the outward aspect is a pageant. One may see processions of young women riding down on island ponies to collect sand from the seashore, or gathering turf, dressed in their shawls and in their brilliantly-coloured skirts made of material spun, woven and dyed by themselves. . . . Their cottages also are little changed. They remain simple and picturesque. It is only in such places that one gets a glimpse of what Ireland *may become again"* (quoted in Kiberd, "Periphery" 10; emphasis added). The sentimentalized images here are indistinguishable from those in imperialist ethnographies or in Mrs. Hall's sentimental, ethnographic tour books. The striking opening line, "Impoverished as the people are," suggests, as Kiberd has noted, an elision of material poverty, a willing investment in, and acceptance of, an imagined Irishness that is defined as necessarily backward and poor. As Kiberd goes on to argue, "In subsequent Irish politics: rural Ireland was real Ireland, the farmer the moral and economic backbone of the country. That myth was given a further lease on life in each generation . . . [as] Dublin was overrun by unanticipated numbers of rural immigrants, who had no sooner settled in than they were consumed by a fake nostalgia for a pastoral Ireland they had 'lost'" ("Periphery" 16).

Joyce, as an urbanized Dubliner, both felt and saw through the invented pressure of such a romantic-pastoral authenticity. The tension is represented in the *Dubliners* story "The Dead," for example, when Miss Ivors plays the authenticity card with Gabriel, inviting him to vacation in the Aran Islands— and Gabriel is discomfited by her accusation that he is not sufficiently interested in his own country (that is, in the authentic, rural, and primitive West). The Gaelic Revival was funneling tour groups to the Gaeltacht, to learn Gaelic language and dancing and music, to study its folk poetry. Nearly a century and several generations later, the West continues to be the critical marker of Irishness for both Irish citizens and people of Irish descent; it is also where most anthropologists have repeatedly gone to study the Irish. As Taylor, one such anthropologist, reminds us, "In the *Gaeltachts* . . . the 'Irish colleges,' which are not unlike the ethnic summer camps one finds in America, still welcome children from the north and the east, teaching them the language, as well as Irish dancing and singing, in the places where these cultural icons are supposed to be enshrined" (217). "Retribalization centers," he calls them. I am reminded of how the Irish spirit is catching on in the United States, too, with "retribalization centers" now moving onto college campuses—such as the annual summer camps at Boston College ("Gaelic Roots"), Syracuse University, and Notre Dame.

Bendix recalls how, in her early fieldwork in the Balkans, she began by working on a New Year's mumming custom, an event considered ancient if not pagan by natives and folklorists alike—only to discover that it actually began at best a few centuries ago and took on its present form only after World War II. She discovered how in the 1940s the national association for costume preservation embarked on a campaign to "clean up" this "degenerate" ritual and to "reintroduce" the pagan element into the celebration, then to advertise this newly laundered version in the newspapers as the "authentic" ritual which it has now grown to be accepted as.

Examples of this phenomenon (what Eric Hobsbawm calls "the invention of tradition") abound in Irish studies, too, untroubled by any challenge from a carefully recorded Gaelic past. Some of these mythologies are parodied and skewered by Joyce in the "Cyclops" episode of *Ulysses*. A particularly interesting example of such retrospectively invented authenticity is the tradition of the Celtic kilt, a garment embraced by the Revivalists "with its connotations of aristocracy, of Scottish chieftains and pipers marching into battle." But, as Kiberd points out, the kilt was never even Celtic: "subsequent historians have shown that the Irish wore hip-hugging trousers long before the English. . . . The kilt wasn't properly Scottish either, having been devised by an English Quaker industrialist. . . . It was worn by Scottish workers in the new factories [only] because it was cheaper than trousers" (*Inventing* 151).

Unfortunately, the cumulative effect of such "invented traditions" and authenticities often serves merely to further reify or shore up sentimental or stage-Irish stereotypes, such as those so influentially disseminated by Matthew Arnold. Basing his ideas on the theories of Ernest Renan, who had found the quintessential Celtic mind to be dreamy and politically ineffectual, Arnold wrote, "The Celtic genius had sentiment as its main basis . . . with love of beauty, charm and spirituality for its excellence, ineffectualness and self-will for its defect" (quoted in Kiberd, *Inventing* 31)—a general description still believed by many and offered up in many contemporary guidebooks. Arnold

suggested that the Celt was unduly susceptible to emotion and excitement—
"he is truly . . . sentimental"—and, with predictable logic, he thus also argued that "the sensibility of the Celtic nature, its nervous exaltation, have
something feminine in them, and the Celt is thus peculiarly disposed to feel
the spell of the feminine idiosyncracy; he has an affinity to it; he is not far
from its secret" (Arnold 344, 347). This is a kind of "gendered" othering that
has similarly been applied to Jews and to "Orientals," as a way to distinguish them from the sovereign (read: masculine) imperial European subject.

We find elements of such stereotypes of a sentimentalized otherness
reflected in, say, the ideas of Yeats, when he writes of "men born into our
Irish solitude, of their curiosity, their rich discourse, their explosive passion,
their sense of mystery" (quoted in Johnston 56). Or, in the words of another
Yeates, Ray Yeates, writing in a collection of essays about the famine: "Deep
down . . . I think I have always known that to be Irish meant to be a lovable
loser" (195); such widespread beliefs echo Renan's and Arnold's ideas of Irish
ineffectualness—what Arnold callously referred to as "nations disinherited
of political success" in his *On the Study of Celtic Literature*, with its suggestive epigraph from Ossian, "They went forth to the war, but they always
fell" (a line which Yeats also borrowed). Such images only encourage and
reinforce an already internalized Irish creed of noble failure and martyrdom.

We see traces everywhere of such beliefs in a brooding, ineffectual,
dreamy Irish spirit. The Irish American editor of *Irish Hunger*, Tom Hayden
(yes, he of sixties-activism fame and Jane Fonda's ex-husband) writes about
the dark and brooding Robert F. Kennedy as "a raw Celtic spirit" who made
him realize that "there was such a thing as an Irish soul" (287).[4] Even in
contemporary Irish cultural studies we find the continued traces of the
reification of Irish otherness, as in Terry Eagleton's description of Irish writing as "the home of a brooding, isolated subjectivity confronting a recalcitrant world" ("Form" 18).

No intelligent person would, of course, dispute the danger of stereotypes. And yet we can't seem to get beyond stereotypes; as one well-meaning
and intelligent senior colleague commented to me after I delivered a paper
several years ago on the English discourse about the Irish, "But isn't there
some truth to those stereotypes? They *are* often slovenly, drunken, sentimental, poetic, and so on." Or, as Donald Connery writes in his chapter on "National Character" in his 1968 book on *The Irish*, "The trouble is that every
time I am solemnly told in Ireland that the stage Irishman does not exist I
meet one the next day" (91; quoted in Gupta 64).

The trouble is not that the stereotyped traits may exist; the trouble is our confusion, our inability to distinguish between authentic essence and cultural/historical circumstance. The comic vein in Irish literature, for example, may be very real and very particular, very specific to an Irish cultural history—as is, say, the scatological vein in Irish literature (what Lloyd calls "writing in the shit"); but these are frequently the complex and symptomatic results—and sometimes even coping strategies—developed (individually and communally) in reaction or response to external circumstances *imposed* on a people and not a measure of innate essences or racial character. Irish pub culture and drinking, for example, can be interpreted variously as a response to the hopelessness of the poverty and destitution wrought on the Irish by the English or also—as Lloyd argues—as a populist and potentially subversive set of practices which could not be governed by English modes of order and discipline, including the activities of collective treating on the round system, oral traditions and musical performances, and a premodern, communal valuation of the individual ("Counterparts").

The clearest and starkest examples I can marshal of such confusion between essence and circumstance come from nineteenth-century studies of scientific racism, such as the immensely popular and influential *The Races of Men* (1850) by Robert Knox, M.D. Knox writes about "the barbarous Celt" that "the Celtic race does not, and never could be made to comprehend the meaning of the word liberty. . . . Furious fanaticism; a love of war and disorder; a hatred for order and patient industry; no accumulative habits" (27)—a description that might better be interpreted in light of the enforced circumstances of longstanding colonialism: the Irish have never been allowed to "comprehend the meaning of the word liberty"; they are thus fanatic and rebellious in their desire for self-rule and independence (hence "a love of war and disorder"); they hate English order and have never been allowed an opportunity for either patient industry or accumulative habits. Nevertheless, the conclusion drawn by Knox is that such enforced circumstances are conclusive evidence of defining and authentic essences: "that character which I now know to be common to all the Celtic race, wherever found . . . under every circumstance . . . is precisely the same, unaltered and unalterable" (213). This is the process by which stereotypes derive their discursive authority and authenticity, encouraging even well-meaning people—like my senior colleague—to interpret the circumstances one observes as innate essences.

Unfortunately, there is a long tradition of such authentic stereotyping of the Irish spirit in academia, too, and I'm going to focus briefly (and very selectively) on Joyce studies.[5] In 1932 Charles Duff wrote in *James Joyce and the Plain Reader*: "[Joyce's] mind is abnormally Irish—that is to say, he has the qualities that make up the typically Irish mind"—which Duff enumerates as "a restless and often fantastic imagination, a keen sense of realism and the comic, a tendency to sombre, mystical brooding, which often finds compensation in either genial or sardonic wit" (23). Such a description turns Joyce into the typical stage Irishman since it is based on a stage-Irish otherness. Similarly, Joyce's early biographer Herbert Gorman wrote that the "Irishman has been so coloured by romance" and is "a creature of emotions"—and that, although it might not be immediately obvious, Joyce is "essentially Irish" (62). Finally, Frank Budgen, as Suman Gupta has convincingly demonstrated, was—in spite of his loyalty and friendship to Joyce—a believer in biogenetically predetermined racism; among other rather repulsive comments, Budgen wrote: "We must suppose that part of Stephen's [Stephen Dedalus's] physical recoil was due to their difference in race. The Jew sometimes hates the Gentile, and the Gentile occasionally hates the Jew but, religious and political differences apart, there exists also a physical chemical repulsion and this is felt only by the Gentile for the Jewish man" (255). It is in such a discursive context and intellectual history that the turn in Joyce studies toward investigating multiple discourses of Irishness, race, and coloniality presents a welcome and overdue corrective.

*A*fter its founding in 1922, the Irish Free State instituted a Gaelic language revival, in correspondence with the ideology of the Gaelic League, as government policy, an authenticating nationalist effort "to help establish its legitimacy" (Brown 47). This officially authenticated the notion of a narrowly definable Irishness—in tandem with the "Irish Ireland" movement, led by Daniel Corkery among others. Corkery, in his influential study, *The Hidden Ireland* (1925), encouraged the Irish "to seek their cultural heritage in an exclusively Gaelic past" (Foster, *Modern* 167), evolving the notion of an "Irish mind." Ireland, Corkery claimed, was "a land dark, scorned, and secretly romantic"—and that the real, hidden "Irish Ireland" was "a peasant nation, with no urban existence and no middle class, oppressed by an alien gentry" (Foster, *Modern* 195). For Corkery, the "Irish mind" was characterized by Catholic religion, republican nationalism, and a deep connection to the land.[6] Consequently, the Irish Ireland movement tended to exclude as un-Irish any thing or anyone that lay outside the pale of its categories of Irishness.

This legacy is reflected in subsequent Irish literary history, including Joyce criticism. For example, Vivian Mercier's important 1961 study, *The Irish Comic Tradition,* endorses the notion of an "Irish mind" by associating the supposedly Irish traits of fantastic humor and verbal wit with a history of magic and mythology, an essential mind-set that supposedly worked its way into a writer's sensibility without his or her awareness; Mercier argued that Joyce was essentially Irish in this sense. In response to Mercier's book, Conor Cruise O'Brien insisted on distinguishing between circumstance and essence, arguing that "Irish wit is a political contingency as words are the weapons of the disarmed"—rather than an innate essence of the Irish mind: "The idea," O'Brien wrote further, "that there is 'an Irish mind' . . . with its own peculiar quirks, not shared even by other Europeans, from medieval times to the days of Samuel Beckett, seems to me implausible. . . . There is probably no continuous and distinctive 'Irish mind,' but there has been since the sixteenth century at least an Irish predicament: a predicament which has produced common characteristics in a number of those who have been involved in it" (104). The distinction lies between innate essences and historical/political circumstances.[7]

So is there an "Irish spirit"? Rather than endorse any such notion of an inherent Irishness, I would prefer to cite Stuart Hall's definition of "cultural identity": "Far from being grounded in a mere 'recovery' of the past, which is waiting to be found, and which once found, will secure our sense of ourselves into eternity, identities are the names we give to the different ways we are positioned by, and position ourselves within, the narratives of the past" ("Cultural Identity and Cinematographic Representation" 70). Such a definition allows for analyses of the discursive processes by which identities are formed in response to real-world situations and political contingencies. A number of Irish literary scholars have been working fruitfully with just such a discursive understanding of cultural identity. For example, Lloyd reminds us of Frantz Fanon's distinction between "culture" and "custom," in which Fanon makes the important point, as I understand it, that colonial cultures are teeming, complex, and perpetually in motion, while custom and tradition construct static and oversimplified essentialisms that only hint at the multifarious complexities of the hidden life of a people. What ensues and survives over time are cultural forms that carry both the traces of the violence and trauma of the colonial encounter as well as counter-mechanisms of survival and adaptation; as Lloyd concludes, "This unevenly distributed relation of damage and survival forges the recalcitrant grain of cultural difference" ("Counterparts" 141).

Luke Gibbons has also argued that we should be skeptical of simple generalizations about a cultural identity: "it is important not only to re-think but to *re-figure* Irish identity, to attend to those recalcitrant areas of expertise which simply do not lend themselves to certainty, and which impel societies themselves towards indirect and figurative discourse" (18)—for "there is no prospect of restoring a pristine, pre-colonial identity," Gibbons writes; "instead of being based on narrow ideals of racial purity and exclusivism, identity is open-ended and heterogeneous" (179). Gibbons argues that Irishness, indeed, rather than being characterizable as essentially premodern, is in fact modern before its time because of the circumstances of its history, one "seared as the record is by the successive waves of conquest and colonization, by bloody wars and uprisings, by traumatic dislocations, by lethal racial antagonisms, and indeed, by its own nineteenth-century version of a holocaust" (6). As a result, Gibbons argues, "Irish society did not have to await the twentieth century to undergo the shock of modernity: disintegration and fragmentation were already part of its history so that, in a crucial but not always welcome sense, Irish culture experienced modernity before its time. This is not unique to Ireland, but is the common inheritance of cultures subjected to the depredations of colonialism" (6). And Joyce, Kiberd argues, was in touch with this "modernity" in the Irish experience: "[Joyce] did not become modern to the extent that he ceased to be Irish; rather he began from the premise that to be Irish was to be modern anyway. . . . It was the politicians who, in cleaving to tired, inherited forms, failed to be modern and so ceased being Irish in any meaningful sense" (*Inventing* 267). Joyce himself had written, "To tell the truth, to exclude from the present nation all who are descended from foreign families would be impossible" (*Critical Writings* 166). "In the face of such variousness," Kiberd concludes, "a unitary racial nationality could never be [for Joyce] more than 'a convenient fiction'"— and Joyce tried, instead, to develop in his fiction open-ended forms "hospitable to the many strands that made up Irish experience" (*Inventing* 337).

Quite a few scholars in Irish studies have been at work demonstrating how Joyce's texts in fact do just that and how they reflect symptomatically the various grains of influence and heritage in Irish history. Lloyd, for example, has argued that *Ulysses* "circulates not only thematically but also stylistically around adulteration [as opposed to purity] as the constitutive anxiety of nationalism" and that an episode like "Cyclops" "dramatizes adulteration as the condition of colonial Ireland at virtually every level" (*Anomalous* 106). *Ulysses*, Lloyd contends, refuses to fulfill the narrative demands consistent with the socializing functions of national identity formation, and its radicality comes from its insistence "on a deliberate stylization of dependence and *in*authenticity, a stylization of the hybrid status of the colonized subject as of the colonized culture, their internal adulteration and the strictly parodic [and hybrid] modes that they produce in every sphere" (110; emphasis added). And, in a compelling set of readings of the "Circe" episode, Andrew Gibson has demonstrated how that episode is full of English idiom and Anglicized voices, English forms revealing a cultural desire for Englishness, exposing "the anglicized or imported nature of Irish popular culture": in this way, the episode dramatizes the reality that "the characters in 'Circe' are necessarily divided against themselves" ("Strangers" 197), a self-dividing doubleness that is at the very heart of an Irish culture long dominated by the hegemony of English discourse and desire. As Gibson concludes, "Joyce's point has to do with a culture caught in a specific historical configuration. . . . It remains adulterate, compromised — 'infected,' to use one of Seamus Deane's terms. It fails to move beyond the anglicized nature of the context from which it sprang. . . . This particular colonized culture is inevitably a culture of imposture" (201).[8]

In other words, and in conclusion, rather than being based on a narrow authenticity, the specific culture of a late-colonial Ireland might be theorized indeed as a mongrel culture — even a culture of imposture, adulteration, and inauthenticity: modern and diverse in its variety and complexity — rather than primitive, premodern, and ineluctably other by virtue of a narrowly defined, authentic otherness. As Joyce himself wrote, "Our civilization is a vast fabric, in which the most diverse elements are mingled. . . . In such a fabric, it is useless to look for a thread that may have remained pure and virgin without having undergone the influence of a neighbouring thread" (*Critical Writings* 165–166).

In *Remembrance and Imagination: Patterns in the Historical and Literary Representation of Ireland in the Nineteenth Century*, Joep Leerssen has suggested that *Ulysses* marks the end of the Irish nineteenth century precisely because Joyce "dared to describe an Irish setting in terms of its *normalcy*" (231) — rather than its ineradicable alienness. Leerssen punctuates this point by noting that the last word of *Ulysses* is not, in fact, "Yes" — but rather "Trieste-Zurich-Paris 1914–1921." In this way, "Joyce carefully situates the fictional universe of Dublin, 16 June 1904, not in a Celtic never-never land or in a stagnated out-of-the-way backwater, but squarely in the space-time of the Joyce family and its vagaries across Europe" (231). In spite of Joyce's efforts, however, Leerssen can only ruefully conclude that "the acknowledgment of normalcy is still very rare in Ireland-related discourse" (231) — a discourse still deeply enmeshed in a rhetoric of authenticity and in a narrow effort to catch, pin down, and codify into national dogma an authentic "Irish spirit." Nevertheless, Leerssen's own efforts, as well as those by many others involved in contemporary Irish cultural studies, suggest that the portals of Irishness are beginning to open up somewhat.

Nation without Borders: Cosmopolitanism and the Inauthentic Irishman

I begin this section by invoking a line from *Finnegans Wake*, to my knowledge the only direct reference in Joyce's published works to cosmopolitanism: "ruric or cospolite, for much or moment in dispute" (309.10). Ensconced in a passage (at the very beginning of Book II, chapter 3) clearly concerning the nature of Irish identity, both ethnic and national—"it is Hiberio-Miletians and Argloe-Noremen, donated him, birth of an otion" (309.11, with references to Hibernia, Iberians, Milesians, Norsemen, Anglo-Normans, and the birth of a nation)—Joyce's comment makes clear his awareness that the position of the rural and rustic ("ruric") versus that of the cosmopolite ("cospolite") were very much "in dispute." The positions of the rural and the cosmopolite are still very much in dispute today, not only in the political and ideological debates surrounding Irish identity and nationness but also in contemporary global and cultural theory.

This binary of the rural/local versus the cosmopolitan/global plays itself out in a number of parallel variants (each side of which can be conveniently glorified or vilified): country versus city; peasant versus urban dweller; primitive folk culture versus modernity and metropolitan culture; rude primitives versus suave and urbane city dwellers. After all, the term *cosmopolitan* contains (as part of its etymological identity) the *polis,* the city—and thus also the various qualities of metropolitanism associated with city-ness. A cosmopolitan, then, is a citi-zen of the cosmos, a member of the world city. This key concept in Western culture is usually attributed originally to the Stoic philosopher Diogenes Laërtius, who, when asked where he came from, answered, "I am a citizen of the world." Worldliness and city-ness are so closely connected within this concept that to be a "citizen of the world" implies a number of features and qualities long associated with both city life and cosmopolitanism: urban, urbane, urbanity (from *urbis,* Latin for city); polite, polished, political (from *polis,* Greek for city); it is perhaps thus inevitable that the term also has come to suggest suave, smooth, sophisticated—even at times disingenuous, dissembling, sybaritic, and degenerate. Opposed to these are the diametrically contrasted qualities long associated with country folk and the peasantry: primitive, provincial, naive, unpolished, ingenuous, straightforward, honest, moral, and pure—all qualities that have been frequently claimed for the Irish peasant. Notice how what Timothy Brennan cites as the "relentlessly positive" connotations of cosmopolitanism—"free from provincial prejudices," "not limited to one part of the world," "sophisticated, urbane, worldly" (19)—can, in point of fact, be just as easily turned inside out and rendered into relentlessly negative connotations: sophisticated, urbane, worldly, smooth, deceitful, degenerate, and so on. As we will see, this has indeed often been the case.

With a country like Ireland, there is a further twist to this binary contrast between the rural and the cosmopolitan—and that is the longstanding context of colony and empire. As Raymond Williams suggested in his classic study, *The Country and the City*, the categories of "country" and "city" can be functionally extended into the realms of global imperialism and economic neocolonialism—with the position of "country" being occupied by the colonies and the Third World, and the position of "city" being occupied by the empire and the imperial city. Indeed, these are precisely the relative valences we have in mind nowadays when, in contemporary postcolonial studies, we employ the contrasting terms *colonial* and *metropolitan*. Thus, the contrast of country and city, of rustic and cosmopolitan, of colonial and metropolitan takes on the important binary also of nation and empire, of national versus imperial—as particular manifestations of the local and the global.

Is the genuine, authentic culture of a people—and thus its cultural identity—local and national? Or is it global and transnational? A question so crudely framed is, of course, already limited and limiting in the very range of answers possible. But it is also the central controversy in the contemporary debate over cosmopolitanism and globalism. This ongoing debate is vexed, complex, and important—involving, among others, such critics and theorists as Bruce Robbins, Timothy Brennan, Martha Nussbaum, Paul Rabinow, David Miller, Arjun Appadurai, Kwame Anthony Appiah, James Clifford, Edward Said, and Mary Louise Pratt. I won't try to summarize here the various aspects and positions within this lively and ongoing debate, but will touch on the key points important for the present discussion of Joyce and Irish identity.[9]

So, is culture local or global? Is identity national or transnational? This is a very Joycean question, too, for Joyce's works—especially *Ulysses* and *Finnegans Wake*—are ones that try to negotiate the complex and mutually dependent relationship between the universal and the particular; between the lived particularity of 1904 Dublin and the nature of "universal" human experience as shared by, for example, Odysseus, Telemachus, Penelope, Bloom, Stephen, and Molly; between the local microcosm of a publican's family in

Chapelizod and the archetypal family of universal history in *Finnegans Wake*. In some obvious ways, though, the question itself (i.e., is culture local or global?) seems immediately wrongheaded, for surely we would all agree, prima facie, that any not purely premodern culture is necessarily (although to varying degrees) *both* local and global, both national and transnational; after all, one would be hard pressed to name many (if any) cultures (modern or premodern) that have been continuously and totally isolated, not touched by any influences (trade, cultural exchange, intermarriage, and so on) outside its borders. Thus, if culture is both local and global, any theories of global culture would have to account for local and national specificities; as Brennan puts it, "A cosmopolitanism worthy of the name, in other words, would have to give space to the very nationalism that the term is invoked to counter" (25). I would suggest that the opposite should also be true—that any nationalism worthy of the name would have to give space to the global contexts and cultures in which *it* operates. In that vein, and in response to exclusivist claims for the primacy of local specificity as the only "real" measure of ethnic or national culture, Robbins has argued for the viewpoint "of culture as neither exclusively inherited nor exclusively national" (19).[10] In its stead, Robbins argues persuasively for a version of cosmopolitanism and internationalism that is more ethical and nonelitist than Brennan's dismissal of cosmopolitanism as essentially the drive for a "specious mastery of the whole" (27) by privileged elitists with the luxury of international mobility.

Such a current debate, however much situated in the contemporary global culture of McDonald's and CNN, has important ramifications for the ongoing negotiations and debates, for the past century, over the nature of Irishness and authentic Irish identity. The discrepancies and tensions between city and country life have long been crucial in the construction of Irishness. The English imperial discourse had long fashioned the Irish as a primitive and uncivilized Celtic other that served as a convenient foil for the supposedly "civil" and "civilized" English "citizen" (all terms derived from *civitas*, Latin for city). In response, the Gaelic Revival searched for many of the same elements (of rural primitivism) in the authentic Irish self, thus mirroring the English stereotypes of the Celt.

What resulted, as we have seen, is a construction of Irish national identity around the idealization of a rural and primitive West, the sentimentalized national mythology about rural Ireland as the authentic Ireland. The discursive result is that, in such an ethos, the real thing, the authentic culture and ethos of the tribe/people, can be found only in the rural and primitive countryside of an Aran or a Connemara, and certainly not in the modern cityscape of a Dublin.

The critical problem, as I noted earlier, with such a discursive logic, is that the concept of rural authenticity implies and mandates the existence of its opposite, the inauthentic, the fake, the nonauthorized—that is, the urban, metropolitan, cosmopolitan, and non-Celtic. In his seminal and influential 1892 lecture, "The Necessity for De-Anglicising Ireland," Douglas Hyde had helped shape the subsequent discourse of the Gaelic Revival and the Gaelic League about the Irish nation in terms that were quite explicit, essentialist, exclusive: as Hyde wrote famously, "We must strive to cultivate everything that is most racial, most smacking of the soil, most Gaelic, most Irish, because in spite of the little admixture of Saxon blood in the north-east corner, this island *is* and will *ever* remain Celtic at the core" (169). This rhetoric linking soil, nation, and race—as in the epigraph of the nationalist newspaper, *The Nation*, "racy of the soil"—is a quasi-religious discourse in which the rural countryside is transcended into a holy ground of originary and inherited sacredness. As Seamus Deane remarks: "Soil is what land becomes when it is ideologically constructed as a natal source, that element out of which the Irish originate and to which their past generations have returned. It is a political notion denuded, by a strategy of sacralization, of all economic and commercial reference. . . . The apotheosis of the peasant and of the Celt readily allied itself with the notion that the soil was a sacred possession, mystically owned by the dispossessed (the peasantry) or disgracefully betrayed by the owners (the landlords)" (*Strange* 70–71, 78). In such a discursive schema, there is no room for those others living not on the authentic and racy soil but on the consequentially "inauthentic" and deracinated pavements and cobblestones of the un-Irish city.

This sacralization of the land as race and "soil" was picked up as a central tenet by the "Irish Ireland" movement, led by Daniel Corkery among others, soon after the founding of the Irish Free State in 1922. For Corkery, in his influential studies *The Hidden Ireland* (1925) and *Synge and Anglo-Irish Literature* (1931), the test for "real" Irish literature and culture was the trefoiled shamrock of Catholic religion, republican nationalism, and a deep connection to the land. Consequently, the Irish Ireland movement tended to exclude any thing or anyone that lay outside the pale of its categories of Irishness—including the cities and their slums—as un-Irish and inauthentic. Such an Irish literature was, in David Krause's words, obviously "not written by Yeats or Joyce, both of whom were summarily dismissed as anti-Irish by Corkery. So was [John Millington] Synge . . . and so was [Sean] O'Casey. None of the best Irish writers fulfilled the dogmatic principles of Corkeryism" and of his "exalted triad of *religion, nationalism, and the land*" (13).

In a sense, the issue here is as basic as the very nature of what we might call genuine human "experience." John Berger has argued that "to dismiss peasant experience as belonging only to the past, as having no relevance to modern life, . . . to continue to maintain, as has been maintained for centuries, that peasant experience is marginal to civilization, is to deny the value of too much history and too many lives" (81); it is also to reinforce an imperial discourse that has long relegated native colonial cultures to a dead or dying past, antimodern and beyond the reach of progress, civilization, and history. Yet to credit peasant life as, conversely, the only sort of experience that can be considered the genuine experience of a people or a nation is to suggest that the lived "nonexperience" of emigration and global dissemination (certainly central to the history of the Irish people) does not qualify as authentic Irish culture. Such a distrust of the lived experience of urbanites and emigrants suggests a cultural anxiety and identity crisis over the metropolitan and the cosmopolitan. Such distrust also mirrors the consciousness of the Englishman Haines in *Ulysses*: to him, the old milkwoman is the genuine Irish artifact; as a result, both Buck Mulligan (who attended Oxford) and Stephen Dedalus (who has lived in Paris), however more familiar they may feel to Haines (or perhaps it is precisely *because* of their familiarity and border-crossing internationalism), can seem but fantasmatic and inauthentic aberrations of the "real" thing. So also would seem that Dublin author James Joyce, he who signed his most famous novel with the defiantly cosmopolitan dateline "Trieste-Zurich-Paris 1914–1921."[11] Indeed, so would all of Joyce's novels (and the characters therein) seem, based as they are on a modern and metropolitan Dublin, the national capital that nevertheless would not qualify as sufficiently and authentically Irish. Such a deep-seated, longstanding, and perhaps even unconscious, discursive national logic may help explain the longstanding Irish distrust of both Joyce and his works—as well as, perhaps, the understandable distrust (at least until relatively recently) by the Irish academy of the discipline of Joyce studies, steeped as it has been for decades in a discourse of international modernism as expounded by a cosmopolitan intelligentsia of foreign professors meeting in metropolitan centers like Paris, London, New York, Zurich, Rome.

Indeed, at times of national anxiety, cosmopolitanism has repeatedly been turned from a generally positive concept denoting worldly and broad-minded sympathy for a common humanity to a viciously derogatory scapegoat of impurity and degeneracy. As Rabinow notes, in earlier eras the concept has been applied to "Christians, aristocrats, merchants, Jews, homosexuals, and intellectuals" (258). Brennan himself admits:

> Any student of the late nineteenth and early twentieth centuries is aware that "cosmopolitanism" was a code word in Eastern Europe for the Jew, where rootlessness was a condemnation and a proof of nonbelonging precisely *there*. Linked in this sense to the sixteenth-century paranoid German Christian legend of the "Wandering Jew" Ahasuerus—condemned by Jesus for his part in the Crucifixion to wander, toiling and wretched, until the Second Coming—the term is one expression of an anti-Semitism that stretches from Luther's diatribes on the "lies of the Jews" through the Russian pogroms to the Warsaw Ghetto, and may originally have been connected to the migration of Sephardim from Spain following the infamous fifteenth-century expulsion. (20–21)

In this way cosmopolitanism itself can be made into the target of racism and xenophobia, thus becoming part of the history of anti-Semitism; as Knox, writing about the Jews in 1850 in *The Races of Men*, the most popular and influential scientific study of race in nineteenth-century England, claimed, "Wanderers, then, by nature—unwarlike—they never could acquire a fixed home or abode. . . . They never seem to have had a country, nor have they any yet" (Knox adds, conveniently, that "they are becoming extinct"; 138, 140). Or as Deasy remarks about the Jews in the "Nestor" episode of *Ulysses*, "They sinned against the light. . . . And you can see the darkness in their eyes. And that is why they are wanderers on the earth to this day" (2.361–363)—a logic that mistakes "wandering" and shiftlessness and mobility (the very essentials, after all, of cosmopolitanism) as innate and essentialized traits of the Jew. In the twentieth century, Stalin was able to harness populist anger against his opponents within the Russian Communist Party by labeling them "cosmopolitans," with the same ugly implications of Jewishness, shiftiness, homelessness, and degenerate foreignness—but "also and very differently as 'intellectual' in the bad sense—as fine-liver, aesthete, soft-handed trader[s] in literary niceties" (Brennan 21). It is very ironic that the term was subsequently and conveniently used in these same ways in Senator Joseph McCarthy's *anti*-Communist witch hunts in the mid-century United States, with "cosmopolite" now coded instead as Communist, but with otherwise the same negative connotations intact: Jew, foreigner, wanderer, urbane, dissipated, fine-liver, aesthete, intellectual.[12] Significantly, these are the very qualities that, in *Finnegans Wake*, Shaun accuses Shem of (especially in I.7, the "Shem" chapter)—echoing charges that had also been lobbed at Joyce himself over the years. It is this anxiety of national identity concerning the inauthentic urban/cosmopolitan Irishman—whether a Joyce, Yeats, Wilde, Buck Mulligan, Stephen Dedalus, or Shem—that is my focus in this part of the chapter.

*J*oyce's *Dubliners* and *A Portrait of the Artist as a Young Man* both play out, symptomatically, these tensions within the discourse of Irish identity—tensions between country and city, as well as the parallel tensions between colony and metropole, between nation and empire.[13]

The conflicting desires and demands of the local/national and of the cosmopolitan/international are played out perhaps most clearly in "The Dead," in the torn allegiances and consciousness of Gabriel Conroy, an urban intellectual with cosmopolitan pretensions. The Gabriel who advocates the wearing of "goloshes" because "everyone wears them on the continent" (181) and who vacations in "France and Belgium or perhaps Germany" (189) is confronted by the ardent nationalist Miss Ivors with an invitation to vacation in the Aran Isles instead: "—And why do you go to France and Belgium, said Miss Ivors, instead of visiting your own land? . . . And haven't you your own language to keep in touch with—Irish?" (189) In spite of Gabriel's annoyed retorts that "if it comes to that, you know, Irish is not my language" and that "I'm sick of my own country, sick of it!" (189)—both comments, incidentally, that the young Joyce would have agreed with—Gabriel cannot help but be discomfited by the sacral power contained in words like "your own land" and "your own language." For this is the rhetoric of authenticity, the discursive terrain in which "land" is transformed into sacred, native "soil" and in which "language" evokes Hyde's argument for de-Anglicization as a necessary step to becoming "racy of the soil." Such a challenge is destined to evoke urban guilt in Gabriel, precipitating (as it does later) his final epiphany—given the national discourse at the turn of the century that had already defined Irish identity as the culture of a rural, peasant, authentic Ireland. Thus, in the story, it is perhaps inevitable that such authentic Irishness gets represented, even in Gabriel's mind, by his "country cute" wife Gretta from Connacht (187, 189), by her dead young admirer Michael Furey (from Oughterard), and by the song he used to sing to her, "The Lass of Aughrim." Furey and his song are especially appropriate vehicles for such a loaded representational cargo, for they literally embody the urban nostalgia for a *dead* (and thus authentic) past—since Furey, cut off in his youth and frozen into symbol, cannot ever (unlike Gabriel or Stephen or Buck Mulligan) be further touched by other external or hybrid cultural influences, and since Aughrim, as the site of the bloodiest Irish defeat (a year after the Boyne), which finally and fully sealed English domination of Ireland, becomes itself a poignant symbol of "that murdered Irish past, the dead, the bodies of, as Yeats wrote, 'long ago / Men that had fought at Aughrim and the Boyne'" (Cheng, *Joyce* 144). In this light, Gabriel's epiphany at the end of the story can be seen as an attempt by the Irish urban psyche to negotiate and come to terms with these two competing urges within Irish culture and identity, the discourses of the local and the global, of the national and the cosmopolitan—a tension symptomatically played out within Gabriel's own mixed urges and consciousness.

Within this nationalist discourse about peasant purity and authenticity, the fear of the urbane, the sophisticated, the modern—and the consequently degenerate—is encapsulated in the final pages of *A Portrait of the Artist as a Young Man* by the story of the old man in the West:

> 14 *April*: John Alphonsus Mulrennan has just returned from the west of Ireland. (European and Asiatic papers please copy.) He told us he met an old man there in a mountain cabin. Old man had red eyes and a short pipe. Old man spoke Irish. Mulrennan spoke Irish. Then old man and Mulrennan spoke English. Mulrennan spoke to him about universe and stars. Old man sat, listened, smoked, spat. Then said:
> —Ah, there must be terrible queer creatures at the latter end of the world. (251)

These apocalyptic "terrible queer creatures" of modernity in the larger universe beyond one's rural enclave, incomprehensible to the peasant mind, suggest the fears and threat to a national discourse of authenticity represented by the cosmopolitan world of Paris, the Moulin Rouge, and the bohemian Latin Quarter, the very world Stephen Dedalus desires to inhabit. Such a discourse of national anxiety can conceive of the urbanity and hybridity of the international only as "terrible queer creatures," immoral and degenerate. Stephen realizes that he, too, like Gabriel Conroy, will have to come to terms with this avatar of authentic Irish identity, the old peasant in the West speaking Gaelic: "I fear him. I fear his redrimmed horny eyes" (252).

Stephen, rejecting the maternal—at once his own mother May Goulding Dedalus, Mother Church, and Mother Ireland (as symbolized in part by the pregnant, bare-breasted peasant woman offering Davin milk in *A Portrait*)—leaves instead for cosmopolitan Paris. In the opening episode of *Ulysses*, we find another woman offering milk, the old milkwoman who similarly represents Mother Ireland: "Silk of the kine and poor old woman," Stephen thinks, "names given her in old times" (1.403–404). Offering the maternal sustenance associated with the natal and the native, she stands for the local, the racy soil, the national, the authentic Irish. This is certainly how Haines also understands her, as he approaches the milkwoman with some words in Gaelic, performing, as I have suggested elsewhere, an act of pseudo-ethnographic research (see Cheng, *Joyce* 156). But there is another "mother" in this episode, the sea, what Buck Mulligan (after Algernon Swinburne) calls "our great sweet mother" ("*Thalatta! Thalatta!*"; *U* 1.80). These are the two competing maternal allegiances present in the episode: one, the old milkwoman, who, as "poor old woman" and "silk of the kine," connects those who drink her milk to the local and the provincial; the other, the sea, is the medium by which Stephen (and many other Irish wild geese and *émigrés*) left Ireland for foreign lands, for which the Martello Tower serves as omphalos to the global. These are Stephen's choices, as well as the forces competing to define Irish culture.

Whereas the Englishman Haines can feel comfortable with the milkwoman as a museum piece that can stand in for the comfortable stereotypes of Irish peasant folksiness, he has a harder time making sense of the urban and increasingly urbane and cosmopolitan Stephen Dedalus. As Mulligan points out, "You know, Dedalus, you have the real Oxford manner. He can't make you out" (*U* 1.53–54). Haines can't make sense of the hybridity of a brooding and sardonic urban intellectual with "the real Oxford manner" who has been living in Paris—for such a figure does not fit within the discursive parameters of the authentic Irishman as a naive and provincial peasant, a stereotype maintained by both the imperialist discourse of the English and the nativist discourse of the Gaelic Revival and nationalist movement. Nor can such a discourse make comfortable sense of an Irishman like Buck Mulligan, who quotes Homer in the Greek and wants to Hellenize the Celtic island, and who (like Oliver St. John Gogarty, on whom he is modeled) attended Oxford's Magdalen College (*U* 1.165–169). This is the Mulligan who can actively *parody* Irish folk art—"—That's folk, he said very earnestly, for your book, Haines. Five lines of text and ten pages of notes about the folk and the fishgods of Dundrum. Printed by the weird sisters in the year of the big wind" (*U* 1.365–367)—rather than merely *stand in* for it and passively *represent* it; he is thus (in postcolonial parlance) a hybrid subject, not merely a representative and representational object. Similarly, rather than merely suffering oneself to be studied and taxonomized (unlike the milkwoman), Stephen—when Haines expresses interest in making a collection of his sayings and thus turning him into folk art too—responds by asserting his personal agency within this ethnographic encounter: "—Would I make any money by it? Stephen asked" (*U* 1.490).

Indeed, Haines's expectation that "we ought to speak Irish in Ireland" (*U* 1.431–432) is part of the shared construction of Irishness maintained, in mirrored discourses, by both English imperialists and the Irish Revival—for it would freeze Irishness within Corkery's triad of peasant connection to land, Roman Catholicism, and Irish nationalism; and it would freeze Irishness in the nostalgic purity of a dead past, doomed to extinction in the face of modernity and history. These are discourses of authenticity that leave no room for the "inauthenticity" of figures like Stephen Dedalus, Buck Mulligan, or Oscar Wilde—with their familiarity with the salons of Paris, the society of London, and the dining halls of Oxford; it certainly leaves no room for an Irish Jew of Hungarian descent such as Leopold Bloom. How then can such a discourse deal with emigration—so important, after all, in Irish cultural history—unless it demand that (in Robbins's words) the eyes of the emigrant "can only be trained on his lost home" (95)? It is the native "soil" and the homeland (so consecrated in Irish songs as "the holy sod," "the holy ground," "the wee bit of green," and so on) that have to remain the only touchstones possible, the only images that can be allowed to be in one's mind continually, in order to maintain a nostalgic cultural identity that denies the existence of any other sorts of experience as genuine and acceptable.

This logic presents a real dilemma for the Irish exile—whether wild goose or emigrant—who is away from home but who wishes to maintain his or her "Irishness." "The wild goose, Kevin Egan of Paris," in *Ulysses* (3.164) is a case in point: a portrait of the Fenian Joseph Casey, who was imprisoned for his involvement in acts of Fenian violence in England (see Gifford and Seidman 52), Joyce's Kevin Egan is a Fenian espousing the discourse of Irish nationalism and authenticity, but ironically stranded in the center of internationalism and cosmopolitanism, Paris. This is an irony not lost on his son Patrice, Stephen's friend, who tells Stephen: "—*C'est tordant, vous savez. Moi, je suis socialiste. Je ne crois pas en l'existence de Dieu. Faut pas le dire à mon père*" (*U* 3.169–170; my translation: "It's hilarious, you know. Me, I'm a socialist. I don't believe in the existence of God. Don't tell my father that"). Like Patrice, Stephen too is a freethinker living in Paris, eating *mou en civet* in his "Latin quarter hat" "when I was in Paris, *boul'Mich*'" (*U*

3.174–179). The Boulevard Saint-Michel, a major boulevard in the Latin Quarter on the Seine's Left Bank, was of course "the cafe center of student and bohemian life at the turn of the century" (Gifford and Seidman 53). In such an environment, the Fenian Kevin Egan tries to hold on to "home": at Rodot's patisserie (9 Boulevard Saint-Michel; Gifford and Seidman 54), he speaks to Stephen "of Ireland, the Dalcassians, of hopes, conspiracies, of Arthur Griffith" (*U* 3.226–227). And he complains about the degeneracy and sexual excess of Parisians: "Licentious men. The *froeken, bonne à tout faire*, who rubs male nakedness in the bath at Upsala. *Moi faire*, she said, *tous les messieurs*. Not this *monsieur*, I said. Most licentious custom. Bath a most private thing. I wouldn't let my brother, not even my own brother, most lascivious thing . . . lascivious people" (*U* 3.234–238). The repeated refrain of "lascivious"—in the context of massages and baths—suggests a paranoid fear of the foreign and the degenerate, all embodied in the Parisian bohemianism and cosmopolitan freethinking indulged in by Stephen and indeed by Egan's own son Patrice. For these modern Parisians are the "terrible queer creatures at the latter end of the world" that the premodern and peasant mind of an authentic Irish discourse distrusts and can comprehend only as cosmopolitan degeneracy. Rather, Egan tries to teach his son "to sing *The boys of Kilkenny*" (*U* 3.257) and to keep his mind focused on "home," as defined by a discourse identifying Irishness as the agrarian, Catholic, and republican West of Ireland, the discourse glorified by the Fenianism through which he defines himself. As Stephen ruefully notes, "In gay paree he hides, Egan of Paris, unsought by any save by me. . . . They have forgotten Kevin Egan, not he them. Remembering thee, O Sion" (*U* 3.249–250, 263–264). Like the Israelites remembering Zion by the rivers of Babylon, Egan continues to train his eyes on the past and on the native soil of an authentic Ireland, while he is stranded by the boulevards of a latter-day Babylon. Unable to admit or incorporate hybrid and foreign experiences as part of his own complex identity, he lives in an authentic past already frozen in nostalgia.

Even more frightening to such a discourse would be the "terrible queer creatures" who cannot be so conveniently relegated to *external* abjection, that is, to the foreign (such as Parisians)—but who are, indeed, domestic and *internal* to the national self. Such a frightening figure of the inauthentic Irishness within the self would be Leopold Bloom, who (unlike Stephen or Buck) must not even be allowed to claim to be "Irish." Bloom is, in a sense, a hybrid, borderless creature of cultural inauthenticity, lacking anything fixed and local about him: he is a freethinking Hungarian Jew who has been baptized both Catholic and Protestant, an urban dweller of foreign descent with intellectual pretensions—he is, in short, everything that Kevin Egan, Mulrennan's Old Man, and Michael Cusack (head of the Gaelic Athletic Association and model for the "Citizen" in the "Cyclops" episode of *Ulysses*) would repudiate as cosmopolitan, and thus not Irish. Indeed, Bloom's own utopian manifesto—in the carnivalesque humor of the "Circe" episode—confirms his universalist idealism: "I stand for the reform of municipal morals and the plain ten commandments. New worlds for old. Union of all, jew, moslem and gentile. . . . General amnesty, weekly carnival with masked license, bonuses for all, esperanto the universal language with universal brotherhood. . . . Free money, free rent, free love and a free lay church in a free lay state. . . . Mixed races and mixed marriage" (*U* 15.1683–1699). As a "universal language," Esperanto (meaning "hopeful") was a popular hope among international idealists at the turn of the century, who saw it as a solution to national sectarianisms. "Union of all," "universal brotherhood," "free love," "a free lay state," and "mixed races" are all, of course, major elements of an internationalist ideal, a cosmopolitan utopia. In espousing these, Bloom is revealing himself as a "citizen of the world" promoting a cosmopolitan and internationalist agenda—one in direct contrast to the Irish Ireland agenda of an insular Catholic and nationalist peasantry.

In the "Cyclops" episode, our "citizen of the world" has a confrontation with the "Citizen" of a narrowly defined Irish nation, based on Michael Cusack, founder of the Gaelic Athletic Association. The Citizen exhibits the same fear and distrust of the foreign we have seen already in Mulrennan's Old Man and in Kevin Egan: he refers to Bloom as a "bloody freemason" (*U* 12.300), much like old Cotter's reference to the "Rosicrucian" in "The Sisters" (*Dubliners* 11) as a sect steeped in ineffably alien, exotic, and degenerate otherness. The Citizen needs to believe in a distinct and separable binary opposition between the pure and the hybrid (the "mixed middling" in *U* 12.1658), between friend and foe, between the self and the other, the Irish and the non-Irish: "—*Sinn Fein!* says the citizen. *Sinn fein amhain!* The friends we love are by our side and the foes we hate before us" (*U* 12.523–524). In citing the slogan of the Fenian movement (*Sinn Fein amhain*, "ourselves alone"), the Citizen is also reflecting the Irish Republican Army's exclusivist rejection of Irish hybridity and polyculturalism, its fear and distrust of difference, its relegation of even some Irish citizens born in Ireland (like Bloom, Yeats, and Synge) to being "strangers in our house" (*U* 12.1151). Bloom is seen instead as dissembling and inauthentic: "—A wolf in sheep's clothing, says the citizen. That's what he is. Virag from Hungary! Ahasuerus I call him. Cursed by God" (*U* 12.1666–1667). Here we have, once again, the distrust of the Wandering Jew so long associated with cosmopolitanism and world citizenship, that race of shiftless exiles cursed by God to roam the earth, never having a home to call one's own, barred from any legitimate claim to nation or citizenship.

In contrast to the Citizen's exclusivity about authentic Irish citizenship, Bloom defines a nation as "the same people living in the same place. . . . Or also in different places" (*U* 12.1417–1431). As I have written in *Joyce, Race, and Empire*, "While [Bloom's] flustered answer is one the men make fun of, it is nonetheless significant (and powerful) in its tolerant breadth: by defining a nation simply as a people generally within a geographical location, Bloom's answer refuses . . . [to deny] the status of 'citizens' or 'nationals' to anyone within the community" (211–212). Furthermore, one might note that, however mockable and hapless a vacillation Bloom's definition of "nation" may be, it is a position which, as I suggested earlier, seems less hapless and rather more viable today, after the Good Friday agreement on Northern Ireland. As David Cairns and Shaun Richards write about Bloom, "As one who, literally, farts [in "Sirens"] on the indulgence of self-sacrifice, the Bloom to whom Molly assents in the sensual conclusion is the living antidote to all denials and exclusions; as an advocate of passion he embodies a sense of nation celebrating the sensual rather than the sacrificial and, as Jew, presents a cosmopolitan alternative to an Ireland whose sense of self was increasingly locked into the conservatism of the Gaelic homeland" (135).

Since Cusack was the founder of the Gaelic Athletic Association and "the man . . . that made the Gaelic sports revival" (*U* 12.880), it is appropriate that one of the arguments the Citizen and Bloom engage in is over Irish and English sports: "So off they started about irish sports and shoneen games the like of lawn tennis and about hurley and putting the stone and racy of the soil and building up a nation once again all to that" (*U* 12.889–891). By 1904 the Gaelic Revival had extended the issue of Irish identity and the cause of "building up a nation once again" even into the realm of sports, "by labeling particular games as 'racy of the soil' and 'Irish,' and by 'banning' particular others as un-Irish or shoneen or English" (Cheng, *Joyce* 206). At this point, the men in the pub join in singing "the immortal Thomas Osborne Davis's evergreen verses (happily too familiar to need recalling here) *A Nation Once Again*" (*U* 12.916–917).

Indeed, both "racy of the soil" and "A Nation Once Again" are attributed to Davis, an Irish poet and patriot who founded *The Nation* and who composed the "evergreen verses" of "A Nation Once Again," long the unofficial anthem of the IRA.[14] But the Citizen's invocation of Davis's slogan and song is very ironic, for, as Cairns and Richards note, "in the prospectus for *The Nation*, Davis addressed 'a nationality which may embrace Protestant, Catholic, and Dissenter, — Milesian and Cromwellian, — the Irishman of a hundred generations and the stranger within our gates'; hence, the motto of *the Nation*, to foster Irish Nationality and make it 'racy of the soil,' pointed to a nationality based on residence and willingness to acknowledge Irish rights and duties" (35). Which is to say that Davis, as one of the founding fathers of the nationalist movement and the author of the IRA anthem, espoused, ironically, a notion of "A Nation Once Again" that was very much a Bloomian sort of nation, rather than the kind of nation espoused by the Citizen. A further irony is that Davis, as a Protestant, would have been barred from Irish citizenship within the narrowly constructed definition of the Irish nation espoused by the likes of Cusack and Corkery. As Cairns and Richards note further, "Davis's writings continued to disseminate the ideas upon which he had hoped to construct a new nationalism, and in particular the concept of intersectarian co-operation for which he personally became an emblem" (41). Such a version of Irish nationalism would have looked very different from the one codified later by the nationalist movement, and a lot more like both Bloom's and that of the Good Friday agreement.

The discourse of Irish authenticity, based so much (as we have seen) on the embrace of the local and national and on the rejection and disavowal of the hybrid and cosmopolitan, results in yet a further irony with significant ongoing implications. After all, it has long been the desire of those millions who have, for centuries, worked for the unquestionably righteous cause of Irish home rule — from the Young Irelanders to Davis to Parnell to the Gaelic League to the IRA — that Ireland should join the brotherhood of nations as "a nation once again." Or, in the memorable words of Robert Emmet, "when my country takes her place among the nations of the earth, then, and not till then, let my epitaph be written" (see *U* 11.1284–1291). This has certainly been the ultimate goal of Irish home rule and Irish republicanism: to be recognized as one of the nations of the earth and not as just a colony of England, to be part of the brotherhood of nations, to be part of the world community, to be — in short — citizens of the larger world. Yet, according to the logic of Irish identity, Emmet's epitaph must never be written, must be forever deferred and postponed, for there is an intrinsic and self-defeating contradiction in this discourse of nationalist authenticity: after all, the authentic Irish self has already been narrowly defined as, and has petrified into, a rigid version of Celtic peasant purity; whereas actually to join the community of nations would naturally necessitate opening up one's borders (literally and metaphorically) to cultural and economic exchange, to hybridity, to difference, to an ongoing renegotiation and reconstruction of the developing nation and of Irishness. In order for this to happen, any rigid notion of an authentic self and national identity must be put under erasure and constantly rethought. This inherent contradiction between avowed purpose and internal logic can perhaps help explain the seeming reluctance of militant groups like the IRA (or Hamas and Hezbollah) to allow what they have so long fought for to actually come about, as seems to be the case now with the paramilitary splinter groups on both sides of the Troubles in Northern Ireland, for to do so would mean having to dismantle the very identities they have long constructed for themselves—the exclusivist notions of a pure and local Irishness, in counter-definition to the impure and hybrid inauthenticity of the transnational—which have given them for so long their very raison d'être. At the point that their Holy Grail would be finally achieved, they would—by this discursive logic—cease to exist or to be real in any meaningful sense. Thus, if one imagines that (to paraphrase Edward Said's memorable line about the "Orient") the *self* is also a career, then the maintenance of that self becomes all-important to one's authenticity; in this way, a rigid republican nationalism must unconsciously work against the very agenda that it consciously espouses and toward which it has worked so long.

I would like to conclude this chapter by telling a joke I once heard at a Jewish studies conference. A Jew, stranded on a desert island, managed to keep himself alive for five years until he was finally rescued by a fishing boat. His rescuers were astounded to discover that he had built on the island, by himself, not one but two synagogues. "Why would you need two synagogues when you are all alone here on this island?" they asked. He answered, "One *shul* for me to worship in on the Sabbath—and one which I wouldn't be caught dead in." My point in citing this amusing story is not to make any observation about Jewish factionalism, but rather to point out the important and simultaneous roles of both identification and *dis*-identification in the construction of a self and an identity. Both processes enter into our understanding of ourselves, and, rather than being contradictory, they are complementary and necessary to each other. As Naoki Sakai writes, "Contrary to what has been advertised by both sides, universalism and particularism reinforce and supplement each other; they are never in real conflict; they need each other and have to seek to form a symmetrical, mutually supporting relationship by every means in order to avoid a dialogic encounter which would necessarily jeopardize their reputedly secure and harmonized monologic worlds" (105). *Both* the fear of worldliness as well as the disdain of the provincial are positions that neglect to take into account that, in reality, culture is *both* local and global, both national and transnational, both particular and hybrid, both native and cosmopolitan. As Eagleton notes, "Local atavisms and predatory transnationalisms are sides of the same coin; the answer to whether the world is getting more regional or more global is surely a resounding yes" ("Ideology" 8).

These issues surrounding cosmopolitanism and globalism have, as I have been trying to suggest, some important and pressing ramifications for contemporary Ireland (both North and South) and for its own national and international identity/identities. After all, how well can the essential centrality of the Irish peasant—as a discourse of authenticity—hold up in a contemporary Ireland that is increasingly nonagrarian and urban; that has grown into an international economic powerhouse nicknamed "the Celtic Tiger"; that has a strong presence both economically and politically within the European Union and an even stronger presence in the cultural realms of international music, film, literature, and dance; and whose best-known and model citizens include such international figures as Bono, Neil Jordan, Seamus Heaney, and Mary Robinson? After all, we live at a point in time when the recent president of the Irish Republic, Robinson, a Catholic married to a Protestant, a woman and liberal feminist lawyer, now heads the very prototype of cosmopolitan idealism, the United Nations Commission for Human Rights.[15]

CHAPTER 4

International
Adoption and Identity

THE ANXIETY OVER AUTHENTIC CULTURAL HERITAGE

⌒•

I don't think I'm tangible to myself. I mean, I think one thing today and I think another thing tomorrow. I change during the course
of a day. I wake and I'm one person, and when I go to sleep I
know for certain I'm somebody else. I don't know *who* I am most
of the time.
—Bob Dylan (*Newsweek* 10/6/97: 64)

Wait. Five months. Molecules all change. I am other I now.
—James Joyce's Stephen Dedalus (*Ulysses* 9.205)

*A*doption, it is clear, is "in" nowadays
in the United States. The most visible sign of this reality is the increasingly
frequent sightings, on city streets, of white parents walking around with their
children of a race or ethnicity different from their own. Indeed, international
adoptions, most frequently involving a nonwhite child, more than doubled
in the 1990s—to 16,396 in 1999, up from 7,093 in 1990; at the same time,
open domestic adoptions are also on the rise (*New York Times* 3/12/00: AR
24). In previous generations kept in the closet as a dark family secret often
not known to either the adoptee or to other close family members, haunted
by what one adoption expert calls "the indelible brand of a bastard" (Pertman
4)—adoption is now increasingly a status displayed publicly and discussed
openly. If not yet chic, adoption is quickly becoming at least normative and
unremarkable.[1] The number of adoptions in the United States is rising fast
each year, and it is increasingly rare for anyone not to be personally familiar
with at least one family with an adopted child. The secrets and lies that had
been hidden in the closet previously now even qualify, in the United States,
for a government tax break, the Adoption Tax Benefit (instituted in 1998,

during the Clinton Administration), which adoptive parents can claim on their income tax returns: surely anything that is rewarded with a tax break can no longer be considered controversial. Furthermore, in February of 2001 a new law passed by Congress went into effect: the Child Citizenship Act grants automatic and immediate citizenship to most adopted children born abroad, provided that they are under eighteen and at least one parent or legal guardian is a U.S. citizen; previously, such applications for citizenship with the Immigration and Naturalization Service typically took about two years and involved complicated paperwork and bureaucracy. In short, in the United States adoption has been legitimized, not only in everyday culture but also formally and legally through public law and policies regulating citizenship, immigration, and taxes.

This sea change in popular attitudes toward what had previously been considered troubling or even shameful is reflected also in the popular culture at large. I first realized this in December 1998 at the annual Modern Language Association Convention, held that year in San Francisco. This is a scholarly conference I have been attending regularly since 1979. In reviewing the program for the convention, however, I was startled by something I had never seen before: there were four different panels listed that year on adoption and literature/culture; I don't recall ever noticing a single one before. Indeed, the visibility and proliferation of adoption in our culture were soon hard to miss, especially in popular film and television. As the *New York Times* reported a year later, "Today, the theme of adoption is familiar in movies, from madcap comedies like 'Flirting with Disaster' and 'Mighty Aphrodite' . . . to provocative dramas like 'Losing Isaiah' and 'Secrets and Lies' [one could add many others]. And now, . . . it also permeates television, cropping up on weekly series [such as *M.Y.O.B., Time of Your Life,* and *Party of Five,* all of which feature protagonists who are adoptees] and made-for-TV movies with startling frequency" (*New York Times* 3/12/00: AR 22). *Secrets and Lies*—a brilliant British film (from director Mike Leigh) about the reconciliation between a white mother and her long-lost, adopted black daughter—was nominated for several Academy Awards. One should also note the striking number of novels and short stories being published these days concerning adoption and adoptees. This explosion of adoption tales in popular culture surely reflects a healthy new openness toward this previously troubled social issue. Meantime, high-profile adoptions by celebrities and public figures such as Steven Spielberg, John McCain, Judy Woodruff, Tom Cruise, Jamie Lee Curtis, and Rosie O'Donnell repeatedly send the implicit message that adoption is now a normal, even laudable, way of making a family. As the *New York Times* went on to note: "With such openness, the phenomenon of adoption is no longer being regarded as an anomaly but as a human experience to which everyone can relate. 'The whole subject is out of the closet,' said Betty Jean Lifton, an adoption counselor and author of *Lost and Found* and *Journey of the Adopted Self.* 'It is now part of our general social reality'" (3/12/00: AR 24).

Whereas this new attitude of openness in matters of adoption is certainly a salutary development, it opens up some new concerns of its own. As "open adoptions" begin to be more common; as individual states (like Oregon; see below) begin to pass new laws opening up previously confidential adoption records; as adult adoptees increasingly embark on quests to find their roots and their birth parents, culminating often in reunions with birth parents (sometimes joyful, but sometimes unwanted and painful), this increasing openness is also a Pandora's box that has let out some complex and unforeseen concerns. Not only are there issues of privacy and confidentiality, which had been promised to both birth parents and adoptive parents, but such openness also highlights questions concerning one's "true" identity, prompting a search for one's roots and "real" heritage. These are questions and matters not without problems or controversy, many of which have to do with what I would call issues of "authenticity"—on both the personal and the cultural fronts. In this present chapter on adoption and identity, I want to focus particularly on issues involving race, ethnicity, and cultural heritage in adoption: on the concerns over how to be true to an authentic cultural, ethnic, or racial heritage. Consequently, my primary concerns here are with the two types of adoption designated by adoption experts as transracial adoptions and inter-country adoptions, particularly the latter (which most frequently involves adoptions of very young babies rather than older children in the U.S. foster-child system). As will be soon clear, the issues and topics here are messy, complicated, and frequently controversial; nor can I promise that my own analyses and positions will be the most popular or comfortable for the many thousands of parents (including myself) involved in such adoptions. But these same issues are, I believe, important reflections of Western cultural attitudes toward cultural identity and authenticity.

*M*any families have secrets they want to keep just that, secret—sometimes involving mental illness, criminal records, homosexuality, and AIDS in the family. Adoption still belongs to such a list, but certainly less so than before. The increasingly open attitude toward adoption means that more children are being told that they have been adopted, and frequently families are completely open to friends and acquaintances about an adoption in the family. Nevertheless, adoption continues to be a common family secret, and the opening of secrets is never uncontroversial. An adoptee seeking his or her birth parents is not always a welcome prospect to either the adoptive family or the birth parents.

In some ways, the search for one's birth parents by adoptees is part of a larger contemporary U.S. ethos and *Zeitgeist* that has witnessed a general explosion of interest in seeking one's roots and family ties, a measure of our collective belief in genealogical authenticity as a measure of who we really are. The Mormon-operated Family History Library in Salt Lake City, where I now live, houses the world's largest genealogical database and is often the first stop for those (Mormons and non-Mormons alike) searching for their genealogical roots and family trees. As *Newsweek* reported in 1997, "By some accounts tracing family histories is second only to gardening as a recreational activity for Americans. PBS is now running a new 10-part series on family-history research called 'Ancestors.' From African Americans searching the manifests of slave ships to the descendants of the first families of Vladivostok plying the Internet, Americans seem determined to pull on their roots" (2/24/97: 27). And surely adoptees have just as much right to know about their roots as other U.S. citizens. Some adoptees have even organized into an activist group called Bastard Nation, which has distributed leaflets at screenings of films such as *Secrets and Lies* and which notes that (unlike Britain) most states in the United States still deny adoptees access to the records of their own birth. But the debate over open adoption records pits the rights of adoptees—seeking to learn the truth of their birth and the details of their parentage and background, even to meet their birth parents and relatives—with the rights of both birth parents (especially birth mothers) and adoptive parents, many of whom participated in the adoption process only because they had been guaranteed confidentiality and sealed records.

On May 30, 2000, eighteen months after the state of Oregon passed the country's first voter-approved law giving adoptees access to their (previously sealed) birth records, the Supreme Court rejected an emergency request for a delay from a group of Oregon birth mothers who had sued to block the law—thus allowing the law finally to take effect, after an emotional and turbulent legal-appeals process. The Oregon law, Measure 58 (approved in November 1998), gives adoptees absolute access to the records, granting the rights of adoptees precedence over the rights of the birth mothers. Most states, under their current laws (though Oregon's new law may lead to similar changes in other states), however, still maintain prohibitions that keep adoption records sealed. While Oregon is the only state in the nation to have a voter-passed initiative on this issue, four other states—Tennessee, Alaska, Delaware, and Kansas—do have legal provisions which retroactively open birth records to adult adoptees without the consent of the birth mother. At the time (May 30, 2000), Oregon's Health Division had already received requests from over twenty-two hundred adoptees for their records under Measure 58; by the end of that week, the state began mailing out copies of these birth records.

It is a telling observation that, in the debates on this issue, both sides—adoptees seeking their birth records and birth mothers trying to deny them those same records—equally and repeatedly buy into the notion that your birth certificate and your birth records constitute "your identity." That general equation—that is, that what we loosely call our roots indeed constitute our identity—is one of the myths of authenticity we often take for granted. Western literature and myth tell us that stories of quests and searches—whether the medieval quest for the Holy Grail or the Odyssey or the Divine Comedy or Marlow's trip up the Congo in Joseph Conrad's *Heart of Darkness*—are ultimately really a search for one's self, for one's own identity and heart of darkness. As Christopher Keyser, creator of the popular TV series *Party of Five* and its spinoff *Time of Your Life,* notes about his character Sarah (played by Jennifer Love Hewitt), an adoptee who is featured in both series, "Sarah's search for her birth parents is essentially a metaphor for her search for herself" (*New York Times* 3/12/00: AR 22). But such a quest—when the acknowledged expectations (unlike the quests in past literature) are to find one's self and one's identity—is freighted with tremendously great expectations. This chapter explores the degree to which the finding of such a self or identity or heritage is even possible, or is itself a myth. Perhaps one could more safely conclude, as does a *New York Times* story on Oregon's Measure 58, that "the law properly extended to adoptees the right to gather information about the most basic of questions: where did they come from?" (5/31/00: A16). After all, "Where did you come from?" is a very different question, and perhaps not to be confused with the much more charged "Who *are* you?" which lies behind the expectations of finding one's identity.

This expectation—as I will discuss later in the chapter—is one also shared at times by a child's adoptive parents, whose sense of guilt may lead them into the belief that the adopted baby's cultural roots and heritage—as manifest by the racial, ethnic, or national background of the birth mother—are a vital and functional key to the child's innate identity and need to be cultivated with great pains. Such parents, no less than adoptees who expect to find their identity from their birth records, share in and participate in the need to believe in an essential and authentic identity handed down by one's cultural, racial, ethnic, or national "heritage." Such identities thus get "naturalized" and "essentialized" as innate and "natural." But I am more interested in the question of what these seekers will find: What is it they are looking for? Is it their heritage? Is it their identity? Will it tell them who they are? Will they then feel more real and authentic?

I would like to highlight these issues first by briefly discussing the striking case of Madeleine Albright. Although she herself was not adopted, her case—and other cases like hers—put these issues of authentic identities in stark relief. Unlike the stories of individuals who created (and then lived) invented identities for themselves quite different from the demonstrably "real" identity they had grown up with—like F. Scott Fitzgerald's Jay Gatsby, like the "Talented Mr. Ripley" (in the film by that name), like the many African Americans who have chosen to "pass" as whites (such as the protagonist of Philip Roth's novel *The Human Stain*)—stories like Albright's involve a past "identity" that the individual has not been at all aware of nor is trying to hide. In early 1997, Albright began her tenure as the first female Secretary of State of the United States, having been appointed by then-President Bill Clinton. The divorced mother of three adult daughters, she was already serving as the U.S. ambassador to the United Nations, and was already widely respected as a tough and principled stateswoman. A February 10, 1997, *Newsweek* feature story on Albright described her background and childhood thus: "Born in '37, she fled the Communist takeover of Czechoslovakia with her family in '48 and immigrated to the U.S. . . . Her rise is a great immigrant success story. In 1948 Madeleine Jana Korbel arrived in America. The girl was only 11 but had been a refugee twice—first in 1938, when the Nazis rolled into Czechoslovakia and forced her father, a diplomat, to flee to England. The second time came 10 years later when a Communist coup forced the Korbels to flee once again, this time to America. The family settled in Colorado" (24, 26).

Two weeks later Secretary Albright was once again featured on the cover of *Newsweek*, but this time it was because her biography needed to be revised, quite spectacularly: the family history, which had consistently portrayed the Korbel family as Catholic refugees from Czechoslovakia, had never mentioned (even to the three Korbel children, of whom Madeleine was the eldest) that the grandparents had been Jews killed in the Holocaust. As *Newsweek* now reported, "Thanks to the disclosures of the last fortnight, she is no longer—publicly or privately—merely the stunningly successful daughter of brave Czech immigrants. Now she is also the child who was kept in the dark of secrecy—never told that her grandparents were Jews who perished in the smoke of Auschwitz and Terezín; raised falsely on a glorious but invented history of Prague Easters and peaceful Catholic deaths" (2/24/97, 26). In spite of *Newsweek*'s assertion that Secretary Albright "is, after all, too accomplished, too mature, too busy, to have her identity reshaped at this late date" (26), Albright's own comments suggest that she herself is more aware and thoughtful about the complex implications of such revelations to the concept of a personal "identity." Indeed, she responds to the *Newsweek* interviewer by bringing up the analogy to adoption: "I've seen the questions from people wondering why I didn't put it together[,] . . . but let me say if it never occurred to you that you were adopted, why would you think that you're adopted? It was not a question" (26). If you didn't know you were adopted and didn't think you were adopted, then would your life—as you had lived it—be any less genuine or authentic? Does the past or the heritage you didn't know about change the solidity or reality of the life you did actually experience? Indeed, we might extend Albright's question further even to those who did know they were adopted at a young age but who never have lived as part of the birth parents' culture in any substantial way: Does the past or the heritage you *are* aware of (as that belonging to your birth parents) but did not share in any substantial way change the solidity or reality of the life you *did* experience? How important, then, is such an unlived past or heritage to your own authenticity and identity?

Indeed, examples like Albright highlight starkly a key question for all adoptees: "Who are you, *really*?" Is Albright, brought up Catholic, really Jewish? Is her Jewishness a past and a heritage that is her real, authentic self and identity, which she should now cultivate as much as possible (and make up for lost time)? Does her Jewishness in any way invalidate the identity she had heretofore felt comfortable with? It is interesting to note that, in both her mind and the public's, her identity will now henceforth be connected with Holocaust victims and the Holocaust, arguably the ultimate marker in our times of Jewish identity and authenticity (see Chapter 5). As Albright said, "I have been desperately sorry for victims of the Holocaust since I've been a conscious human being. But now that it's part of my story, it has even deeper meaning" (*Newsweek* 2/24/97: 31). Furthermore, her own story had already contained the outlines of the alienated condition of displacement that we traditionally ally with both modernity and with Jewishness (think Joyce, Paul Celan, and so on)—exile, refugee, diaspora, displaced modernism: "I had felt always in coming to America that my life and my parents' life was a reflection of the turbulence of the 20th century" (31). Her particular relationship with Jewishness makes Albright a singularly interesting cautionary tale in terms of Jewish authenticity, an issue I return to in Chapter 5. But her story is one of many real-life examples that ask these same questions about identity and authenticity. For example, the well-known Catholic novelist Mary Gordon (whose novels repeatedly rely on Catholic themes and issues) discovered, in the process of writing a biography of her beloved father (who had died when she was only seven), that her father was really a Jew who had converted to Catholicism, whose life and career were based on lies, and who had himself been a virulent anti-Semite. Or, for example, John Silber, the controversial former (and now reappointed) president of Boston University, grew up in a devout Presbyterian family, the son of German immigrants. Many years later, as an adult in Germany on a Fulbright scholarship, Silber met a cousin who first told him that his family was Jewish: he later learned that one of his father's sisters had been killed at Auschwitz and that his great-grandfather had been a famous Jewish scholar and artist in Berlin. In fact, Silber's father had kept his own Jewish past a secret not only from him but even from Silber's own mother, who was equally shocked by these revelations. One last example: in his book of memoirs titled *The Color of Water*, African American author James McBride tells the story of his mother, a rather light-skinned black woman—or so he thought. As an adult, he learned from her not only that she was white but that she was the daughter of an Orthodox rabbi; after marrying his black father, she had chosen to "pass" as black—in a stunning and subversive reversal of the dynamics of "passing"—so as to make the life of her family and her children less turbulent and racially fraught.

All of these examples (of nonadoptees) highlight starkly the question of what it is that composes our genuine, authentic personal identity. Is it our lived experience, the sum total of how we each have lived? Or is it our cultural, ethnic, or racial heritage, an inherited past but not one that has been necessarily lived or experienced—or, as in the above instances, even known about?[2] Does the knowledge of a past or heritage that you did not share in invalidate or de-authenticate the years of actually lived experience? Does such knowledge of another heritage or past add an important and undeniable authenticity to your life? As Silber said in the aftermath of learning about his father's Jewishness, "I am who I am, and that is not altered by this" (*Newsweek* 2/24/97: 29).

In July of 1997, Albright visited Prague, the city of her birth, for the first time since learning that she was born Jewish. Visiting the city's 550-

year-old Jewish cemetery, whose Pinkas synagogue contains, inscribed on the walls, the names of over seventy-seven thousand Czech Holocaust victims, she read the names of her grandparents among them. Having had several months to digest the implications of the revelation of her Jewish heritage earlier in the year, Albright was intelligently thoughtful about the implications of such knowledge, reading—at the end of her visit to the cemetery—a carefully considered statement she had composed early that morning. She commented, "Now that I am aware of my own Jewish background—and the fact that my grandparents died in concentration camps—the evil of the Holocaust has an even more personal meaning for me and I feel an even greater determination to ensure that it will never be forgotten." This "more personal meaning," was, however, tempered by her awareness that identity is a much more complex mix of elements than a past heritage that she had not actually shared, however authentic or inauthentic: "Identity is a complex compilation of influences and experiences—past and present. I have always felt that my life has been strengthened and enriched by my heritage and my past." And again: "I have always felt that my life story is also the story of the evil of totalitarianism and the turbulence of 20th century Europe." Finally, she concluded by noting that, "to the many values and facets that make up who I am, I now add the knowledge that my grandparents and members of my family perished in the worst catastrophe in human history. So I leave here tonight with the certainty that this new part of my identity adds something stronger, sadder and richer to my life" (*Los Angeles Times* 7/04/97: A9). To admit to a heritage and a past that strengthens and enriches one's present life, that adds something stronger and richer to one's ongoing identity formation, an identity that is a complex compilation of ongoing influences and experiences—grants the past a role in informing and enriching one's identity, while still acknowledging that one's identity is based largely on the complex compilation of lived experiences and influences. It does not collapse or conflate the two (heritage and identity).

Few of us would dispute that, in spite of her family's Jewish heritage, the lived experiences of a Madeleine Albright (or a John Silber) make up her (or his) real identity. But the relevance of these questions to adoption—especially to children adopted as infants or babies—should also be clear, for such adoptions make a radical mockery of any notions of an authentic identity. Children adopted as infants or babies have almost no experience of their birth parents and of the culture of their birth parents; rather, they grow up, like Albright or Silber, as members of their adoptive parents' community. Whether adoptees know they are adopted, whether the adoption records are open or closed, whether the family even knows who the birth parents are—adoptees' experience with their adoptive families in their adoptive homes, cultures, and nations is their actual lived experience, and—one might argue—their true identity. But when it comes to transracial adoptions and intercountry adoptions, these issues become—as we shall now see—much more controversial and problematic.

*I*n the rest of this chapter, I discuss some identity issues involving what in adoption studies and legal documents is referred to as ICA, inter-country adoption—which very often also involves TRA, transracial adoption. I want to distinguish the argument that follows from the particular issues surrounding domestic U.S. TRAs, even though those issues are also very interesting. There are three reasons why domestic TRAs (involving mostly African American and Native American children) are very different from ICAs: (1) The issue of African American adoptions is extremely and peculiarly charged because of the unique place of African Americans in U.S. history and culture, and the long, troubled historical baggage involved; (2) Native American adoptions are also a unique and extraordinarily emotional topic, in which the concern about "cultural genocide" is arguably quite real, given the precarious survival of contemporary Native American culture to begin with; (3) but, most important, there is the age issue. Adoptees from domestic foster care typically are older and have spent some time living with their birth mothers; as Adam Pertman notes, "Their sensibilities and sensitivities therefore can differ markedly from those . . . of children adopted as infants from abroad" (19). The questions involving identity and cultural heritage are consequently very different; as R.A.C. Hoksbergen writes, "Obviously . . . the age of the child when placed in the [adoptive] family is of importance" to the way in which issues of identity and cultural heritage take shape (81). The older the child is when adopted, the stronger his/her sense of an already-established identity and familial/cultural background derived from the birth family. In the case of ICA, however, the majority of adoptees are infants or very young children—and the questions of identity and culture are consequently quite different from those in domestic adoptions. I wish to address specific issues involving identity in international adoptions.

*P*ertman notes that "white men and women, married and single, are forming transracial families at an unparalleled pace" in the United States today (159). The main reason for this is the startling jump in ICAs noted at the beginning of this chapter. Indeed, Americans adopt more children internationally than the rest of the planet combined (Pertman 51). Most of these are infants or very young children (in fact, the availability abroad of young infants is one main reason for the ICA explosion, since most adoptive parents wish to adopt as young a child as possible). Most of the adopting parents are white: over 90 percent of parents adopting infants outside the domestic child-welfare system are white (Pertman 22), whereas 60 percent of ICAs involve children who are *not* white (Pertman 159). Which is to say that, in large part, the adoption revolution has been fueled by white U.S. parents adopting foreign, mostly nonwhite, babies. As Rita Simon and Howard Altstein, two of the most respected, longstanding experts on adoption, write, "[Today] ICA is a story of global race relations, where nonwhite, free-for-adoption Third World children are adopted by white families living in the West" (6).[3]

Whereas no systematic records are kept for domestic adoptions, international adoption is tracked very precisely because everyone who enters the United States must fill out legal documents with the Immigration and Naturalization Service. So we know, for example, that in 1999 there were exactly 16,396 ICAs ("and the trend line looks like an upward slope for the foreseeable future"; Pertman 23). Whereas the breakup of the Soviet Union in the early 1990s provided a large number of Russian children for adoption, and during that time the number of adoptions from Romania and Central America were also on the rise, the ICA explosion since then is, to a large extent, a tale of Asia and the United States. Ever since the Korean War, South Korea had been the major source of young ICA adoptees until the 1990s (with well over one hundred thousand Korean-born children adopted by Western families during that period; Simon and Altstein 7); in 1989, for example, the Republic of Korea provided the United States with 3,552 adopted children, almost half of the 7,948 ICAs recorded that year. Since the Vietnam War, Vietnam has also been a significant source for ICAs. But the main reason for the ICA explosion has been mainland China: in the 1990s, China opened its doors to the adoption of its children, especially the huge number of unwanted little girls as a result of the one-child policy in a culture that values boys over girls. Such adoptions, one should note, consist of a collective international act of mercy: it is estimated that about 150,000 girls are abandoned every year in the People's Republic of China, not counting the unknown number who are drowned or otherwise killed (Simon and Altstein 11). In 1990 there were only 28 adoptions from the People's Republic of China into the United States; in 1998, there were 4,206, easily surpassing the 1,829 Korean adoptions that year. "As the twentieth century closes, adoption of Chinese orphans is one of the most preferred forms of intercountry adoption" (Simon and Altstein 9). In 1998, two-thirds of all ICAs came from just three countries: Russia (4,491), People's Republic of China (4,206), and South Korea (1,829). The other countries with significant numbers of adoptees were Guatemala (911), Vietnam (603), India (478), and Romania (406) (Simon and Altstein 19).

During the previous ten years, annual adoptions from Asia had risen by more than 50 percent, from 5,112 to 7,827; but the real explosion was from China: in this ten-year period, the number of children adopted annually shot from 33 in 1989 to 4,206 in 1998! In New York City alone, about one thousand Chinese girls under the age of five were adopted during the 1997 calendar year (Simon and Altstein 112). As a result, white parents accompanying their young Chinese girls to the playground or supermarket have become, in the past few years, a typical and normal part of our daily landscape.

One big issue such a huge number of transracial ICAs raises is the question of cultural "heritage": such a contemporary cultural reality has spawned a palpable anxiety among white parents over how to provide their adopted, nonwhite foreign babies with an authentic cultural heritage. But as Barry Richards, another longstanding expert on adoption, notes, "Alongside the term 'identity,' another unexamined rhetorical category in the literature [about adoption] is 'heritage.' Transracial placements, it was argued, destroy heritage, or take it away from the child" (108). It is this assumption, in the context of ICAs, that I want now to address.

*T*he concern, on the part of white adoptive parents, over losing the authentic cultural heritage of their adopted children has resulted in attempts at retrieval and preservation that, in many ways, parallel the dynamics and problems of attempts by nationalist movements to preserve a lost national culture (whether the Gaelic Revival, the Aztlan movement, Hindu nationalism, and so on). In the case of ICA, this quest for an authentic heritage takes the form of what I call a "roots mania." Now I want to be clear that I am not trying to criticize this well-meaning and mostly salutary impulse. Many white U.S. couples adopting foreign, transracial babies are genuinely trying to take the roots and cultural heritage of their adoptee babies very seriously. There are regular gatherings of children adopted from the same country, often from the same adoption agency or orphanage; for example, in the San Francisco Bay Area a number of families who have adopted over the years from the same small Taiwanese orphanage my own son was adopted from gather regularly for Fourth of July picnics and Christmas parties. More and more frequently, such parents attend cultural festivals with their children and send them to "culture camps" so that they can immerse themselves in their "cultural heritage." Especially in the case of Asian adoptees, this is now becoming something of a cottage industry, what one adoption expert refers to as a "heritage industry" (Richards 108), teaching the children about their homeland, its customs, its traditions. This seems especially true of the parents of Chinese girls; says Maureen Evans, the former executive director of the Joint Council on International Children's Services: "as a group, the parents of the Chinese girls have been more educated and more sharply focused about their children's heritage from the start" (cited in Pertman 57). Many adoptive families nowadays are much like Russell and Susan Correia, a white couple who "started their multiethnic parenting the minute they brought their ten-month-old daughter home to Portland, Maine, dressing her in clothes they had bought in China and decorating her room with artwork from her homeland" (cited in Pertman 58; I might add that these details suggest to me an unacknowledged Orientalist urge to preserve the girl as an exotic little China doll); meantime, the Correias are not only learning to cook Chinese at home but are learning Mandarin in order to speak Chinese to a little girl who was probably never able to speak it to begin with — and will likely not have many occasions to do so in Portland, Maine. As Pertman puts it, "The adoptive mothers and fathers are most often willing, even eager, to learn their children's native language, take them to cultural festivals, and engage in a host of other activities to ensure a sense of connection" (54). Years later, many such families will take what the adoption literature refers to as "roots journeys" — group tours organized by adoption services or organizations taking adoptive parents with their adolescent adopted children to visit the child's country of origin (Hoksbergen 75).

I first began thinking of these issues when, right after my wife, Maeera, and I had adopted a six-month-old baby from Taiwan, Maeera joined an email chat group of parents in the United States who had adopted Chinese babies, the local Los Angeles chapter of Families with Children from China: in reading over the members' often frantic email exchanges, most of which had to do with how to provide themselves with authentic Chineseness, I was astonished by the palpable anxiety and, indeed, feverish mania about ensuring that their adopted children received an authentic Chinese cultural heritage. Surely such anxiety suggests some repressed or unacknowledged deeper issues at stake. (At one point the group decided to organize a dragon-boat race around the time of Chinese New Year's: which led me to wonder, since I was born in China and speak Chinese and was raised Chinese, what it meant about *my* Chineseness that we had never bothered with dragon-boat races; or was this merely another packaged, consumable version of Chineseness, like fortune cookies?)

Oddly (at least oddly to my mind), there has been no controversy or dispute or even mild criticism over this mania for authenticity and the notion of a "heritage industry." I have read all the adoption literature I can get my hands on, and all the experts agree; as Pertman puts it, one of the characteristics of what he calls the "adoption revolution" is that adoption agencies and social workers now all "advise . . . parents to incorporate their children's heritage into daily life" (53). But this very notion—of being able to preserve a baby's authentic identity through some immersion in his/her cultural "heritage"—carries with it some unexamined assumptions which I would like to now interrogate.

*F*irst of all, whose identity is really at stake here? Whose anxiety is at issue, whose concern over authenticity? After all, as Simon and Altstein admit in their longitudinal studies of adoptive families, after years of such attempts at such cultural immersion, "it was the children rather than the parents who were more likely to want to call a halt to these types of activities" (67). One wonders, then—in the parents' honest attempts to deal with the challenge of raising a child so visibly different from themselves—if perhaps the identity problem and the challenges at issue are not really the parents' own unacknowledged struggles with the challenges of difference. What that repressed and unacknowledged problem is is a matter I will return to shortly.

Second, this unexamined notion of cultural "heritage" is, in most adoption literature, naively and unquestioningly equated with cultural "identity." Now, contemporary cultural studies and postcolonial studies (and gender studies, queer studies, and so on) have repeatedly troubled the very notion of what "identity" means to begin with.[4] But, whatever it means, a person's identity, to my mind, has to be related to his or her lived experience—that is, to the ongoing life experiences that shape one's self, one's identity, whereas, for a child adopted as a baby, the cultural "heritage" of one's birth mother can only be a dead past detached from one's actual lived experience (and presumably from the actual lived experience of the adoptive parents); and the immersion in such a past culture, like that of a nationalist search for origins and like nationalist "revivals," can only seem an act of "reviving" what is already lost (more than actual "preservation"), an exercise in cultural nostalgia and sentimental Orientalisms.

Let's look at three specific case studies of such efforts, all culled from the national media and all of which follow the universal consensus in praising such exercises in cultural retrieval. The October 4, 1999, issue of *Newsweek* ran a story (titled "Culture by the Campfire: Families with Kids from Overseas Share Their Stories") focusing on two "culture camps" for foreign adoptees, one for Chinese kids in Maine, and one for kids from India in Snow Mountain, Colorado. "Hidden Valley looks a lot like the dozens of other camps that dot the woods of central Maine. There's a lake, some soccer fields and horses. But the campers make the difference. They're all American parents who have adopted kids from China" (75). Hidden Valley was started by the Boston chapter of Families with Children from China, which—in 1999—listed 650 families on its membership roster. Activities at the camp include not only swimming and riding horses but also "singing Chinese songs or making scallion pancakes" (75). The story cites one parent, Diana Becker of Montville, Maine, watching her three-year old daughter dancing to a Chinese version of "Twinkle, Twinkle Little Star" (how is *that* "Chinese"?), commenting that while her daughter "may be growing up American, her soul is Chinese" (75). Comments like that always make me nervous. What does it mean to say that her "soul" is Chinese? As with the previously discussed claims about an Irish spirit or an Irish soul, such statements are essentialist and stereotyped, whether in the form of sentimental blarney or genuine affection. The *Newsweek* story goes on to note that the camp is a continuation of classes in Chinese language, dance, art, and calligraphy that many of the kids attend during the year. One of the parents notes that "when we rented out a theatre [in Boston] for 'Mulan,' it was packed"; one of the art teachers is then quoted as saying that "our mission is to preserve the heritage" (75). I have no question that a good teacher of Chinese language or calligraphy can teach something useful to anyone—native Chinese, Chinese American, white, or otherwise. But what heritage is being preserved here? The traditional Chinese story of Fa Mu Lan is a fascinating and important literary work which has been variously interpreted, including the Asian American riff done on it by Maxine Hong Kingston in *The Woman Warrior*; but if showing Disney's film *Mulan* to young children is part of the mission to "preserve the heritage," then we are really in trouble, mistaking Orientalism-for-consumption for cultural "authenticity."

On July 26, 2000, the *New York Times* (page A21) ran a story about a conference held the previous weekend in Hasbrouck Heights, New Jersey, for adopted Koreans and their families. As the children learned Korean-style brush painting, one of the organizers (Thomas Grove Masters, himself a Korean adoptee) advised parents on the importance of learning about their children's native culture: "Adoption is also a sense of loss—loss of their roots, parts of their personal identity. . . . For the most part, the children don't even realize that they have lost this part of themselves until much later" (one wonders if, like nationalist nostalgias, that loss is an "invented tradition" that one then later "rediscovers"). The story cites the visits (the "roots journeys") many Korean adoptees take to the "homeland" when they become teenagers; the story's writer notes, however, that "the journey back to Korea, whether metaphorical or actual, can be rough. In Korean society, adoptees are seen as victims of misfortune, and adoptees say Koreans there and here sometimes reject them for being too Western or for not speaking better Korean." Such a Catch–22 should ring a bell of recognition with any hyphenated person confronting his or her parents' cultural heritage: indeed, it seems to me that the issue of cultural retrieval here is hardly any different from the dynamics confronting a Korean American or Chinese American (or whatever) child, born in the United States to native Asian parents, who is visiting his or her parents' Asian country for the first time—a topic frequently explored in Asian American literature and film (for example, Wayne Wang's movie *A Great Wall*); nor, for that matter, are such "culture camps" for adoptees any different from the summer camps Irish American students often attend ("retribalization centers," as one anthropologist calls them), camps that teach Gaelic language, Irish step dancing, and Irish music (such summer camps exist, for example, at Boston College and Notre Dame), often in conjunction with visits to the home country. The writer of the article also quotes one of the organizers (another Korean adoptee) as warning that "some parents clung to their children's ethnic identity as if it were their own, or treated their forays into Asian culture as an exotic adventure. She cautioned against forcing culture camps and language lessons on a reluctant child" (A21). This cautionary observation raises not only the question of cultural Orientalism/exoticism/tourism, but again the question of whose identity and whose anxiety is really at stake here.

Finally, that same month the *San Diego Tribune* published, on the front page of the Sunday paper (July 9, 2000), a story on international adoption. The piece focused on a white couple who decided to adopt from Vietnam: "The Busches . . . learned some of the language, toured the Southeast Asian country and in April went to an orphanage near Hanoi to bring home Ha Thi Thu Yen, then 6 months old." Now the Busches "shop at Asian markets and dine at Vietnamese restaurants. And Michelle Busch speaks to [her daughter, renamed] Allison in Vietnamese on occasion. '*Uong sua*,' she says to her daughter. Meaning 'drink milk,' it is one of many Vietnamese phrases she learned." The story goes on to quote Jo Rankin, co-founder of the Association of Korean Adoptees, as saying that "what the Busches are doing should be required of all parents who adopt children from another culture." Yet eating Vietnamese food and mouthing some Vietnamese phrases in a dislocated context that is not organic to your lived experience seem to me the exact recipe for what we might call "cultural tourism," which—like much actual tourism (or even the cultural tour groups involved in "roots journeys")— merely replicates the dynamics and exoticism of colonialist ideology.

Finally, one more question about authentic cultural "heritage": *Which particular heritage is that? How does one decide?* After all (as Chapter 3 argues), an authentic culture is itself an elusive and arguably fantasmatic notion to begin with. How are white parents in the United States then to discern and retrieve an authentic culture that even native cultural theorists argue about? Take the case of my young son, Gabi, for example. Any Chinese culture I or my wife introduce him to at least has (and will have) a lived component and experience—not only because I myself was born and raised Chinese, speak Mandarin, and so on, but because half of Gabi's relatives— that is, my whole side of the family—are Chinese speakers who visit him regularly and are very much part of his continuing lived experience. However, should Maeera and I decide to further introduce Gabi to authentic Chinese culture, I am confronted with the question of what and which Chinese culture(s). Both my parents were from the Chinese mainland (which by tradition as well as upbringing makes me a mainlander), but I myself was actually born in Taiwan. So should Gabi get mainland Chinese culture or its very different contemporary Taiwanese variant? Should he speak Mandarin, since that's the national language (on both the mainland and Taiwan) and is my mother's native dialect (she's from Hupei and thus grew up speaking a different dialect and eating very different foods from my southern Chinese father, who was Cantonese [so in fact which cuisine should Gabi get?])? Or should Gabi learn Cantonese (since my father was Cantonese and by Chinese patrilineal custom I am Cantonese, too, regardless of where I was actually born)? But then again my father was actually from Chao-zhou, a distinct part and separate ethnicity within Canton province with its own peculiar dialect that hardly anyone else I know (including my mother and myself) speaks or understands; surely I must not have to teach *that* dialect to Gabi. But then again Gabi was born in Taiwan (as was I), and his birth mother was, I think, of native Taiwanese stock—not of mainland Chinese roots like myself. The native Taiwanese have their own language and history and customs (and cuisine), with which I have very little familiarity. Is that the culture that I have a responsibility to maintain as Gabi's authentic identity?

As you can see, these are very complex and real choices—even for a Chinese native like myself. Even if the parents meticulously introduce a child to Chinese culture and language, if the avowed purpose is to be true to your child's authentic heritage, how can you be sure you've chosen the *correct* heritage? How are white parents in the United States supposed to negotiate, discriminate among, and make choices about different authentic Chinese cultures—when they are often not even aware of such differences and subtleties? Hence such choices are not likely or frequently to be made, however scrupulously, on the basis of actual lived experience, but rather on the basis of cultural stereotypes about China dolls and women warriors. Not knowing enough perhaps makes it convenient and possible to make such choices; but a little knowledge is a dangerous thing, resulting most frequently (and unconsciously) in Orientalisms and fetishizations of an exoticized otherness, evocations of an exoticized but dead past, or exercises in what the late anthropologist Renato Rosaldo has so aptly coined "imperialist nostalgia."

I want, at this point, to insert some caveats and clarifications, for I want to be very careful to make clear that I am not criticizing the basically ethical and responsible impulse behind this urge for authenticity on the part of adoptive parents and adoption experts: the attempt to be sensitive to the issues of difference is an important, responsible, and honest response to the challenges of raising a foreign child. Everyone's heart is in the right place here: it's not the heart I am worried about. Nor do I want to provide any ammunition for the cultural right, which repeatedly has tried to erase cultural, ethnic, and racial difference and specificity under the banners of universalism, assimilation, and triumphalist globalism; I have, in my own work, long been committed to a careful, anti-universalizing, anti-essentialist elaboration of racial and cultural identities. So I don't want to make this chapter in any way sound like the right wing's mantra that "race doesn't matter": because my argument is precisely, as you will now see, that this issue is in fact all about race.

In fall 2001 I was watching the season's final episode of the hit HBO comedy series *Sex and the City*: in the episode, New Yorkers Charlotte and Trey, a married couple having trouble conceiving a baby, consider adopting a "Mandarin baby" (as Charlotte puts it). Charlotte starts trying to learn Mandarin—for "her heritage" ("her" indicates a still hypothetical but very clearly female Chinese baby). A bit later in the episode, Charlotte and Trey attend a

Scottish fling, since Trey is of Scottish American ancestry. This hypothetical question then occurred to me: if, say, a typical white American couple (not of Scottish ancestry) happened to adopt a little white baby from Scotland, would they feel the same anxiety, even hysteria, about authenticity—and drag that baby (and themselves) to Gaelic lessons, bagpipe playing, kilt wearing, and highland flings? Or another hypothetical example: in the unlikely scenario that some white parents in the United States happen to adopt a white baby who also happens to be a Chinese national born in China (say, of white missionaries or business people who went to China and then stayed), would anyone feel it was their ethical obligation to make this white baby take Mandarin lessons and lessons in Chinese culture? Why not? He or she is a native Chinese national, after all. Indeed, why does no one seem overly concerned about providing the thousands of Romanian or Russian babies adopted every year by American parents with Slavic language lessons or making them eat borscht instead of macaroni and cheese?[5]

What questions like this suggest is that what is really at issue here is not cultural heritage at all, not even national identity, but a form of difference that is even more threatening, a general category that Irish scholar David Lloyd calls the "unrecognizable" (*Anomalous* 10), that blind spot in any particular cultural discourse which must remain unrecognized and repressed. And in this case it is, of course, race—for it is clear that we would not apply the same dynamics of authenticity when there is no racial difference involved—that is, with white babies. The real parental guilt at stake here is not over cultural or national difference, but over that old bugaboo of a reified difference that can't even be defined (and really doesn't even exist), that tragic accident we have learned to call "race" (or really, here, skin color). By continuing to make the assumption that race is what determines difference in cultural identity (which we then smoke-screen by convincing ourselves it is really a matter of cultural and national difference), we are buying into racialist judgments and into the flawed and dangerous constructions of racial difference. How else to explain the fact that it is only the 60 percent of foreign adoptions involving *non*white children which seems to elicit this anxiety over cultural authenticity? It is our *own* guilt and anxiety that is operative here: the white liberal guilt of white parents having to come to terms with the realities of racial difference in their own family units—and, in doing so, reaching for that old saw, that familiar and convenient balm, the knee-jerk instinct to believe in identifiable and simple national or racial authenticities, the essentialisms of absolute difference. Rather than think through and struggle with the complex and troubling reality that we are, each one of us—

white/black/yellow/whatever—messy and complex mixes of things (including different races and cultures), we become anxious about authenticity, and this anxiety itself reflects—and is part of—a broad fear of cultural complexity and messiness. The reality is that we like it simple, but we are all in fact messy mixes: as Ward Connerly—the African American University of California regent and prominent opponent of affirmative action, who is actually half Irish American and thinks of himself as mixed-race—said, "If I talk about my Irish heritage, whites laugh and blacks accuse me of trying to be white" (quoted in Page, A19). It is easier to want things simple, to think that we each have one, definable authentic identity and cultural heritage; it is much harder to think through the implications of cultural hybridity and mixedness. As Orlando Patterson at Harvard put it (also in the context of blacks and Irish), "The real paradox here is that the one-drop rule succeeded all too well, so much so that its most devoted adherents today are African Americans, in spite of its devastating role in their own history of exclusion" (Patterson 16). Similarly, the implicit message we are teaching our children—adopted and otherwise—is that those who are racially different must remain different, are authentically and irremediably other, must always remain marked as different (no matter how Americanized), have a different identity (by sheer essence) from the rest of us.

Keep in mind that Asian Americans and Chicanos, for example, even when they were born in this country, are often mistaken as and treated as "foreign" and not-belonging—merely because of their skin color. As educated, liberal-thinking people, we abhor this practice of labeling such citizens as ineradicably other and alien, of marking them by their skin color even though they may be as American as we are; we call it "racial profiling." Then why are we so willing, on the basis of a few months of an infant's life spent in a different birthplace, to eagerly label and mark an adopted baby on those same terms—as innately, essentially, and authentically foreign and other?

I am not recommending that adoptive parents be blind to the realities, in the United States, of both racial and national difference. We *do* need to prepare our adoptive children to learn how to deal with a world in which racial difference still matters, and in which Americans who don't look white (Chicanos, Asian Americans, and so on) are still considered foreign. It is still useful—and laudable—for both adoptive parents and adopted children to learn about the child's country of origin (not least because it teaches everyone greater understanding and tolerance of difference). It *is* important, indeed essential, to instill a bicultural awareness in a child who will likely, at some point in his or her life, need or want some sense of connection to the history, language, and culture of the birth parents' heritage. But all of this applies equally to any Asian American child, as well as to any child of hyphenated or mixed-race heritage; these unfortunate realities are not peculiar to foreign adoptees. Indeed, the challenges the foreign-adopted, transracial baby will face are, in many ways, the same challenges which any hyphenated-American minority child or mixed-race child faces, with all the attendant liabilities of ethnic/racial minority status and cultural double consciousness. Most of them will also try to learn something about their parents' cultural heritage (whether it's Vietnamese, Cuban, whatever)—but will likely do so without mistaking that heritage for their current, real-life identity; and without imagining that that heritage is who they "really are." And if everyone involved in international adoptions can be aware that this anxiety over heritage has as much to do with race (and racial difference) as with culture or nation, then the pursuit of such a "heritage" or "mother culture" can perhaps take place in a more sensible and productive, less essentialist, perspective.

Indeed, it is in the best interests of the child to be exposed to others who are like him or her. As Hoksbergen points out, "As the child grows older, the number of groups to which he belongs will expand and the child will grow more conscious of differences between groups and of the groups to which he belongs. In sociological terms, the latter are called 'membership-groups.' These 'membership-groups' are of great importance for the formation of identity consciousness"(80). In the case of, say, adopted Asian babies, some of the appropriate membership groups—or "identity groups," we might prefer to call them—might be specific, local Asian American communities and group activities, not only because other Asian Americans face similar challenges (being hyphenated or mixed-race in a white-dominant country), but because these groups are live and growing, real communities that can provide a lived and shared and particular Asian American (Chinese American, Korean American, and so on) experience for its members. These groups, too, are concerned with keeping in touch with their cultural heritage.

In other words, to my mind the ICA baby presents to adoptive parents a double challenge and a double responsibility, in terms of the child's identity. The first part involves the identity issues in *any* adoption—whether white or transracial, foreign or domestic: any adopted child, in addition to needing help with all the emotions and struggles that may result from coming to grips with one's adopted status, will need help sorting out and accepting the distinctions between his/her adopted family life (that is, the life and identity he or she now has) and the birth parents' identity and their particular backgrounds. The second part involves the challenges of growing up mixed or hyphenated in the United States—whether foreign-born or native-born, adopted or not adopted. Now, I am not trying to say that there is no difference between the situation of an Asian American child born in the United States and the situation of an ICA child adopted by white parents; but those differences do not justify imagining their identities as so radically different. Nor are the challenges they will each face so dissimilar, including being repeatedly treated and considered "foreign" because of skin color. The challenges for adoptive parents are, first, to *not* imagine that the child's birth parentage and "roots" (whether foreign or domestic) actually define the child's identity, and, second, in the case of ICAs, to not imagine that either race or foreign birth inherently defines the child's identity. Rather, identity is a constantly shifting, progressively accumulating, individually varying thing, based on the lived experience of live individuals in live and growing communities. Such personal *identity* can, of course, also be enriched, inflected, and informed by an awareness of the cultural *heritage* of one's birth parents. But the two things are not the same.

CHAPTER 5

The Inauthentic Jew

JEWISHNESS AND ITS DISCONTENTS

~.

*T*he vexed cultural debates surrounding difficult questions such as "What is Jewish literature?" or "What constitutes Jewish American culture?" are strikingly complex and difficult[1] —in large part because they all depend on an even more vexed and basic issue: "What is Jewishness?" As a category of identity, Jewishness is notoriously hard to pin down, since it is difficult to determine even what *type* of identity designation "Jewishness" is: Is it a religion? a nation? a race? an ethnicity? a peculiar history? a distinct culture? As a composite, omnibus term in general popular usage—and it is popular usage and perceptions I am mostly concerned with in this chapter—"Jewishness" is surely a bit (actually a lot) of each of these things. But if we have a hard time even specifying what *type* or *sort* of thing "Jewishness" is, how are we to determine with any clarity who qualifies as "Jewish" and thus who can authentically speak for Jewishness?

I can at least begin by saying that I am clearly neither of these things: neither Jewish nor one who can authentically speak for Jewishness. My own particular relationship to Jewishness is an especially tenuous, precarious, and complex one. I am a literary and cultural critic, currently writing a book on issues of authentic identity; Chinese by birth and upbringing (and now a naturalized U.S. citizen), raised Roman Catholic, married to a Jewish woman who is herself a literary scholar and an expert in Jewish studies and literature. Consequently, many of our closest friends are Jewish studies scholars and experts. A typical *Shabbat* dinner at our house might find Jewish scholars, theologians, rabbis, poets, etc.—many of whom are also our close personal friends—around the table. The guest list at our wedding included what someone referred to as a Who's Who of Jewish scholars on the West Coast. Our son, a Chinese boy adopted as an infant from Taiwan, is being brought up Jewish, speaks Hebrew, and is thoroughly involved in religious Jewish life. Whereas I myself have chosen not to convert, in a sense Jewish culture has become for me also an adopted culture, for I have been a thoroughly involved participant for years in the theological, halachic, and cultural discussions about Jewishness that swirl around our home life, our extended family life, and our professional lives. I cannot and would not wish to claim the status of insider or of expert on issues of Jewishness; my perspective, rather, is that of an outsider with a privileged view of the inside. Like F. Scott Fitzgerald's Nick Carraway, I am both "within and without" the story of Jewishness.

In the first half of this chapter, I outline and discuss the labyrinthine complexities and subtle challenges to understanding even the very nature of "Jewishness," especially in popular usages and contemporary understandings of that term among U.S. Jews. For that reason, I am contextualizing this initial discussion less around the extensive and sophisticated scholarly studies of such issues within academic Jewish studies, and focusing rather more on popular understandings, public surveys and statistics, and journalistic accounts of these matters. These popular perceptions and cultural disseminations result in complex situations which produce certain cultural anxieties and insecurities: in the second half of this chapter I explore, and speculate about, some of the implications of these complexities and anxieties, focusing particularly on the cultural and ideological work being performed in contemporary Jewish culture by both the Holocaust and the state of Israel. In these ways, the very complexities and resultant anxieties surrounding Jewishness serve almost as a test or limit case of the troubling paradoxes inherent in popular notions of "identity."

What Is Jewishness?

According to Genesis, Jacob, the son of Isaac and grandson of Abraham, spent twenty years in the desert in exile. One night, alone and alongside a river bank, he met a stranger with whom he wrestled until dawn. Since Jacob would not give up, the stranger broke Jacob's hip at the socket, leaving him with a limp for the rest of his life. Before he left, the stranger—an angel according to many sources—renamed Jacob, calling him "Isra-el"—that is, one who wrestles with God. This story, then, is a foundational story for Israel and for the Israelite, the person who wrestles with Elohim.

Biblical scholars have, ever since, debated the meaning of this story: Whom did Jacob wrestle with—man, angel, demon, or God?[2] If he was alone, wasn't he actually then wrestling with himself? And what is the meaning of the painful limp he carries with him for the rest of his life? Says Rabbi Alfred Wolf, founding director of the Skirball Institute on American Values and rabbi emeritus of Los Angeles's Wilshire Boulevard Temple, "The message is that Jews have always been people who wrestle with God. They ask tough questions. They don't agree with the prevailing wisdom. They're skeptical." He adds, "Jews have historically been outsiders, and the limp of Jacob is what truly sets them apart. It's a mark of being different" (*Los Angeles Times* 4/23/98: A26). As a foundational story of the origins of the Jewish people, the naming of "Israel" is a richly suggestive one in terms of how an "Israelite" is defined: Are Jews those who wrestle with God, questioners and skeptics who thus grapple with Scripture and with the Word, people always interested in "learning" and in "*shul*," the People of the Book? Are they people who wrestle with themselves, and with their own identities and consciences? or with the world itself? If Jacob's limp is "what truly sets them apart" and is "a mark of being different," what is that particular difference which needs to be marked upon the Jewish body? Is it (as Wolf says) that they are "outsiders"? Is the role of the wanderer—the exile, the outsider, even that of the victim—the mark of their difference? If so, is this difference something Jews should accept and even embrace with pride? What exactly is the mark—and meaning—of Jewish difference and authenticity?

Is it a matter of race or ethnicity? Is it a matter of religion and religious observance? Is it a matter of a particular history and culture? Is it a matter of nation? On the one hand, I should clarify that this chapter is written specifically from the perspective and within the contexts of contemporary Jewish American culture; at the same time, the issues cannot be so narrowly construed, since "Jewishness" is also a category that claims to transcend national boundaries and cultures. One should further note that all of these broad terms and categories—race, ethnicity, religion, culture, history, and nation—are by themselves contested terms that elude clear definition: think particularly of the debates since the mid-twentieth century, within various intellectual disciplines, over the very meaning of the concepts of "race," "nation," and "culture." Since it is hard to pin down what each of these terms actually means, and since Jewishness as a category of identity keeps slipping and sliding between each of these four broad and hard-to-define registers (race/ethnicity, religion, culture/history, and nation), it is no wonder that it is so difficult to know what Jewishness means. The result is a peculiar and insistent anxiety about identity that itself (at least in contemporary Jewish American culture) is sometimes recognized as a symptom of Jewish insecurity, a crisis of identity. After all, how can Jews know who they are if they cannot even know if they are really and authentically, sufficiently, "Jewish"? As Alain Finkielkraut points out in his provocative and evocative study of

The Imaginary Jew, "You can rarely pick out a Jew at first glance. It's an insubstantial difference that resists definition as much as it frustrates the eye: are they a people? a religion? a nation? All these categories apply, but none is adequate in itself" (165).

The indeterminacy of the Jew and the lack of a clearly visible or recognizable Jewish difference have made possible the successful mimicry of French, U.S., and English Jews, for example, in "passing" as typical Frenchmen, Americans, or Englishmen; one devastating irony of this situation is not only that the Jews suffer a great anxiety about identity and a consequent search for self-definition but that anti-Semites continually have to, in turn, "create" a visible difference by which to mark and know Jews—whether in the form of yellow stars, tattooed numbers, or other "marks of difference." Indeed, anti-Semitism is in good measure fueled by the lack of a visible difference, and the consequent fear of racial mixing on the part of a dominant culture—that is, since "they" (Jews) can actually look like us, they might actually become part of us, and so we need to mark and label and ghettoize them in order to know and recognize their difference. But the result is, on both the Jewish side and the side of the anti-Semite, a quest for definition and notable/visible difference, since "Jewishness" doesn't clearly fit any other comfortable designations (like race or nation). As Jon Stratton writes in *Coming Out Jewish* (9–10), "The claim to authenticity, the feeling that one 'really is' an Italian or whatever, and can speak as such, is dependent on a belief, and indeed a feeling, of identification, a certainty of identity. For Jews, where there is no national site for identification, identity comes in many and varied forms. For example, even subscribing to Judaism is not necessarily enough to be accepted as a Jew because there are divisions within Judaism on the issue of who might be identified as a Jew. For those wishing to identify as secular Jews, identification, and the possibility of feeling authentic, is even more uncertain."

Let's look at each of these four broad categories—which I have arbitrarily designated as religion, culture, nation, and race/ethnicity—separately, starting with religion. Certainly most of us would grant that active practitioners of Judaism, those who are of the Jewish faith and who are religiously observant, are Jews. My own Roman Catholic upbringing left (for me) the issue of religion and belief very clear: if you believed in, and followed the rules and practices of, Catholicism, then you were a good Catholic; since I cannot in good faith continue to do so and am thus a lapsed Catholic, I no longer identify myself as Catholic. Oddly, one of the striking things about Jewishness as a category of identity is that, unlike most membership categories or identity formations, you can never really stop being Jewish. Even if you should choose to renounce both the religion and the culture(s) of Judaism, you never cease being a Jew: that status is conceived (in mirrored collusion with anti-Semitic racism) as an essentialized category or stigma that you are forever branded with, that marks you indelibly. With Jewishness, continued religious practice or observation hardly helps define or clarify (or limit) the category of Jewishness: to begin with, there are various branches within Judaism, most notably the Orthodox, Conservative, and Reform movements, Hasidic groups, and Reconstructionists. At times the more fundamentalist groups (Orthodox and Hasidic) question the legitimacy of the other branches (especially of the Reform branch), and thus the status of some practitioners as "real Jews." Furthermore, unlike Catholicism, if a Jew stops observing the rites and rituals of the religion, he or she does not stop being a "Jew." Indeed, much of the Jewish world is populated by what are commonly called "secular Jews"—those who do not observe the religion but who retain their Jewishness through cultural practices and a lived Jewish culture (what Raymond Williams called "a whole way of life"). So perhaps we need to look beyond religious affiliation to the broader notion of "culture."

When Americans think about "Jewish culture" (or Jewish humor, Jewish life, and so on), they are on the whole thinking about *Yiddishkeit*, the traditional Jewish culture of Central and Eastern Europe, of Ashkenazi Jews, who were the largest group of Jewish immigrants to the United States, especially the Yiddish-speaking *Ostjuden*. These were the Jews who migrated from Eastern Europe in the nineteenth and twentieth centuries, who formed the Bund, who dreamt of migrating to Eretz Israel, and who formed the core of the Zionist movement. Theirs was the culture of latkes and blintzes, of *Funny Girl* and *Fiddler on the Roof*, of klezmer music and Borscht Belt comedians. Indeed, a *Los Angeles Times* survey in 1998 revealed that 79 percent of Jews in the United States identify themselves as Ashkenazi—followed by 8 percent listed as Sephardi, 8 percent as unsure, 3 percent as mixed, and 2 percent as other (4/22/98: A16). Yet English and South African Jews (to cite two examples), while largely also Ashkenazi, have a very different culture from the Jewish American way of life. At the very start of his book of meditations on Jewish identity, *Thinking in Jewish*, Jonathan Boyarin writes, "The phrase ["Thinking in Jewish"] alludes to the use of the term 'Jewish' to designate the language otherwise known as Yiddish. This usage is peculiar to a certain intermediary generation, child immigrants and the children of immigrants from Jewish Eastern Europe. It is a partial translation, a failed translation, evidence of a barely possible attempt to display attachment and competence in an ancestral idiom on the one hand, while demonstrating an educated, responsible awareness of the new idiom on the other: to claim identity without being claimed by it"(1). However, to equate Jewish identity with a Yiddish mind-set is from the start to make a troubling equation, naturalizing Jewishness as Yiddishness; as Stratton notes, "Boyarin does not talk about the transformation of the usage into a way of naturalising the dominance of Ashkenazi and Yiddish Jews in the social order of the West. This hegemonic formation has marginalized other Jewish groups, most importantly Sephardi and Mizrahi Jews" (4). I follow up this point in the discussion on race and ethnicity below.

Another problem with this formulation—that is, the popular equation of Yiddish culture with Jewishness—is that traditional Yiddish culture has been (except for a few small neighborhoods in a few places such as Brooklyn) virtually wiped out, the horrific consequences of the Final Solution and the Holocaust in Europe. (For example, the popular U.S. Jewish newspaper the *Forward* was originally a Yiddish newspaper, but eventually switched to English in order to maintain a real audience and readership.) As a result, the continued reification of Yiddishness as "Jewish culture" does not represent the real presence of a lively and ongoing living culture and way of life, a set of daily practices, but rather a sentimental construct bathed in nostalgia and resulting in Borscht Belt stereotypes that are, in themselves, as essentialist and racist (and often exactly the same) as some of the negative stereotypes behind anti-Semitism.

Finally, even if one were to grant the importance of Yiddish culture in defining Jewish identity, there is still the inherent problem of defining identity through cultural adherence and practice. Is a person who is not Jewish by halachic definition (that is, someone whose mother was not Jewish) and who is also not a convert but who subscribes to Judaism, whether religiously or culturally (or both), a Jew?[3] As Stratton asks, "What would it mean, for a person to subscribe to Judaism but not be a Jew?" (9) After all, what do we mean by a "secular" or cultural Jew? (Or "Sunday Jews," as in Hortense Calisher's novel by that name)? What is the difference between those two positions—a non-Jew adhering to Jewish cultural practices, and a secular Jew? If a (halachically defined) Jewish person chooses not to be religiously observant but is very much a part of a specifically Jewish culture—for example, traditionally Yiddish neighborhoods in Brooklyn—he or she is, of course, still considered Jewish. If such a Jewish person chooses not to be religiously observant and becomes wholly assimilated into the dominant culture (attending Christian schools, observing Christmas, and so on), he/she is nevertheless still considered a Jew (by both Jews and non-Jews); in that case, should we not consider a person who is *not* halachically Jewish but who is very much immersed within Jewish cultural life—and thus whose lived experience is much more "Jewish" than the thoroughly assimilated Jew—also a Jew? One way of putting this is (and here I am echoing a Jay Leno comedy routine): Aren't all native New Yorkers (eating at kosher delis and employing Yiddish words as part of their daily vocabulary) "Jews"? But can anybody from Kansas or Oklahoma ever really claim to be "Jewish"? My older sister, herself very much imbricated in New York Jewish life, knows a lot more about Jewishness than many assimilated Jews; for that matter, so do I, and I can certainly claim to live a much more real "Jewish" cultural and religious life (via my wife, son, friends, and in-laws; via our weekly religious practices in our home life) than many secular Jews I know. And yet no one, myself included, would claim that I should be considered a "Jew." So then does the determination of Jewishness finally really just come down to race/ethnicity and genetic heritage?

But before we move to the issue of race/ethnicity, I want to look briefly at the category of "nation" (and then return to it much later in a discussion about Israel). When we speak about French or Belgian citizens, it is assumed that we are talking about a national affiliation. But even in the Hebrew Bible "the people Israel" is a term that has always encompassed more than one "nation" or "state." In the twentieth century, the creation of the state of Israel was accompanied by the Law of Return, granting all legitimate "Jews," anywhere in the world, a legitimate national status as potential citizens of the state of Israel. Indeed, Finkielkraut argues that the dream of Zionism was to put to rest the indeterminacy surrounding the term: "What Zionists . . . wanted . . . was for Judaism to put an end to its undecidability and become a categorizable difference. . . . False hopes" (166). Instead, the nation of Israel finds itself increasingly enmeshed in an explosive internal debate about the definition of Israel and about who should be allowed to be called its citizens. A major part of this controversy involves the rift between the nation's Jewish and Arab citizens, Israeli Arabs who increasingly demand to be known as "Israeli Palestinians." Even as the state of Israel in the 1990s tried to move toward making peace with Palestine and the Palestinians, it also continued to turn away from confronting the internal problem of "the million Palestinians who live as second-class Israeli citizens" (Sontag 48). Indeed, Arabs now make up 18 percent of the population of Israel, a figure which is likely to rise further (in view of that community's very high birthrate); nevertheless, the consensus among the dominant Jewish population is that the Israeli Arabs

are illegitimate citizens, and every Arab must be treated as a "potential terrorist": "What most unnerves Israeli Jews is a series of bills that seek to nibble
at the Jewish identity of Israel. One challenges the national anthem, another
proposes that Israel pronounce itself a multicultural state. . . . To American
ears, this sounds innocuous, but to those Israelis who consider this the Jewish homeland, it sounds treasonous" (Sontag 53).[4] The problem originates
in the fact that Israel invokes, for Jews, both a secular nationalism and a religious entity at the same time; the difficulty of distinguishing between religion and state is at the heart of this debate in the Knesset: "Inside and outside
the legislature, the debate is already raging, a national soul-search about
Israel's identity and just how central Jewishness — much less Judaism — should
be" (*New York Times* 12/06/99: A1). After all, statistics released in October
of 1999 showed that, for the first time, over half of immigrants to Israel in
the previous twelve-month period were not Jews according to Jewish law:
that is, 53 percent of that year's immigrants did not have a Jewish mother
nor had they undergone a Jewish conversion. Indeed, of the one million immigrants who have made up the great wave of emigration to Israel from the
former Soviet Union since 1989, 208,000 have not been Jewish. In fact, the
original Law of Return, guaranteeing Israeli citizenship to Jews, read that
"every Jew has the right to come to this country"; but, in 1970, that law was
amended — in a deliberate rejection of the Nazi definition of a racialized
Jewishness (of *mischlinge*, part-Jews, in which even one bit of "Jewish" blood
would be a contamination, a Nazi version of the "one-drop rule" in the United
States) — to include those with Jewish connections and heritage: non-Jewish
spouses, children, and grandchildren of Jews. Which is to say that the Law
of Return was amended to "embrace those who might not consider themselves Jewish but might nonetheless face anti-Semitism" (A12) in a non-
racialized, nonethnic, nonreligious definition of a secular nation-state.
Nevertheless, this matter continues to be deeply controversial in an Israel
whose politics are increasingly under the influence of the Orthodox right,
and — the Law notwithstanding — the debate about the nature of Israeli identity is far from settled. As Yuli Tamir, Israel's former immigration minister
(1999–2001), says, "I see this as a deep, profound debate going way beyond
our immigration law. . . . What will the nature of Israel be? A religious Jewish state? A state of all its citizens? A secular, democratic and Jewish state?
It is a debate that will engage us for many, many years" (A12).

If neither the observance of religious practice nor "Jewish culture" nor
a national citizenship comes close to being able to define authentic
Jewishness, how about the presumably more "natural" and "real" categories

of race and ethnicity, of a genetic lineage? First, it should be obvious that Jews come in every "race" and ethnicity (my own son, ethnically Chinese, is one obvious example). Second, to define Jewishness as a matter of blood and genes runs the perils of racism—of mirroring precisely the attempt by Adolf Hitler to define Jews along bloodlines, as some sort of natural and eternal essence, so that one drop of "Jewish blood" (no matter what one's actual lived culture or citizenship) would be enough to deserve a yellow star and removal to Auschwitz. As Benedict Anderson points out, "The fact of the matter is that nationalism thinks in terms of historical destinies, while racism dreams of eternal contaminations, transmitted from the origins of time. . . . Jews, the seed of Abraham, forever Jews, no matter what passports they carry or what languages they speak and read. (Thus for the Nazi, the *Jewish* German was always an impostor.)" (149). Indeed, the notion of defining Jewishness through racial status is provocative and offensive to Orthodox Jews, for whom there is no such thing as a "part-Jew" or as a "half-Jew": if your mother is Jewish, you are a Jew, period; if not, you are not. Even Reform Judaism, willing to accept patrilineal descent, requires all subscribers to accept a full Jewish identity. As James Shapiro notes, "The last ones to call people half-Jews or *mischlinge* were Nazis; they divided identity up so neatly because they saw Jewishness in racial, not religious or cultural terms" (18). In direct contradistinction, as I noted earlier, the 1970 amendment to Israel's Law of Return refuses such a racist and essentialist definition of Jewishness.

Nevertheless, in Israel itself this argument about lineage (versus multiculturalism) is being hotly debated. Many Jews would prefer to deny the rights of citizenship to Arabs and Sephardim. But is it even possible to distinguish an ethnic/racial heritage of Jewishness? After all, while Ashkenazi racism toward Sephardic Jews certainly exists, it is contestable whether white Ashkenazi are themselves direct descendants of the Israelites. The term *Semite* includes many near-Eastern peoples, some of whom are clearly of much darker skin color. Scholars have long argued and debated the ethnicity of various Biblical figures (including Solomon, David, and even Jesus).[5] Was King David himself even a Jew? As Jack Miles points out, "For decades, [some] scholars have quietly entertained doubts"; for a variety of reasons, including linguistic evidence in the Hebrew Bible, "the possibility has loomed for a long while that the greatest Jew in the Hebrew Bible may not have been born Jewish." Whatever his actual origins, he was, in Miles's description, "a cross-cultural adventurer . . . and, in his wild early years, a virtual border bandit" (11).

An episode of the PBS series *Nova*, titled "Lost Tribes of Israel," featured the research of British anthropologist Tudor Parfitt and his study of the Lemba tribe in South Africa. This is a black tribe who claim to be descendants of Abraham and Isaac, who adhere to kosher dietary practices, who circumcise their males, who practice ritual slaughter and sacrifice (not otherwise a common African practice), and who have apparently done so since time immemorial. Are the Lemba one of the "lost tribes"—the ten northern tribes carried off into exile after the Assyrian conquest (and presumably scattered and assimilated across the Middle East)? Parfitt, taking advantage of sophisticated contemporary genetics, had the Lemba tested for genetic markers, with the samples then sent to the University of London for laboratory analysis. The results were startling. The "Cohen" Y chromosome, the gene of the Cohanim, the priestly line of the tribe of Levi directly descended from Aaron and Moses, is a hereditary marker whose presence occurs much more frequently in Jewish populations than in the population at large. It occurs in about 10 percent of Jews not of Cohanic descent, but in about 50 percent of Jews of Cohanic descent. In the genetic test of the Lemba, the analysis revealed almost the same high frequency of Cohanic markers in the Lemba as in the Jewish populations tested. In one particular clan of Lembas, the premier clan and the oldest, known as the Buba, the frequency was almost 50 percent—nearly the same as with the Cohanim Jews! Could the Buba be Cohens? The Buba are taught daily that they are a people in diaspora, that they must never forget who they are, that they must remember the way back to their origins in "Sena" in the north. Parfitt noted that Ezra and Nehemiah both mention "the children of Senna" near Jericho; Parfitt was then able to locate and visit a place in what is now Yemen that was traditionally known as "Sena," and is very close to the Indian Ocean current on the eastern coast of Africa traditionally used by ancient sailors to travel down the African coast; this current could presumably have brought such a "lost tribe" from the Mideast down to South Africa.[6]

If, as Parfitt's genetic evidence would seem to suggest, the Lemba are, by genetic lineage, Israelites (even Levites), is heredity enough to prove their authenticity and Jewishness? One should note that despite the Lembas' tribal practices and their claims of Hebrew descent, the white Jews of South Africa have rejected them as fellow Jews. It is all too easy to reject others based on their perceived racial or ethnic difference—even if genetic evidence would suggest a different conclusion. By the year 2000, there were, in Israel, over seventy thousand Ethiopians as a result of the waves of immigration since the mid–1980s: Ethiopian Jews, some of whom—like the Marrano Jews in medieval Spain—became outwardly Christian about fifty years ago during a period of Christian harassment of Jews in Ethiopia, are considered one of the lost tribes of Israel. But to be allowed to emigrate to Israel, to be accepted as authentic Jews qualifying for "return," Ethiopians have to clear a higher bar than white Russians do. As the *Los Angeles Times* notes, "Some earlier Israeli governments questioned their Jewish origin and did not allow them to immigrate under Israel's Law of Return, which allows all Jews to claim Israeli citizenship" (7/9/98: A4). As the *New York Times* comments further, "Israel has accepted thousands of Russians, not all of them Jewish by Jewish law, a fact that the Ethiopians have noticed. 'Since we are black there are serious investigations,' Mr. [Mitiku] Yalew [chairman of the Addis Ababa Beta Israel Community] said. 'For Russians, they don't do the same thing. That is racism'" (4/19/00: A3).

In Israel itself, the Sephardic population is referred to as "the blacks" of Israel. Yet there have been strides in the status of the Sephardim—with the rise of the ultra-right, religious Shas party, with Sephardic members of the Knesset, and with marriage between Ashkenazi and Sephardi no longer an uncommon practice. Indeed, DNA research (published in May 2000 in *The Proceedings of the National Academy of Sciences*) suggests that the Y chromosome found in Jewish men may go back to a common pool of Middle Eastern ancestors, presumably a genetic link between Jews and Palestinians, suggesting a common ancestry dating back four thousand years and supporting the tradition that Abraham fathered both the Jewish and the Arab peoples. "The study compared the male, or YT, chromosome—which is passed from father to son—in 1,371 males from seven groups of Israeli Jews of various origins and 16 non-Jewish groups in the Middle East, Africa, and Europe": the results, suggesting a genetic link between Jews and Arabs, give further credence to the biblical story in Genesis of how Abraham fathered two sons: Ishmael by his wife's maid Hagar, and then, when Sara was at last able to conceive, Isaac. The line of Ishmael, according to tradition, resulted in what we call Arabs. As Batsheva Bonne-Tamir, a geneticist at Tel Aviv University and one of the scientists involved in the study, notes, "Eventually people will realize that they are not that different" (*Salt Lake Tribune* 5/10/00: A1). Indeed, while postcolonial and cultural critics constantly remind us that people on different sides of a racial or cultural divide—like Israelis and Palestinians—often actually share the same culture, the same foods, the same words, similar ritual practices, and so on, in the case of Arabs and Jews, such studies argue also that they are, genetically and ethnically, actually the same people.

Who/What Is a Jew?

The difficulties discussed above in defining Jewishness along each of the available identity registers—religion, culture/history, nation, race/ethnicity—are reflected also in the popular culture and in the views of the public at large. In an important broad survey of U.S. Jews conducted by the *Los Angeles Times* in 1998, when they were asked, "How, primarily, do you define your own Jewish identity?"—15 percent defined it as religion, 17 percent as ethnicity, 48 percent as history/culture, 16 percent as "all of the above," and 4 percent as "other" (4/20/98: A10). Obviously, these difficulties and confusions in defining Jewishness bring with them the corollary challenge of defining who or what is a Jew. How can one know or define a Jew? Halachic definitions and popular conceptions vary greatly, as do differences in such perceptions between different Jewish populations. For example, on this sensitive issue of defining who is a Jew, the same *Los Angeles Times* survey asked both U.S. Jews and Israelis "to choose the person they considered 'more' Jewish: someone with a Jewish mother who doesn't practice the religion, or a person whose mother is not Jewish but who attends synagogue regularly." The Israeli respondents sided with the Orthodox matrilineal interpretation of a Jew, even a nonpracticing one, by 43 to 13 percent; whereas the respondents in the United States chose, by 50 to 27 percent, the person who attends synagogue. However, U.S. Jews are more likely to view Jews as defined by ethnicity or culture rather than religion (52 percent, as opposed to 39 percent of Israelis); while 42 percent of Israelis view Jews as a group defined by religion, only 32 percent of U.S. Jews subscribe to a religious definition. And while both groups said that defining themselves as Jewish is important, 27 percent of Israelis say that it is "the single most important part of their identities," while only 13 percent of Americans feel that way (4/19/98: A36).

So who or what is a Jew? Who can be a Jew? Who can't be a Jew? How does one become a Jew? How does one stop being a Jew? Indeed, *can* one stop being a Jew? Finkielkraut describes Jewishness as "an eternal identity that [the Jew] can neither reject nor recast" (5). While a halachically defined Jew may be an eternal Jew no matter what he or she does, some others are perhaps simply not eligible for Jewishness. For example, as Stephen Whitfield, author of *In Search of American Jewish Culture*, notes (10–11), "In planning an encyclopedia on the history of American Jewish women, its two editors wondered about including Marilyn Monroe. She had converted immediately prior to her third marriage [to playwright Arthur Miller], after submitting to two hours of religious instruction. Was that sufficient? To solve this conundrum of identification, Paula E. Hyman of Yale asked her adolescent daughters, 'who were tuned in to popular culture'; and Deborah Dash Moore of Vassar asked her 'similarly situated sons.' Exclusion was the unanimous verdict, which the editorial board of the encyclopedia upheld (though, in any Reform synagogue, Monroe was eligible for an aliya—the honor of being called to the Torah)." Is someone who is so clearly the Platonic ideal of a *shikse* simply ineligible for authentic Jewishness? In a country in which about half of the Jewish population defines that status in terms of culture and history (and only 15 percent in terms of religion), definitions of Jewishness can be very pliable, contestable, and simply weird. Arguably, no Midwestern Jews (like the gossip-columnist sisters Pauline and Esther Friedman, better known as Dear Abby and the late Ann Landers) can really be considered Jews.

According to halachah, however, a person's legal status as a Jew is based on matrilineal lineage; this is the traditional and Orthodox viewpoint. In the West Bank in February 2002, Staff Sergeant Michael Oxman and five of his comrades died when Palestinian gunmen attacked the Israeli outpost they were manning (*New York Times* 2/24/02: A7). But the six comrades were not buried together: Sergeant Oxman, a twenty-one-year-old Ukrainian immigrant who considered himself Jewish, like his father, did not qualify for burial in a Jewish cemetery under Jewish law because his mother was not Jewish. But by Israeli law, the Law of Return, Sergeant Oxman had been allowed to come to Israel at the age of fifteen and was granted Israeli citizenship; as an Israeli citizen, he was liable for service in the nation's armed forces, and indeed died for his country; nevertheless, he was (amid much controversy) denied the right to be buried with other Jews, the very compatriots he lost his life for.

Reform Jews are willing to accept a patrilineal definition of Jewishness, in contrast to the matrilineal hard line espoused by the Orthodox. In strict halachah, however, if a Jewish mother becomes pregnant as a result of adultery, incest, or rape, her child—while a Jew—is considered a *mamzer*, a bastard, and is forbidden to marry a Jew of legitimate birth. It is, of course, possible for individuals whose mothers were not Jews to convert according to Jewish law—and I address conversion below. But such a matrilineal definition makes the conditions of intermarriage very troublesome and perilous—and intermarriage is the issue that has, among Jews in the United States, become the greatest anxiety and obsession.

As Egon Mayer, professor of sociology at the City University of New York's Graduate Center and director of research for the Jewish Outreach

Institute, puts it, "Intermarriage is not threatening to individuals. But the phenomenon is threatening to our collective well-being" (*Los Angeles Times* 4/21/98: A14). In his book *Does the World Need the Jews?* Rabbi Daniel Gordis, a former dean at the University of Judaism in Los Angeles, suggests that, for the first time in Jewish history, a large part of a whole generation, the baby boomers, is rejecting a committed Jewish life "without even giving it much thought, lured away by the currents of a culture that makes Judaism seem of little consequence" (*Los Angeles Times* 4/20/98: A10). And the main reason for such anxiety among Jewish leaders is the high rate of intermarriage, an option strongly opposed by traditional Jewish culture. This is an issue that has divided the U.S. Jewish community since 1990, when a controversial survey suggested that half of all Jews were marrying non-Jews (*Salt Lake Tribune* 5/19/01: C1). According to the 1998 *Los Angeles Times* survey, in the United States, 33 percent of married Jews are married to non-Jews; indeed, among those under forty-five years of age, the rate goes up to 47 percent. This particular trend is likely to accelerate, since only 21 percent of unmarried respondents said that they would marry only a Jew, while 57 percent said the religion of their partner would not make any difference in their choice of spouse. Furthermore, only 33 percent would object to a child of theirs marrying a non-Jew, while 58 percent said that it would not matter whom their children marry (4/20/98: A10). These figures were confirmed in a separate survey by the American Jewish Committee two years later (in 2000; *New York Times* 10/31/00: A18), which clearly showed that most U.S. Jews are willing to accept intermarriage. This study found that 56 percent disagreed with the statement "It would pain me if my child married a gentile," while 80 percent agreed with the statement "Intermarriage is inevitable in an open society"; 50 percent even agreed with the opinion that opposing intermarriage between Jews and non-Jews is "racist." Fewer than one in four of those surveyed felt that a rabbi should refuse to officiate at such marriages. Mayer found these survey results, especially about whether rabbis should officiate at interfaith marriages, "stunning"—and a clear reversal of attitudes just ten years earlier (in the 1990 survey). As Rabbi Eric Yoffie, president of the Union of American Hebrew Congregations, noted about this new survey, "Like it or not, intermarriage is a reality in our society" (*New York Times* 10/31/00: A18).

One can understand why these numbers are worrisome to rabbis and Jewish leaders in a culture that defines its identity through matrilineal continuity, in a population historically under attack by dominant host cultures from the time of Moses to the present,[7] and in a contemporary global context in which the Final Solution came horrifically close to its goal of exterminating

Jewish populations altogether. Yet while the historical memories and worries are perfectly understandable, the actual populations of Jewish communities are in fact growing. Whereas the estimated worldwide Jewish population in 1940 was 15,750,000, by 1960 it was only 12,800,000, largely as a result of the decimation of European Jewry during the Holocaust; however, by 1995 the worldwide population had rebounded to 13,059,000. During that same period (1940 to 1995), the Jewish population in the United States grew continually, from 4,831,000 to 5,690,000 (*Los Angeles Times* 4/22/98: A16).[8] Which is to say that, rather than overall Jewish populations declining because of intermarriage or loss of faith, Jewish populations are growing; the feared loss of Jews is being more than replaced by conversions of non-Jews, most frequently non-Jewish partners of marrying Jews and interfaith children raised as Jews. So why the deep and pervasive anxiety in the United States today about the threat of intermarriage to the future of Judaism? Indeed, some Jewish thinkers are now beginning to advance the startling notion that intermarriage could actually be regarded as an opportunity, rather than a danger, to the Jewish faith and to its continuation, for intermarriage allows the possibility of expanding the population pool of practicing Jews: "There may be 600,000 kids in the United States who aren't being raised Jewishly. If we could get 70%, or even 50% . . . that's 300,000 kids," says Steven Foster, a rabbi in Denver. The *Los Angeles Times* reports that Foster "founded a program to offer two years of free Jewish education to interfaith families; a University of Denver report found that 67% of participants chose to continue Jewish study after graduating" (4/20/98: A11).

But the controversy and sharp disagreements surrounding this trigger-hot topic of intermarriage also have to do with the internal clashes between Jewish denominations around the question of Jewish identity and who can actually be considered authentically Jewish. The American Jewish Congress survey in 2000 revealed sharp disagreement between Orthodox and non-Orthodox Jews: 64 percent of Orthodox respondents strongly disapproved of intermarriage, as opposed to 15 percent of Conservative Jews, and only 3 percent of Reform Jews. At the center of these disputes are basic theological differences between Orthodox and Reform Judaisms, including the issues of intermarriage, conversion, and matrilineality (especially whether a child born of a Jewish father and a non-Jewish mother can be considered Jewish). In both the United States and Israel, such differences have come to a head over the issues of conversion and intermarriage. Currently, only conversions performed by Orthodox rabbis are considered valid in Israel; the same is true for religious marriages and divorces. But, even in Israel, according to the *Los*

Angeles Times survey, 58 percent approve of allowing Reform and Conservative rabbis to perform marriages and religious conversions, while 36 percent are opposed (4/19/98: A36).

The issue has been the subject of bitter controversy, led by Orthodox rabbis arguing that traditional Jewish law applies in all instances. The Orthodox leadership in Israel refuses to recognize the Reform and Conservative movements as legitimate Judaism. Orthodox practitioners adhere rigorously to halachah, to the laws of Judaism handed down from God, as they believe. They keep strict kosher dietary rules; they will not work or even use electricity or machinery on the Sabbath. They are opposed to interfaith marriages, to women being allowed to become rabbis, even to men and women praying together. These rules are interpreted differently by Conservative Jews, who—for example—ordain women as rabbis. Reform Jews (who also ordain women) regard these rules more as loose moral guidelines than as absolute laws, with a broad range of both adherence and dissent. The status of these more liberal versions of Judaism threatens to divide Jews in Israel (who are largely either secular or Orthodox) from those in the Diaspora, most of whom belong to the Reform and Conservative movements. And these divisions have come to a head around the issue of conversion. For example, when in January 1998 the Israeli government and Jewish leaders tried to draft a compromise proposal on the explosive issue of who can conduct religious conversions, Rabbi Ovadia Yosef, spiritual leader of the Shas party, responded angrily: "When darkness covers the land and the Reform and Conservative sects, the destroyers of religion, attempt to dig their claws into the Holy Land, they should not be recognized" (*Los Angeles Times* 1/27/98: A4).

Such debates also reflect, of course, fundamental issues in Israel as to what kind of nation the Jewish homeland should be—whether a secular democracy or a religious state in which halachah is predominant even in matters of national and public policy. That debate and conflict between the secular Israeli majority and the influential ultra-Orthodox wing has deepened with a number of Supreme Court decisions—ending a blanket exemption from military service for students in Orthodox seminaries, permitting kibbutz stores to open on the Sabbath, and requiring that Reform and Conservative Jews be allowed to serve on local religious councils (*Los Angeles Times* 2/15/99: A4). But the most sensitive issue confronting the Court is whether Jews converted by non-Orthodox rabbis should be recognized as Jews—for the Orthodox rabbinate is afraid of losing its traditional monopoly on performing conversions in Israel, and consequently on deciding and defining who can be a Jew.

In the United States, a group of Reform, Conservative, and Orthodox rabbis established, in 1977 in a meeting in Denver, a set of common criteria for conversion; but by 1983 the Orthodox rabbis renounced the agreement, claiming that their standards had been compromised. As Whitfield observes about such disagreements among branches of Judaism, "At stake is the very definition of who is a Jew, and whether an ultra-Orthodox definition will prevail. The eclipse of secular and ethnic forms of identification hints at a future when religion alone will be decisive: a Jew will be a practitioner of Judaism. But whether that faith can remain pluralistic or will be reduced to a single denomination, [no one] can prophesy" ("Jewish Wars" 22).

Reform Judaism is willing to accept children of a Jewish father and a non-Jewish mother as Jews. In traditional Jewish practice, however, when the mother is gentile, the child must be formally converted to Judaism; this is also true of a non-Jewish partner whom a Jew may wish to marry. Conversion is a ritual rebirth in which the individual's status (as Jew) can be established only at the moment of conversion. For a legitimate conversion, Orthodox and Conservative rabbis require, with males, *brit milah* (ritual circumcision), immersion in a kosher *mikveh*, and a naming ceremony, in which the individual takes on a Hebrew name. While Reform practice does not require formal conversion via circumcision or *mikveh*, there is a growing trend among Reform rabbis to encourage such traditional rituals as part of the conversion process.

Indeed, in June 2001 the Reform movement's rabbinical union proposed a tightening of standards for Reform conversions, including greater emphasis on ritual immersion and circumcisions, and the encouragement of those wishing to convert to observe elements of rabbinic law. As the Jewish American newspaper the *Forward* reported:

> The document, in arguing for a more traditional approach, points out that the incorporation of ritual immersion and circumcision helps strengthen Jewish unity because the Conservative movement only recognizes Reform conversions that involve these ancient rituals. At the same time, however, Reform leaders continue to pledge their support for the patrilineal-descent decision, which flies in the face of an ancient precedent . . . that says a child must be born to a Jewish mother to be considered Jewish. The decision has been characterized by many non-Reform religious leaders as the most divisive single step in the recurring "Who is a Jew?" debate. (6/22/01: 12)

According to these newly proposed guidelines, Reform converts should be urged to follow dietary regulations, Sabbath observances, and some other traditional religious practices that are largely disregarded by most Reform Jews. As the *Forward* goes on to note, "It appears that the proposed conversion guidelines would, in theory, encourage converts to select and commit themselves to a more specific set of specific observances than other reform Jews" (12). Which is to say, ironically, that converts have to become more "authentic" and "Jewish" than Jews by birth. In other words, the only way for a non-Jew to really become an accepted Jew is not only to mark the body as Jewish (through circumcision and *mikveh*) but to prove yourself even more Jewish than the Jews.

One particular and increasingly visible manifestation—and challenge—in the arena of conversion, at least in the United States, is the matter of adoption (see also Chapter 4). Adoption is fast becoming an accepted part of the landscape in the United States, a not-uncommon way of making a family—especially among white Jewish parents. Many of these adoptions take place under the auspices of Stars of David, an information and exchange network for Jewish (and interfaith) adoptive families. Susan Katz, director of Stars of David, reports that Jews adopt at a significantly higher rate than non-Jews. The 1990 National Jewish Population Survey registered sixty thousand adopted children; as Katz notes, if one factors in their parents, one set of grandparents, an aunt, uncle, and two cousins, then at least half a million U.S. Jews are members of an adoptive family (Musleah 12). Given the explosion in international adoption since 1990, the numbers of adopted Jewish children in this country have no doubt also skyrocketed.

The identity status of children adopted to Jewish parents is never a simple one, a fact I have discovered with the adoption and conversion of our own Taiwanese son, now a five-year-old who can recite many Hebrew prayers, who loves his Jewish life and is a very active participant in the local *shul*, but who hardly looks "Jewish" and who has a hard time being accepted as Jewish in some congregations we have attended (though certainly not in our own present one in Salt Lake City, where he is quite beloved).[9] The challenges facing Jewish parents of adopted children, in addition to the matter of a racial or ethnic authenticity, begin with the challenges to any one attempting conversion. Furthermore, children adopted by Jewish parents must negotiate two sets of authenticities: that of a new identity according to the laws of nations and states, and that of a new identity according to Jewish law, halachah.

Yet adoption itself is as old a Jewish practice as the Hebrew Bible. As Rabbi Michael Gold reminds us, "Unable to have a child of his own, Abraham adopted his servant Eliezer to be his heir. Jacob adopted his two grandsons

Ephraim and Menashe. Pharaoh's daughter adopted Moses and raised him in the house of Pharaoh. Mordecai provided a home for his orphaned cousin Esther. And King David's wife Michal, herself childless, raised the five sons of her sister Merab. The Talmud says: Merab bore them and Michal brought them up; therefore they are called by her name. This teaches that whoever brings up an orphan in his home, Scripture ascribes it to him as though he had begotten him (Sanhedrin 19b)" (14). It is perhaps especially (though certainly not intentionally) appropriate that the Jewish adoption network should be called "Stars of David," since some contemporary Biblical scholars doubt whether King David himself was an Israelite by birth. While there is no word in the Bible for adoption, the word in modern Hebrew is *ametz*, meaning to be firm or strengthened. Adoption, thus, might be seen as "the raising and passing of one's values to a new generation, and thereby strengthening the Jewish future"; as Gold reminds us, the Talmud (Sanhedrin 19b) states, "He who teaches a child the Torah, it is as if he were the parent" (14).

An episode of the immensely popular and Emmy Award–winning NBC drama *Law and Order* depicted, for its prime-time television audience, some of the halachic intricacies of Jewish adoption and conversion, as well as the need to simultaneously negotiate both legal and religious authenticities. In this particular episode, the detectives and district attorneys in the series investigate a murder in New York City, and suspicion eventually alights on the son of an elderly Jewish couple; when the police show up to arrest the son, they learn that he has fled the country to Israel. Since under the Law of Return the son is an Israeli citizen, the Israeli consul-general, although he would like to bring the murderer to justice, feels that he is constrained by the Law of Return and refuses to extradite the accused. The matter is resolved only when the younger female district attorney, clearly a *shikse*, discovers through court records that the accused murderer was an adopted child; she then bones up on halachic law surrounding conversions and discovers that although the boy had been circumcised and there had been a ritual naming ceremony, there is no record that a *mikveh* had ever been performed. She then requests a hearing—a *beit din*—with a panel of Orthodox rabbis, and presents her case. After careful questioning and deliberation, the *beit din* agrees that the adopted child had not fulfilled the necessary conditions of Jewish conversion and declares the accused a non-Jew. At this point, the Israeli consul is able to extradite the accused murderer to stand trial in New York City.

Certainly one of the cultural truths suggested by this piece of popular media entertainment concerns the complexities of authenticating Jewishness, especially when—as with adoptions and conversions—the status of Jew-

ishness is not obvious from the very start. In such instances, it becomes necessary to make visible the signs of an authentic Jewish difference, including
the physical marking of the Jewish body (ritually and literally, through immersion and circumcision). Arguably, as with Ethiopian Jews wishing to emigrate to Israel, the standards for authentication are higher and stricter for those
who have to prove their Jewishness, who thus need to become more Jewish
than the Jews.

As we can see, authenticating who is a Jew and who is not a Jew is
not a simple matter. And it is perhaps understandable why, in Jewish culture, there has long been much anxiety about issues of identity and difference, about what constitutes Jewishness, about who is a Jew and who is not,
and indeed about one's own identity, about "who am I?" I am especially interested in popular disseminations of the diasporic Jewish experience because
they help us understand the problematics of authenticity for Jews in general
and for diasporic Jews in particular; these cultural understandings result in
particular but widespread insecurities and anxieties, which are the topic of
the subsequent half of this chapter.

Imaginary Jews, Inauthentic Jews, and Jewish Envy

In the context of such complex problematics of authenticity, it is especially hard for diasporic Jews—including U.S. Jews—to have a clear sense
of an authentic identity. Not only do they, like most of the contemporary
world, suffer (as I have argued in previous chapters) from a general feeling
of vacated authenticity because of the effects of a globalism that is reducing
everything increasingly to global sameness and inauthenticity; but, furthermore, the loss of what in the United States has long been considered genuine Jewish culture—that is, *Yiddishkeit*, the traditional Jewish culture of
Central and Eastern Europe—creates a vacuum that results in a desire for a
real, concrete, specific cultural Jewish difference. With the loss of the specificity of a particular Yiddish way of life, nowadays even the performance of
Jewishness (by such as New York Jewish comedians), Adam Gopnik suggests, is now practiced "as something learned rather than as something felt"
(128). Whereas it was possible before to be a nonobservant Jew (in terms of
religious practices) and still feel thoroughly and authentically Jewish because
one was immersed in *Yiddishkeit,* now, in order to feel Jewish, one has perhaps to resort to other means of feeling authentic, including a return to strict
religious observance. As Gopnik goes on to note, "While Yiddishkeit as a
practice had nearly disappeared from New York, one of the things that were

replacing it, paradoxically, was Judaism. A number of our friends are what I have come to think of as X-treme Jews, who study Cabala or glory in the details of the lives of Jewish gangsters, and even like to call themselves 'Hebes', in the manner of young black men calling each other 'niggas'" (129; there is now, in fact, a Jewish periodical for young adults called *Hebe*).

Indeed, many diasporic Jews today fit the category that Finkielkraut has dubbed "imaginary Jews": feeling inside like inauthentic frauds, Jews who secretly question their own Jewish authenticity, deprived of a sense of real Jewish culture and specificity, comfortably secure in diasporic culture and no longer persecuted and thus unable even to feel Jewish via a sense of persecution and victimization; inauthentic and imaginary Jews. What, after all, connects all Jews and makes them "real"? Who gets to be a real Jew? Indeed, what dues need to be paid in order to claim the title of "Jew"? These are questions that all too frequently get answered with a return to, a falling back upon, the belief in an essentialized "Jewishness," in Jewishness as inevitable "nature."

When one is challenged with a feeling of inauthenticity and a need to authenticate one's identity, the easiest thing to do is to fall back on the stereotypes of an authentic identity, the stereotyped marks of an essential difference. Whereas for Jews many of these stereotypes are of an anti-Semitic nature (miserly, nonspiritual, degenerate, and so on), which contemporary Jews have no trouble rejecting out of hand, one of the traits of an essential Jewishness is a quality embraced (and to some degree a status envied) both by anti-Semites and by Jews themselves: and that is the status of victim, of the inevitable scapegoat.

In *The Imaginary Jew* Finkielkraut recalls a demonstration in Paris in May 1968, a protest against anti-Semitism in which "thousands of people gathered spontaneously in the streets, and began to chant 'We are all German Jews!'" (17). In expressing their solidarity with Jewish victims of anti-Semitism, the protesters shocked Finkielkraut into the realization that "Jewish identity was no longer for Jews alone" (17). This was a troubling realization because it robbed him of what he felt was a proprietary and specific identity of his own: "'We are all German Jews' despoiled me and sullied my treasure, as if the demonstrators, while assuring me of their complete support, had picked my pocket of my special status. 'Hands off,' I felt like saying. 'You can't become a Jew or a dago just like that. You need certification, references. German Jews? With your French-looking faces? What gives you the right to reap the rewards? You haven't paid your dues'" (18). The required certification, the references, the dues are, of course, the status of victimhood and suffering, the wearing of the yellow star, the status of Jews as the perpetual victims and losers, the cult of victimhood so problematic as an essential identity. As James Young notes, "Many years ago, the great dean of modern Jewish historiography, Salo Baron, rejected what he called the 'lachrymose conception' of Jewish history, a 19th-century view of the Jewish past by which only the terrible destructions and martyrdoms were recounted. Such history, Baron believed, necessarily omitted much of what made Jewish life worth living and writing about in the first place" (38).

Similarly, Leon Wieseltier has reminded us of the dangers of such a conception of Jewishness by invoking another Jewish thinker, Simon Rawidowicz, who in 1948 published what Wieseltier refers to as "a great retort to pessimism, a wise and learned essay called '*Am Ha-Holekh Va-Met*,' 'The Ever-Dying People.'" Rawidowicz wrote, "The world has many images of Israel, but Israel has only one image of itself: that of an expiring people, forever on the verge of ceasing to be. . . . He who studies Jewish history will readily discover that there was hardly a generation in the Diaspora period which did not consider itself the final link in Israel's chain. Each always saw before it the abyss ready to swallow it up. . . . Often it seems as if the overwhelming majority of our people go about driven by the panic of being the last" (cited in Wieseltier 19). Wieseltier argues that this sort of thinking is currently making its way back into U.S. Jewish consciousness:

> [It revives] the old typological thinking about Jewish history—according to which every enemy of the Jews is the same enemy, and there is only one war, and it is a war against extinction, and it is a timeless war. This typological thinking defined the historical outlook of the Jews for many centuries. It begins, of course, with the Amalekites, the nomadic tribe in the Sinai desert that attacked the Israelites on their journey out of Egypt. "The Lord hath sworn that the Lord will have war with Amalek from generation to generation. . . . Thou shalt blot out the remembrance of Amalek from under heaven; thou shalt not forget it." From generation to generation: An adversarial role, a diabolical role, was created in perpetuity. And so Amalek became Haman (who actually was an Amalekite), who became the Romans, who became the Crusaders, who became Chmielnicki, who became Petlura, who became Hitler, who became Arafat. The mythifying habit is ubiquitous in the literature of the Jews. In some instances, it must not have seemed like mythifying at all. (20)

But, as Wieseltier reminds us, "it is mythifying, and the habit is back"—

especially as a response to the second Palestinian *intifada* and the concurrent renewal of anti-Semitic violence in Europe.

One of the dangerous results of such thinking is, in Finkielkraut's words, "a split, a schism between the Jew in the abstract, who functioned as a kind of standard measure for comparing all types of misfortune, and the concrete Jew, neglected in favor of the *latest* victims. . . . In short, the Jew was useful as a measuring stick only if he was first stripped of his concrete, living character" (175). Juliet Steyn suggests that this notion of the Jew as "forever a victim" has political consequences: "It is through the very *assumptions* of Jewish identity that past memories are often evoked to legitimate and explain today's defensive nationalism so vividly enacted in Israel by both Israelis and Palestinians, by fundamentalists of either side. These need taking apart lest the Jew remain forever a victim and fail to come to terms with the consequences of power" (5). As Steyn goes on to argue, "The particular problem here for the Jews, as the author Ilan Halevi maintains, is that by making anti-Semitism the sole evil principle, Jews are forever innocent, not only of responsibility for their own sufferings but also for what in other places and other times, they may make others suffer."[10]

It is this abstract and even figurative conception of the Jew as innocent and perpetual victim, stripped of any concrete reality as a specific and living entity, that continually allows Jewishness to function so pervasively as a trope, as an empty signifier that can be objectified into a figure for suffering, alienation, and victimhood. For example, for art critic John Berger, it is Jewish suffering that gives Jews their identity; for Berger Jewish art is "the result of acute suffering and intense yearnings," the prototype of modern angst (quoted in Steyn 16). Similarly, the Russian poet Marina Tsvetayeva appropriated the figure of the Jew as a metaphor for the artist, arguing that "all poets are Jews": this popular observation, almost a mantra in the modern literary world, is a particularly dangerous formulation in its essentializing of Jewishness (see Maeera Shreiber's analysis of this point). Indeed, "the Jew" has become a popular metaphor for modernist exile, cosmopolitan rootlessness, and alienation: consider the cumulative effect of the works of Kafka, of Joyce's fictional figure Leopold Bloom, and of the works of Saul Bellow, among others. As Ruth Wisse has argued about this modernist icon of the cosmopolitan Jew (a Joycean modernism that is equally tempting, she admits, to Jewish writers such as Henry Roth), "A warning bell should toll whenever a social scientist, cultural critic or politician exploits the word 'Jew' to mean the man without a country and turns him into the standard-bearer of yet another theory of 'deterritorialization'—'internationalism' or evaporation by a subtler name" (*The Modern Jewish Canon*, quoted in Schor 17). As Esther Schor points out about Wisse's concern, "Indeed, for Wisse it is not so far from this icon to the Nazi evaporation of Judaism into a racial category; in the chapter 'Shoah, Khurbn, Holocaust' she argues fiercely that scholarship itself has imperiled the plurality of Jewish experiences in the Holocaust" (17).[11] After all, an evacuation of the specificities of Jewish life in favor of figurative tropes—as suffering victim, as rootless exile, as alienated artist—facilitates the essentializing and stereotyping of Jews from specific entities into broad racial categories and types, with a consequent erasure of the textured specificities and heterogeneities of actual Jewish lives. Thus, even well-meaning chants of solidarity—such as "We are all German Jews," "All poets are Jews," or Derrida's suggestion that we are all Jews (see Steyn 11)—are culturally dangerous in their evisceration of real and concrete Jewish cultures and experiences.

Curiously, such a trope also constructs Jewishness as a condition devoutly to be wished for (as in "All poets are Jews"). While Jewish specificity gets evacuated into a metaphor that can be inhabited generally by anyone, it is nonetheless simultaneously reified, in another way, as a specific, concrete identity, a tribal and ethnic community with specific cultural customs and traits that bespeak a "real" (and not fantasmatic) cultural identity. In a world haunted by a sense of millennial inauthenticity and by a pervasive anxiety about identity, Jewishness can function simultaneously as a trope of modernist alienation and rootlessness, and—for non-Jews—as a very concrete and specific cultural otherness to be envied. Jewishness in this latter sense, an ethnic/racial sense, is a desirable and "real" (not whitebread) self, a concrete ethnic identity enviable precisely because it is imagined to still obtain and exist in the modern world—a cultural atavism and essence in conflict with contemporary globalism that has somehow not yet disappeared, something that is not as inauthentically whitebread as, say, the diluted and bleached-out nonidentity of WASPness, in this globalized world of whitebread sameness and alienation, haunted by anxieties of inauthenticity. What results is a sort of Jewish envy and a consequent construction which I call "Jewish chic"—the phenomenon, hardly unusual anymore in First World metropolises, of the "Jewish wannabe." Finkielkraut writes about such envy when he remarks on the "surprising goyim, who are so fascinated with the longevity and unparalleled destiny of the Jewish people that they dream of becoming Jews[,] . . . who are jealous of the Jews!" and "who envy their collective memory, their intense sense of belonging and the immutable bonds that bind them to a unique history and living community; who envy the inherent transcendence that makes them more than mere individuals, that quality of having something extra, in a word, that shatters the repetition of me-me-me, and removes them from the stagnation of an exclusively personal existence. To be Jewish: or, the chance to escape yourself" (92) . "To be Jewish" provides the chance to escape your own whitebread self; Jewish chic and Jewish envy are the direct results of modern alienation and global inauthenticity:

> These sullen members of the majority culture have the white bread blues, feel a woeful lack of belonging. . . . To people such as these prisoners of the egosphere, Jews seem blessed by history: part of their being is not of the self but transcends it, partakes of a vaster group and greater temporal scheme. A patrimony, a faith and a spiritual dimension is theirs. . . . Founded on law, their existence is protected against the vague terrors of contingency. In an era of humdrum lives, Jewishness seemingly provides an enviable reason to live. The image of the Jew is undergoing a kind of reversal of fortune: now he is the one who has roots, and it's the French philo-Semite, that poor wandering goy, who sees himself as deracinated and stateless, a man without qualities. (94)

One striking manifestation of Jewish chic has developed in an unlikely place, Poland, which is witnessing "a remarkable Jewish revival in the country where 50 years ago European Jewry was almost wiped out": as Ian Buruma reports in a cover story (titled "Young Poles, New Jews") in the *New York Times Magazine*, "Judaism is a new form of chic": "As is true in Germany, many bookstores now have well-stocked Judaica sections; Jews and non-Jews in Warsaw are learning Yiddish and sometimes even Ladino; Cracow has an annual Jewish cultural festival featuring klezmer orchestras and kosher cooking classes. A Jewish primary school in Warsaw is already oversubscribed; out of 80 children, nearly a dozen are from non-Jewish families. A Jewish literary magazine, called *Midrasz,* was started earlier this year. More and more people are discovering their sometimes tenuous, hitherto hidden, Jewish roots" (36). Buruma interviewed a number of Polish youths, some with Jewish roots they had not been previously aware of, who decided to interest themselves in Judaism: "It had the attraction of exotic and still almost forbidden fruit. Judaism is more 'intellectual' than Catholicism, Jarek tells me. . . . Jarek adopted the stereotype of the 'clever Jew' as something to aspire to. So now he is studying Hebrew, works for *Midrasz,* sometimes goes to the synagogue and has a Jewish girlfriend" (37).

As with the nostalgias in cultural nationalisms (such as the Gaelic Revival or Chicano Aztlan) that supposedly "*re*-discover" (revivals, renaissances, and so on) that which has been already largely eradicated, such cultural nostalgia is really possible only when the culture in question has been virtually and functionally already wiped out. Consequently, the study by contemporary Polish youths of Ladino or Yiddish in a country where Judaism has been wiped out for over fifty years is a culturally safe exercise in "imperialist nostalgia." Emmanuel Levinas has noted the paradox that the fact of questioning Jewish identity means that it is already lost and past (see Steyn 175). As Buruma muses, "It seems strange to me that these young people are trying to revive a way of life from which my grandparents had escaped. But what else is there to revive? The New Polish Jews have to start from scratch. You can hardly have assimilated Jewry if there is no Jewry to assimilate" (38). In such a case, playing at Jewishness is a safe and defanged, nostalgic exercise because it presents no real threat, since it is not based on any living culture that can threaten the status quo. Rather, it is a function and symptom of the need to alleviate the culture's sense of nonbelonging and nonidentity. As one of the rabbis interviewed by Buruma says, "Young Poles are looking for their identity. We can't live in a vacuum. We have to ask ourselves who we are and where we come from. Jews lived here for a thousand years and contributed so much to Polish culture" (41).

As with most exercises in cultural nostalgia (see Chapter 3, on Irishness), the result is, inevitably, a reinforcing of essentialist and racist stereotypes of cultural (here, Jewish) otherness—for, as Steyn points out, "To seek out the 'identity' of Jewish thought is also to assume a 'pure" identity" (175). Such a logic elides the specific realities and the nonextraordinary, nonother daily lives, the pluralistic and heterogeneous cultures of real Jews (what Steyn calls the "banal" lives of Jews); as Ilan Halevi pointed out, "At the very point when Jewish society was breaking up as an autonomous social system, disintegrating into a host of special social situations, the idea spread among Europeans, as among the Jews of Europe, of a single question: a question which always went back in the last analysis, to the idea that each had Judaism in general" (quoted in Steyn 9). As Steyn concludes, "The Jew is already confirmed in an identity, recognized, characterized and thereby potentially 'known'"—whether characterized as the Jewish spirit, the "Jewish Experience," or whatever, it is an essentialized vision of Jewish difference and otherness, of extra-ordinariness, that casts the Jew as forever inaccessible, other, immutably different from the ordinary and normative (non-Jewish) self.

A particularly striking, controversial, and instructional case study of Jewish envy is the peculiar and complex case of Binjamin Wilkomirski, who wrote the celebrated 1996 memoir *Fragments*, winner of a National Jewish Book Award, about surviving the Holocaust as a child at Auschwitz-Birkenau. As Philip Gourevitch writes about *Fragments* (in his essay on Wilkomirski titled "The Memory Thief"), "Wherever it appeared, reviewers honored it as a classic. . . . Wilkomirski's depiction of an absolute naif adrift in a realm of absolute malevolence was seized upon as a testimonial that delivered what had no longer seemed quite possible: a fresh line of vision on the century's defining moment of inhumanity" (50). But then in 1998 a Swiss writer named Daniel Ganzfried—himself the son of an Auschwitz survivor—wrote an exposé documenting that the author of *Fragments* was actually Bruno Doessekker (born Bruno Grosjean), a Swiss-born gentile impostor who had in reality spent the war as a child in his native Switzerland. Born to an unwed Protestant woman in 1941, Bruno was later given up for adoption and lived for some time as a child in an orphanage, where he was found by his foster parents (the Doessekkers), who legally adopted him.

Gourevitch recounts how he met with the Israeli writer Aharon Appelfeld in Jerusalem to discuss the Wilkomirski case—and Appelfeld told him a story "about his encounter with a woman adopted by non-Jews, who later decided she was a Jew 'lost in the Holocaust'"; Appelfeld's judgment was that "there was no evidence, only strong feeling. I understand why. You are just an unwanted child, and then here you are—a child with an interesting history" (62). An adoptee deserted by a birth mother, living in an orphanage, later adopted by Swiss bourgeois parents, "Bruno Doessekker" was an inauthentic self lacking a clear sense of identity and personal drama; in such an identity vacuum, nothing could seem more real, more specific, more dramatic, more fantastically attractive than to be a Jewish child survivor of a Nazi death camp. As Ganzfried points out, "Here's a complex person with a complex background, and he looks for explanations, and the Holocaust can explain everything. It explains why your girlfriend left you, why you have headaches, why you have school problems. The Holocaust is the key to the universe" (Gourevitch 65). Ganzfried adds that in Wilkomirski he sees someone desiring victimhood and otherness, so that Wilkomirski may actually enjoy the controversy surrounding his unmasking and the attacks on the authenticity of his "memoir": "He's again the victim, the one he always wants to be. So I think he kind of likes me. . . . I was the first real person to challenge him" (66). In reviewing the book about Wilkomirski by Blake Eskin (who really *is* a Wilkomirski), *A Life in Pieces: The Making and Unmaking of Binjamin Wilkomirski*, Jonathan Lear suggests that what "*A Life in Pieces* so magnificently points out—[is] that the hysteric has come forward in the voice of the ultimate victim" (22). To be a Holocaust survivor thus becomes the ultimate badge of suffering victimhood, of Jewish persecution—and the ultimate fantasy (however self-destructive) for those who desire or envy the status of victim or the condition of Jewish otherness.

Holocaust and Authenticity

In this contemporary global anxiety about identity and authenticity, Western diasporic Jews occupy a particularly complex position. Like everyone else, they wonder, "Who are we?" Like everyone else, they long for a specific and concrete cultural authenticity and identity. Yet, ironically, they are also themselves the objects of envy on these very terms, envy by non-Jews for owning a supposed cultural and ethnic specificity which in truth Western Jews really no longer have. Deprived in this century of both the specific cultural lifestyle of Eastern European Jewry—*Yiddishkeit*—as a result of emigration and the Holocaust; deprived furthermore of the status/identity of perpetual victimhood as a result of their late-twentieth-century ascension to a social position of relative security and comfort in First World countries, a position of social acceptance and security unparalleled in Western Jewish history—Jews in the United States and Western Europe today are faced with a double emptiness of cultural identity, doubly deprived of traditional modes of defining their Jewishness, resulting in feelings of hollowness, inadequacy, and betrayal as inauthentic Jews. Into this double vacuum, enter two related manifestations: the Holocaust, and Israel.

Gourevitch points out that part of the initial power of Wilkomirski's *Fragments* was that the story had been presented as an article of faith, "and it had been embraced in a spirit of passionate belief by many of the individuals and institutions that helped to transform Holocaust remembrance into a form of secular religion" (52).[12] Indeed, the Holocaust has become, for many Jews, a secular religion of sorts—along with the cultural and material productions that accompany any religion. The historical trauma of the Holocaust has resulted in thousands of cultural and scholarly (and commercial) productions—memorials, museums, films, books, plays, merchandise, and so on—that could be considered collectively a "Holocaust industry" (or what is sometimes referred to as "Shoah business"). Whereas this general phenomenon has garnered considerable criticism of late, no one—myself included—should dispute the tremendous importance of Holocaust testimony and memorials, the crucial need to remember, to never forget, to ensure that it can never happen again. But Theodor Adorno's famous declaration that "to write lyric poetry after Auschwitz is barbaric" is also, after all, "an interdiction"—as Steyn notes (176)—warning us about the dangers of sentimentalizing and appropriating the Holocaust, anticipating the contemporary cultural industry that has resulted from the Holocaust. One consequence is the way memorializing the Holocaust now shapes Jewish identity: for example, James Young, in discussing the "politics of identity" involved with the U.S. Holocaust Memorial Museum (in Washington, D.C.), points out that the museum has spawned a competition between the "various cults of victimization" (cited in Steyn 183). Another is the way the Holocaust has gotten appropriated as a money-making, cash-raising venture, what the *Times* of London called the "Holocash" campaign (in Bartov 8). In *The Holocaust in American Life*, Peter Novick further demonstrates how the Shoah has also "opened the way for a variety of exploiters and small-time opportunists" (quoted in Bartov 8). Equally crucial is the way the emphasis on the suffering and victimhood of Jews in the Holocaust has homogenized and flattened out the complex, pluralistic, and heterogeneous range of actual Jewish experiences in the Holocaust, as Wisse and others have pointed out.

Any religion, even a secular one, requires its corresponding temples and altars. In addition to the creation of memorials and Holocaust museums, there is now also the question of what to do with the sites of former Nazi concentration camps. For example, the Risiera di Santa Saba (which my wife, Maeera, and I have visited)—the only Nazi death camp in Italy, just outside Trieste—remains virtually (and startlingly) intact and has now been admirably and tastefully converted into a state-sponsored museum to depict and remember the atrocities of the Holocaust and of Italy's own involvement. More controversially, there has emerged a heated debate over what to do with the piece of land that used to be the Auschwitz death camp. The Polish city of Oswiecim has now built a popular nightclub, known as Disco System, over what had been Auschwitz; but as *Newsweek* reports, "Auschwitz survivors, historians and Jewish leaders have joined together in a protest over what they insist is a desecration of hallowed ground" (10/9/00: 49). And yet there is something troubling to me about the site of a death factory being considered hallowed ground that must not be desecrated, for Auschwitz is hardly a Lourdes or a Masada or a Temple Mount, hardly a shrine that must not be desecrated, but rather a detestable and already-damned place that had itself witnessed the desecration of humanity. To enshrine it might only seem to endorse a Jewish self-image of perpetual victimhood and "lachrymose" history, always looking back at a sad past that both defines and imprisons the Jewish future, turning a history of suffering into a sentimentalized nostalgia for a dead past. As one local resident of Oswiecim said, "If we listen to what people tell us we should do, then we'd be a city always in mourning"; and as the owner of Disco System noted, "If they close this place down, then Oswiecim will be a place only for dying" (49).[13]

For some Jews, the Holocaust has provided a secular religion that has allowed them to continue—in spite of the collective loss of *Yiddishkeit* and in spite of not being Judaically observant—to feel somehow in connection with their Jewishness, as if the Holocaust made it possible for them to be Jews again, providing them with a sense of identity and purpose, a continued raison d'être. Stratton refers to this as "Holocaust-Jewishness, the idea that what defines being a Jew for many secular Jews is their relation to the Holocaust" (11). These "Holocaust Jews," as they are commonly referred to, are often held in contempt by religiously observant Jews. Yet, even for religious Jews, there is a teleological pressure exerted by the Holocaust that makes it a particularly compelling marker of Jewish identity and authenticity.

In this form of secular religion, there is a hallowed and priestly role reserved for Holocaust survivors. In this cult, the survivor is the voice of real authenticity, the true Jew. The large bulk of the 6 million Jews slaughtered in the Shoah were Yiddish Jews, the Ashkenazi *Ostjuden* from Central and Eastern Europe, about 5.4 million of them having originated in Poland and the Soviet Union (Stratton 2). The survivors are what remains of a once-vibrant Yiddish culture and way of life. In Israel, for example, there are still about 360,000 survivors of the Holocaust and about 700,000 offspring of survivors (*Los Angeles Times* 1/24/98: A8). Whether at Jewish studies conferences or at conventions of groups such as the American Jewish Congress or at the local synagogue, whenever a survivor stands up to speak, there is an immediate hush in the audience—for his or her words (regardless of the particular individual's character) must be paid full and exquisite attention, as if God's own deputy were speaking essential Truth. As the *Los Angeles Times* noted in a piece about the Holocaust industry, "Many of the survivors now feel comfortable enough to roll up their sleeves in public to reveal the bruise-like concentration camp numbers tattooed on their forearms, or to tell the story of seeing their parents marched off to the gas chambers, to evaporate into smoke and ashes" (1/24/98: A8)—for they are now revered as the voice of essential and authentic Jewishness. This reverence for the Holocaust experience as the defining essence of Jewish modernity is what Steyn criticizes as "those histories which set the Shoah as the founding moment of Jewish history and as the framing identity for the *Jew* in Modernity" (2). While Adorno argued that Auschwitz was the central event of our age, the works of Shoshana Felman, Claude Lanzmann, and others have, in David Suchoff's words, "suggested that the need and simultaneous impossibility of narrating the Holocaust remain the informing and unattended event of contemporary culture" (xvii).

Rolling up one's sleeves to show one's concentration-camp numbers allows the survivor to speak with a special status, to be accorded the halo of authentic Jewish truth; it is to show your defining markings, tattooed onto the Jewish body. In this way, once again—as with circumcision—the Jewish body gets inscribed with the marks of legitimization and authenticity, as if such an "essential" identity had to be made "natural," part of one's body. Indeed, Holocaust suffering and survival nearly become, culturally speaking, "naturalized" as markers of authentic modern Jewishness, something that is "in one's blood" as a Jew. As Ran Kislev wrote in the daily Israeli newspaper *Haaretz*, "Each of us carries something of the Holocaust inside, and it is passed almost in our genes from generation to generation" (quoted in the *Los Angeles Times* 1/24/98: A8). The unimaginable experience of Holocaust suffering, victimhood, and survivorship thus gets naturalized into Jewish essence, and the survivor's body carries the physical markings (and genes) of an authentic Jewish identity. The devastating irony of such logic is—as a friend of mine noted—that Hitler created the authentic Jew.[14] And he (or she) is an Ashkenazi survivor.

Certainly the memory of six million Jews murdered in the Holocaust is a horrific but extremely powerful tie for contemporary Jewry. It is an unspeakable tragedy that should never be forgotten or trivialized. But its legacy is also a complicated and problematic one. As Nobel laureate Elie Wiesel has noted, "If we say this is the single area in which our Jewishness is expressed, we would become a melancholy, paranoid generation. We should not do that" (*Los Angeles Times* 4/20/98: A10). Or, as author Susan Jacoby's father said to her about the limitations of an identity that posits Jews as tragic victims, "It's like letting Hitler define the terms. Holocaust, Holocaust, Holocaust—well, it seems to me that being a Jew has to mean something more" (in Shapiro, 18).

Wishing upon a Yellow Star

Finkielkraut, in his brilliant, important, but extremely controversial book *The Imaginary Jew*,[15] reviews the qualities of the "authentic" Jewish identity that he, as a Jew, supposedly has and which many non-Jews envy: "I am

a Jew, that is, interesting, mysterious, unique; I have a history and countenance molded by twenty centuries of suffering. . . . The world was divided
into torturers and victims, [and] I belonged to the camp of the oppressed. I
had no need of consciousness raising or of a dose of reality: from Spartacus
to Black Power, an instinctive and unconditional solidarity united me with
all the earth's damned. . . . I was an *authentic* Jew" (8–9). It is this status
and identity—the Jew as suffering, innocent victim—that creates the envy
of victimhood exemplified by Wilkomirski and by other "ethnic transvestites"
(to appropriate a term coined by Werner Sollors in *Beyond Ethnicity*).

But Holocaust envy is a problem and condition for contemporary Jews,
too, especially diasporic Jews in First World countries—for they are mostly
not Holocaust survivors nor even of the generations that were forced to undergo the anti-Semitic atrocities of the first half of the twentieth century. These
belated Jews face a double reality in the wake of the Holocaust: first, the
virtual eradication of *Yiddishkeit* as a result of the Shoah means that they, on
the whole, have no sense of a concrete Jewish cultural identity to claim as
their own; second, they missed the Holocaust, and thus cannot even feel that
they are authentic by virtue of having had their Jewishness thrust upon them.
They were not made to suffer; rather, they have grown up secure and sheltered in nations such as France and England and the United States, where
they lead comfortable, middle-class lives generally free of anti-Semitism and
ethnic threat. Thus, they feel inauthentic (and on this point I will quote at
length from Finkielkraut):

> Think of it then: the Judaism I had received was the most beautiful
> present a post-genocidal child could imagine. I inherited a suffering
> to which I had not been subjected, for without having to endure op-
> pression, the identity of the victim was mine. I could savor an ex-
> ceptional destiny while remaining completely at ease. Without
> exposure to real danger, I had heroic stature: to be Jewish was enough
> to escape the anonymity of an identity indistinguishable from oth-
> ers and the dullness of an uneventful life. . . . Judaism for me was a
> way of redeeming the quotidian. My life insignificant? . . . But within
> I was a nomad, a wandering Jew. (7)

As Finkielkraut puts it, "I had all the profit but none of the risk" (12); like
George Meredith's "sentimentalist" (cited in *Ulysses* 9:550–551), "The sentimentalist is he who would enjoy without incurring the immense debtorship
for a thing done."[16]

But Finkielkraut records how, with time, his sheltered life in a contemporary French culture that did not mistreat Jews as in previous generations led to feelings of inauthenticity within himself and his Jewish friends: "As young Jews aching to belong to a people crowned by sorrow, we couldn't wait for someone to treat us like a 'kike'" (162). Such Jews seem but "armchair Jews, since, after the Catastrophe, Judaism cannot offer them any content but suffering, and they themselves do not suffer"; for such victims of Jewish inauthenticity, Finkielkraut proposes the name "imaginary Jews" (15). "In judging others [gentiles chanting "We are all German Jews"] to be usurpers of the Jewish condition, it was impossible not to condemn myself. . . . All German Jews? Come on: we were all imaginary Jews" (21), all rendered inauthentic by virtue of belatedness. As a Jew, Finkielkraut describes the condition in which he and others like himself were themselves appropriating the Holocaust: "Even the affirmation 'I am a Jew' quickly produces a painful sense that I'm *appropriating the Holocaust as my own*, draping myself with the torture that others underwent" (32)—for, as Finkielkraut argues, no one can or should appropriate something so unspeakable that it is not appropriable: "To put it still more bluntly: the Holocaust has no heirs. No one can cloak himself in such an experience, incommunicable, if not the survivors. Among the peoples that constitute our generation, it is given to no one to say: I am the child of Auschwitz" (34).

In discussing Finkielkraut's ideas—which have been the source of much controversy among Jewish intellectuals—Suchoff points out that, for Finkielkraut, Jews had become "the elevated symbols of all who were oppressed, while concrete forms of Jewish culture and their political predicaments in history were forgotten" (xii); the cult of victimhood as Jewish identity initiates the actual erasure of Jewish identity, for "the flaunting of Jewish difference in post-Holocaust France, [Finkielkraut] suggests, enacts a suppression all its own by forgetting the culture of Yiddishkeit" (Suchoff xiv). This inauthentic identity masks contemporary Jewry's longing for an authentic Jewish culture and way of life, in "an era so devoid of significance" that the only form of Jewish identity available for secular Jews was what Finkielkraut calls "symbolic identification" (19, 21). Because "a disaster without precedent cut me off from Jewish culture," previous forms of cultural belonging were not available to him, and "the Holocaust had exiled me from the experience of Jewish collectivity itself"; as a result, now "I am nothing instinctively, unable to claim any specific kind of cultural difference" (37). In recognizing that "the sickness specific to this last quarter-century is the need for roots," Finkielkraut laments contemporary Jewry's radical lack of roots: "This murdered world moves me, haunts me, precisely because I am completely excluded from it. . . . No feeling of recognition ties me to Poland's lost Jewish community" (39): "In twenty years at the most, there will be no more than a handful of professional historians to tell us of the Jewish culture of Central Europe and of the genocide that brought it to an end. We occupy that pivotal moment, that detestable moment, when our past enters into history. . . . The Judaism into which I was born is increasingly acquiring the status of a historical object, marked by a sudden distance making it both a painful and desirable object of reflection" (176) .

Finkielkraut notes that "Jewish life was suddenly reduced to folklore by a specific, singular, and quite recent event: the Holocaust" (36–37). The horrific reduction of a vibrant and pluralistic way of life (for "Yiddishkeit was erased as one of the world's unique cultures") to a folkloric object of study and scholarship renders it a prime subject for nostalgia: "Unquenchable nostalgia for the Jewish life of Central Europe is the entire legacy I have been left. Jewishness is what I miss, not what defines me" (38). Cultural nostalgias, with their typical desire and search for an authenticating and originary native difference, inevitably erase heterogeneous differences and perpetuate stereotypes (as Wisse has also argued):

> [But the reality is that,] between the wars, the Jews of Europe were anything but a homogeneous community, and certainly not a community divided in two, split between a group of doctors-lawyers-bankers and those who wore traditional garb. Yiddish was no exotic dialect, spoken by a few fossil throwbacks as the world left them behind. Three million Jews lived in Poland; their culture was a varied space in which the observant and the secular, Zionists and Bundists, Orthodox and Reform Jews, cosmopolitan citizens and inhabitants of the shtetls rubbed shoulders and confronted one another. You could keep the sabbath without looking like a bearded prophet, enjoy the Yiddish theater as well as Bizet's *Carmen*, study the Torah and play Ping-Pong or volleyball, be fully Jewish and reject the Talmud's rules. Modernity and Judaism were not the two mutually exclusive options, one set against the other, that we have retrospectively made them to be. (41)

The Holocaust, "by reducing Jewish life to something archaic" (42), in a way completed Hitler's agenda to destroy Jewish culture, leaving us only curiosities and objects of nostalgia: "The elegiacally inclined can still visit Mea Shearim in Jerusalem, or certain neighborhoods in Brooklyn and Anvers. There they will see those freaks in flesh and blood: our era's last representatives of the Jewish civilization of Central Europe" (42). Alas, their presence now seems more like mere curiosities or "historical objects" of cultural nostalgia, not parts of a living, growing, functioning, and diverse culture. In such a vacuum, Finkielkraut suggests (in a rather essentializing move of his own), the only choices left for the Jew are religion or cultural emptiness—for now "religion constitutes the sole expression of Jewish life. There's no longer any choice: it's ritual or nothing, repetition or disappearance, the tradition . . . or the void" (98).

Israel and Diasporic Identity

Whereas the Holocaust largely destroyed the vibrant Jewish cultures of Central and Eastern Europe, there *is* another legacy of the Holocaust, which has resulted in the creation of a living and growing Jewish culture—and that is, of course, Israel. Even though the "soul" or "spirit" or identity of Israel as a nation and people is itself constantly and controversially under ongoing internal debate—see, for example, the arguments among historians such as Yoram Hazony (*The Jewish State: The Struggle for Israel's Soul*), Benny Morris (*Righteous Victims: A History of the Zionist-Arab Conflict, 1881–1999*), and Avy Shlaim (*The Iron Wall: Israel and the Arab World since 1948*); see also the first half of this chapter—in the present section I am more interested in the effect and function of "Israel" for the Diaspora, in the cultural and ideological "work" performed by the idea of Israel, especially for contemporary Jewish American culture and identity.

The history and creation of the state of Israel, after all, is importantly and inextricably connected to the Holocaust. Before the rise of Hitler, Zionism and the creation of a Zionist state were fervently argued and espoused by committed Zionists—but lukewarmly received by much of the rest of the world, including many secular Jews themselves. It is highly doubtful that the nations of the world would have agreed to the creation of such a Jewish state in the Middle East had it not been that the horrors of the Final Solution proved the urgent need of a safe haven for Jews worldwide. As commentator Ran Kislev wrote in the Israeli daily *Haaretz,* "It would not be unreasonable to say that the U.N. resolution on the establishment of the state would not have passed were it not for the trauma of the genocide which took place on European soil. Even the mass immigration to Israel might not have occurred without the Holocaust. This is the close political connection between the Holocaust and the state of Israel, part of whose population is Holocaust survivors and their children and grandchildren" (quoted in the *Los Angeles Times*

1/24/98: A8). Indeed, even now, a full 20 percent of the population of Israel consists of Holocaust survivors and descendants, which is to say that Israel is, to a significant extent, populated by those who underwent the horrors of the Holocaust—another way by which the state of Israel came into being largely as a result of the Holocaust. Just as in a sense Hitler created the authentic Jew, in a parallel sense Hitler, as the architect of the Holocaust, was a founding father of Israel. No wonder then that Jewish culture has witnessed the impulse to naturalize the Holocaust as an originary source of Jewish identity, whether in the recognition of tattooed concentration-camp numbers as the voice of Jewish legitimacy or in the argument that the Holocaust is virtually "in our genes."

This reality has also fostered the retrospective argument that the Final Solution was proof of the validity of the Zionist platform, that the Holocaust proved once and for all the necessity of leaving the Diaspora so as to form a nation of one's own with powerful military might. As Tom Segev, author of *The Seventh Million*, a study of Israel's relation to the Holocaust, writes, "The Zionist lessons of the Holocaust are that we ought to be strong and make sure nothing like that ever happens again" (*Los Angeles Times* 1/24/98: A9). Indeed, one might retrospectively argue that if Israel had been established a decade earlier than it actually was, many of the millions of Jews slaughtered in the Holocaust could have been saved via emigration to the Holy Land; as Ehud Barak said in 1992 on a visit to Auschwitz, "We came 50 years too late" (quoted in Reich 13). Nevertheless, the irony is that it was just the reverse: Israel would not have been created without the Holocaust, the founding cause and origin of Jewish statehood. As Finkielkraut observes with pained irony: "Zionism achieved universal acceptance, but it was a somber victory, and produced a tragic split. The Jewish state found its *raison d'être* in the annihilation of those for whom it had been envisioned: the persecuted communities of Eastern Europe. The Promised Land, in other words, would never have come to be if those Jews who had sworn to pursue it had not perished in the Holocaust. . . . For Israel to be born, those who needed it most had to die" (119) .

Although Israel was established to serve as a secure Jewish homeland for those Jews imperiled by the Diaspora, the odd irony is that, as Finkielkraut points out, few Jews from the First World actually move there: "Militant Zionists seem discouraged by their own triumph. Everyone agrees with them and no one moves to Israel. What movement there is now takes place in the wrong direction—New York is not only the largest Jewish city, but also the second-largest Israeli city in the world" (121). Indeed, the statistics bear this out: whereas U.S. Jewish charities and agencies raise millions of dollars each year for Israel and whereas 86 percent of U.S. Jews think that "what happens in Israel is important to them personally," in fact only 7 percent of them say that they can envision ever moving to Israel, while conversely 16 percent of Israelis say they can see themselves moving to the United States (*Los Angeles Times* 2/19/98: A36). Which is to say that on the whole, for U.S. Jews, "Israel" exists more for its symbolic value and presence than as a viable personal alternative; indeed, the predominant story of U.S.-Israeli emigration is toward the Diaspora, not toward Israel, with thousands of Israelis moving each year to cities like New York or Los Angeles, establishing—ironically—Israeli communities and enclaves (some of which resemble ghettos) in the Diaspora, a second diaspora of sorts. In 1995 there were 5,690,000 Jews in the United States, while in Israel there were 4,549,500 (*Los Angeles Times* 4/22/98: A16). Although Israel's population is also growing, this growth is not coming from diasporic Jews in the First World so much as it is largely due to the emigration of Russian Jews and to the explosive birthrates among ultra-Orthodox families. Indeed, Israel is becoming an increasingly ultra-Orthodox nation that few diasporic Jews in the First World really want to move to.

Finkielkraut points out that "the Jewish state and Jews in exile have switched roles, but *discourse about them has not changed in kind*" (129). The reality is that diasporic Jews hold on, as sentiment, to an image and rationale of Israel (in relation to their own lives) that is contrary to actual fact and practice—so that "contemporary Zionism suffers from a split between feeling and expression. Many among us go on as if nothing were wrong, praising the Promised Land for a security that only life in the Diaspora can offer. Unshakable, they keep presenting Israel as a *solution*, when in reality, it is the central site where Jewish existence continues to be a *problem*" (129). The reality is that the continued healthy existence of Jewish life is guaranteed not by Israel but by the Jewish communities in the Diaspora, in places like New York or Los Angeles (including Israeli enclaves), where Jewishness has entered mainstream history and is secure in a way it has seldom been in the long history of Jewish culture; the Diaspora is now the safe haven for Jewish emigration, whereas it is actually Israel that is continually a danger zone, fighting for its existence, and where Jews live an ever-threatened existence. Thus, the roles have been reversed in actuality—but not in ideology, for we can still pretend that the promise of the Promised Land of Zion is what it always was to the ever-threatened Jewry in the Diaspora.

"Next year in Jerusalem" is, Finkielkraut suggests, "a meaningless invocation now that Jerusalem is Jewish" (122). But the teleological, ideological power (backed by thousands of years of telling the Passover story) behind such a phrase is such that the image of Jerusalem as the eternal destination to be always desired needs continually to be culturally enforced and maintained. Consequently, Israeli immigrants living abroad carry with them always the guilt of the *yordim*—a disparaging Hebrew name for those who would dare "descend" from the land of Israel down to the Diaspora. As the *Los Angeles Times* put it, "Their presence—as voluntary immigrants, not refugees forced to leave by circumstances—seems to some to mock the essence of Zionism and the traditional declaration that closes the Passover Seder: 'Next year in Jerusalem!'" (4/22/98: A16). Indeed, for decades both the Israeli government and U.S. Jewish organizations were openly hostile toward Israeli immigrants; the latter were assailed for betraying the hallowed notion of *aliyah*, the return to the Jewish homeland.

Rather, I would argue, for many diasporic Jews—who now have the power to "identify directly with the Israeli image" (Finkielkraut 124)—Israel exists largely as a symbolic avatar, and a convenient scapegoat/carrier, of Jewish identity, suffering, and victimhood. The existence and the ongoing plights of Israel allow diasporic Jews still to cling to a knowable Jewish identity—as the ever-threatened, suffering victim, the world's scapegoat, ever dreaming of a return to Zion, the homeland, with its promise of shelter from the storms of the Diaspora.

As I have already suggested, the general global anxiety over identity and authenticity, in its particular Jewish American manifestation, elicits in some a clinging to the negative stereotype of the Jew as victim. Similarly the state of Israel, legitimized by the horrors of the Holocaust, thus has been able, while simultaneously becoming one of the world's strongest military powers, nevertheless continually to claim the status and high ground of innocent victim (even as it engages in practices that victimize others), shielded for many Jews by an intrinsic immunity to criticism.

This is even more true with the second intifada and the escalating terrorist activity and suicide bombings in Israel. The bombing not only helps consolidate the identity of Jew as victim but also consolidates for the time being a seemingly unified Jewish solidarity that belies all the internal tensions that had become manifestly clear in recent decades. In Israel, one result of the current situation has been a muting of dovish voices in opposition to military action (after all, it is understandably hard to feel dovish when you live in daily fear of being blown up); as historian Tom Segev comments, "It pushes us back into tribal closeness" (*Newsweek* 4/01/02: 29). In the United

States, the bombings have had a similarly unifying effect on Jews; as the *New York Times* reported (4/22/02: A10), "With the intensifying conflict in the Middle East and a cluster of anti-Semitic attacks in Europe, Jews across the country are feeling squeezed, increasingly worried that their homeland, and their people, are under siege. . . . Not since the wars of 1967 and 1973, perhaps not since Israel's founding in 1948, have American Jews been this united—or this unnerved." As a result, synagogue attendance is up in the United States, as well as fundraising for Jewish causes.

One specific illustration of this trend is the rise to prominence of Morton Klein, an anti-Palestinian fear monger who has been generally regarded as an extremist but who is now speaking to packed houses and garnering widespread support, even among liberal U.S. Jews, for his hard-line and essentialist views of Palestinians. In reporting on this phenomenon (in an article titled "Tapping into Jews' Fears"), the *Los Angeles Times* (6/26/02: A1) interviewed David Myers: "David N. Myers, a professor of Jewish history at UCLA, says Klein and others have tapped into what he called 'a deeply felt historical memory of persecution' that has abruptly and spectacularly reemerged among many Jews. Despite American Jews' attainment of unparalleled economic success and social acceptance, [Myers] said, the Sept. 11 terrorist attacks, rising anti-Semitism in Europe and the relentless suicide bombings in Israel have rekindled a sense of collective vulnerability." Myers laments what he calls the "mainstreaming of Morton Klein": "Pressure to present a 'united front,' he says, is having harsh consequences for any dissenting Jewish voice." Similarly, Aryeh Cohen, a scholar of Talmud at the University of Judaism in Los Angeles who had lived in Israel for twelve years and had fought in the 1982 war in Lebanon, bemoaned the fact that critiques of Israel or of Prime Minister Ariel Sharon have been now chilled where there was once open debate: "It's really painful for me to feel completely alienated from a rally in support of Israel. On a day-to-day basis, among colleagues and students, I do find myself in situations where I don't necessarily say what I think" (*New York Times* 4/22/02: A10).

The "sense of collective vulnerability" and "tribal closeness" are encapsulated by the comment of a U.S. Jewish college student: "The same battle they're fighting there, we're fighting here. My identity is threatened. They're taking a piece of who I am and stomping it" (*New York Times* 4/22/02: A10). Michael Kotzin, executive vice president of the Jewish Federation of Metropolitan Chicago, comments: "There is a sense of really being threatened, and there's also a sense the world is ganging up. It's touching something that's deep within people. Their being is at stake" (A10). What is being touched deep within people, what is at stake, is precisely their "being," precisely that their "identity is threatened"—or at least the image of their being and identity that diasporic Jews need to hold on to. The attacks on Israel have tapped into, have reinforced, that need to believe in a Jewish identity of victimhood which can rise, as it is doing now, into Amalekite paranoia. As Wieseltier writes about the escalation of Jewish anxiety among Jewish Americans, "We are [in actuality] the luckiest Jews who ever lived. We are even the spoiled brats of Jewish history. And so the disparity between the picture of Jewish life that has been bequeathed to us [the history of persecution and suffering] and the picture of Jewish life that is before our eyes [security, prosperity, and social acceptance] casts us into an uneasy sensation of dissonance. One method for relieving the dissonance is to imagine a loudspeaker summoning the Jews to Times Square. In the absence of apocalypse, we turn to hysteria" (22).

Israel is, indeed, wonderfully, uncannily, suited to such forms of symbolic identification and hysteria. And never more so than now. After all, Israel—since its inception and founding—has never known security, has always been in a state of siege or emergency, has always been threatened with extinction and surrounded by enemies, has continually felt the need to fight for its very existence. The existence and condition of Israel allow for a continued maintenance of an essentialized Jewish identity—as hated, threatened, ever-persecuted, always as David fighting multiple Goliaths. The contemporary anxiety over the loss of that comfortable and stereotyped sense of a Jewish self is alleviated by the continuing symbolic value of Israel. In a sense, Israel is the sacrificial scapegoat that allows contemporary Jewry to continue to believe in Jewish victimization and in the inevitability of anti-Semitic persecution, allows for the continued "Amalekization" of the universe. Israel is like Dorian Gray's picture in reverse, the carrier of an idealized image that allows the cultural Jewish self to continue indulging in a fantasy of an essential Jewish identity.

The maintenance of this fantasy, via symbolic identification with Israel, of a people perpetually under siege, always victimized and persecuted, helps many diasporic Jews soothe their anxiety over the loss of a specific Jewish identity and living culture—all the while that the individual diasporic Jew sits, comfortable and secure, by the swimming pool of his or her suburban ranch house reading the *Forward*. As Finkielkraut suggests, "Jews on the outside receive a whole series of important benefits from [Israel's] vulnerability. . . . Of the many anxious pleasures they enjoy, the crown jewel for Diaspora Jewry is the lucky stroke of having charged Israel, that country on the globe that *always makes the front page*, with the task of defining and representing them. For it's Israel that's always page-one news, and Israel that always makes the headlines. Such audiovisual permanence allows the Diaspora to survive its own cultural extenuation" (131). While no Jew could consciously, and in good conscience, wish for the continuation of suicide bombings—which are truly horrible—and for the seemingly insoluble cycle of Israeli-Palestinian violence, nevertheless diasporic Jews can unconsciously enjoy certain cultural benefits to their sense of self deriving from the plight of Israel. Such a plight makes the existence of the Diaspora itself—and of their individual, comfortable, and secular selves within the Diaspora—still viable, not yet (by the logic of symbolic identification) culturally inauthentic and historically irrelevant. Such diasporic Jewish identity *requires* the presence of Israel, especially an Israel under threat, so as not to judge itself inauthentic or irrelevant.

No wonder then that, like "Holocaust Jews," so many secular Jews have embraced the unequivocal support of Israel as a neoreligious cause, resulting in what Finkielkraut describes as "this unconditional support for every Israeli policy [, which] is the symptom of a malaise" (131), a secular religion of sorts: "Now there are two types of practicing Jew: the devout who attend synagogue, and the much more numerous group who produce a running (and delectable) commentary on the situation in the Middle East as their form of observance. What do the oil embargo, the Camp David accords or the Islamic revival actually mean to assimilated Jews in Europe or America? Constant recognition, and a regular reminder of their condition. . . . For the problems that make the Jewish state an object of debate are received as a series of gratifying images, becoming material for an authentic religious practice" (132) . Indeed, it is my contention, and my conclusion, that Israel— together with the Holocaust—provide jointly, for contemporary Jews in the Diaspora, a form of secular and ideological religion (and what Finkielkraut 138 calls "Sentimental Zionism") that helps give many Jews a comfortable, continuing, and reassuring sense of authenticity and a Jewish self, one seemingly mandated and justified by both essence and history.

For many diasporic Jews, this reassuring sense of authenticity and Jewishness, brought to them courtesy of Israel and the Holocaust, helps to deflect (and to keep at bay) their anxieties about inauthenticity and a loss of identity. Especially with almost-daily Palestinian suicide bombings threatening the security of Israel and with growing anti-Semitic violence in Europe raising again the specter of the Holocaust, U.S. Jews certainly find themselves concerned— but, at the same time, many of them haven't felt this Jewish in a long time.

CHAPTER 6

Asian American Identity

THE GOOD, THE BAD, THE UGLY—AND THE FUTURE

I begin this chapter with an extended discussion of what we loosely call "mixed-race" identities and dynamics (and what we might mean by that term) and of the increasingly prominent place of mixed-race individuals in contemporary U.S. culture, especially in relation to Asian and Asian American cultures in this country, as a way to initiate a discussion of Asian American identity and particularly of the latter's relationship to mixed-race issues. It is my contention—as I shall argue—that what we call "Asian American" identity is a category that could be more fruitfully thought of, in functional terms, as a "mixed" racial or ethnic category. From there, the rest of the chapter analyzes and discusses the peculiar and "mixed" natures of this Asian American identity still very much under construction, culminating with some speculations about the promising potentials that such a strangely fabricated identity may hold in store.

"Love Your Race" (If You Can Find It . . .)

To begin with, what do we mean by "mixed race"? What do we even mean by "race"? I recently found several sheets of paper, rather crumpled and weather-beaten, blowing in the wind in front of my house in Salt Lake City. The contents of the first one I picked up took my breath away for a moment: over an iconic image of a blond, white woman (with a halolike aura around her head) were three words printed in large bold capital letters: "LOVE YOUR RACE." Below the female image (the white woman as "the banner of race," as E. M. Forster wrote in *A Passage to India*) was the organization's identification—"National Alliance"—along with its telephone number, address, and website information. The National Alliance is obviously a white supremacist organization, and the other pieces of windblown paper were some of its hate literature, blaming nonwhite peoples for all of the social problems in the United States. Such material is troubling and incendiary enough to find floating in one's neighborhood. But it was "LOVE YOUR RACE"—obviously addressed not to me but to white Americans—which I found most arresting and which I could not stop thinking about. Out of context, "Love Your Race" might seem—at a cursory glance—a phrase addressed to anyone, and an innocuous-enough message: after all, we encourage different peoples to celebrate their particular identities and heritages, whether it's during Kwanza, Chinese New Year's, or St. Patrick's Day. Why shouldn't we each take pride in our individual race or ethnicity or culture? However, in the context of racist arguments for racial purity, I found myself muttering, "Yeah, if you can find it. . . . " After all, how do you even *know* if you are white? Indeed, who qualifies as "white" in the United States has shifted continually and has been under debate since the days of the Founding Fathers. How can you be sure what race you even belong to? And is that in fact an actual "race"? Or an "ethnicity"? Such labels are just perceptions, after all, which we tend to accept and which interpellate us: I am a white American of Irish origin; I am a Hispanic male; I am an Asian American woman; and so on. But such categories are hardly set in stone.

For example, is "Asian American" (or "Asian/Pacific Islander")—the identity under consideration in this chapter—a "race"? Are Asians a distinct race? Or is Asian American an ethnicity? In the United States today we tend to, in popular usage, imagine "Asian American" as an ethnicity, comparable to something like Chicano identity—but, in fact, the sociological distinction generally goes something like this: "Race has been used by theorists to refer to distinctions drawn from physical appearance. Ethnicity has been used to refer to distinctions based on national origin, language, religion, food—and other cultural markers" (Mittelberg and Waters 425, quoted in Tuan 21). On the basis of this distinction, then, "Chinese" (or Chinese American) and "Korean" (or Korean American) might designate different ethnicities. But the omnibus term *Asian American* is clearly not an ethnic designation. But would this combined category—Asian, or Asian American—then constitute a "race"? Why should we think so? Do we really imagine that people as different as, say, Sikhs, Samoans, Filipinos, and Koreans, all actually belong to the same "race"?

And what about "mixed-race" identities? As Michael Omi reminds us, "To consider an individual or group as 'mixed race' presupposes the exist-

LOVE YOUR RACE

ence of clear, discernible, and discrete 'races.' But the concept of race as a biological category has been roundly discredited in the sciences, and we are left struggling over the social construction of multiraciality and its cultural and political meaning" (x). At the same time, Omi and Howard Winant remind us that, in the United States, each person needs to have such an identity: "without a racial identity, one is in danger of having no identity" at all (Omi and Winant 62)—and the perceived lack of such a racial/ethnic identity is the source of that cultural anxiety about inauthenticity that I have referred to as the whitebread blues. But how can we talk about "mixed race" without knowing what "race" is? If we don't really believe in race and racial distinctions, if we consider them "social constructions," does the term "mixed race" then really even have any usable purchase? The simple fact is that we clearly don't know what "race" means, since we cannot even determine how many races there are: three (black, white, yellow)? five (black, white, yellow, red, Australasian)? Race has been a convenient fiction we have bought into for centuries and still buy into; but it has no strict and measurable basis and has eluded all attempts at scientific definition. Mostly it suggests popular classifications based on ostensible differences in skin color, facial features, and hair texture; but, in view of the entire broad range of biological and genetic variations within humankind, these are largely superficial differences. Indeed, genetic variations within a "race" are much greater than variations between the "races," and genetic similarities among the "races" are much greater than differences. Most scientists and sociologists have now abandoned "race" as a scientifically meaningful category: for example, in 1995 the American College of Physicians urged its eighty-five thousand members to omit racial designations in patient case files because "race has little or no utility in careful medical thinking" (*Los Angeles Times* 4/15/95: A1); that same year geneticists at the American Association for the Advancement of Science's annual conference confirmed that they considered racial categories to be biologically meaningless (Nakashima, "Servants" 43). Rather, "race" as a term is a relic that has been dangerously used to mean whatever we have needed it to mean. Numerous social scientists—such as Michael Banton, in his comprehensive study *Racial Theories*—have detailed the complex, varied, and inconsistent theories and conceptions of race in Western history and science—in which "race" could variously be confused with issues of sociology, biology, ethnicity, nationality, genetics, lineage, physical typology, animal species, social class, status, and so on—theories that were often backed by the scientific or pseudoscientific imprimatur of the most educated circles of the time. Given all the confusions, "race" as a term has been virtually a Rorschach test, a hopelessly unspecific term that serves as a blank screen or cipher upon which to encode a culture's or an individual's own unacknowledged preoccupations; as Ruben Martinez has written, "Often when we say 'race' we mean 'nationality' or 'ethnicity' or even 'religion' or 'culture.' We say race when we mean class. We say race when we mean fear" (12). As L. Perry Curtis Jr. points out, "The word race always seems to cry out for definition, if only because those who use it so rarely bother to explain their meaning" (*Anglo-Saxons* 2); as Banton concludes, "Were it not that so many members of the general public still thought in terms of race, it would by this time have been possible to dispense with the word" (96).[1]

Love your race? Which race? Are you even sure you are white? After all, what is considered "white" in the United States has been changing significantly during the past century. At the beginning of the twentieth century, Irish, Italians, Jews, and many Central European ethnic groups were considered separate "races." Their supposedly hereditary traits—such as simian features, low intelligence, sexual rapaciousness, propensity for drunken and criminal behavior—were considered such a threat to the common weal that Congress stepped in to impose immigration quotas on such groups (passing a law in 1924 to severely limit immigration of the so-called inferior races of Southern and Eastern Europe). Scholarly work has brought the history of such startling changes to public consciousness.[2] Indeed, as Ian Haney-Lopez, author of *White by Law: The Legal Construction of Race,* argues, Congress and the courts have tried to legally adjudicate—for the purposes of immigration, naturalization, and voting rights—what science has never been able to determine: the difference between races and who qualifies for that most preferred category of "a free white person." As Haney-Lopez notes, "You would expect the courts to come up with a definition for what this phrase 'white person' means." But the courts repeatedly "refuse to do so and instead establish the nonwhiteness of the particular person before them" (quoted in the *Los Angeles Times* 4/15/95: A14). The results have been confusing and inconsistent: at different times, for example, Armenians were both white and nonwhite; Chinese immigrants—but not Japanese—were classified as "colored"; Mexican immigrants were classified first as a separate race and later as white, while today we designate them as "Hispanic." Children of mixed ancestries were variously considered legally white or legally nonwhite, depending on the miscegenation laws of different states (similarly, French tennis star Yannick Noah—whose mother is French and whose father is from Cameroon—notes that "in Africa I am white, and in France I am black"; *Newsweek* 2/13/95: 68). Perhaps the most fickle racial status has been that for immigrants from the Indian subcontinent: "In a series of court rulings and administrative decisions since the 1920s, the racial status of Indian immigrants has gone from 'Hindu'—a religious designation used as a racial label—to Caucasian, to nonwhite, to white—and then most recently to 'Asian Indian,' so [that] Indian immigrants and their descendants could qualify legally for minority status" (*Los Angeles Times* 4/15/95: A14). The definitions are likely to keep changing. Ellis Cose predicts that "we have no idea what 'majority race' will mean half a century from now. . . . Earlier in this century, entry of eastern and Southern Europeans was restricted because of their supposedly inferior racial stock. Now Romanians are considered as white as any other Europeans. By the middle of the 21st century, many of those whom the Census projects to be Asian, Hispanic or black may be considered white—or whatever the new term is for the majority" ("Colors" 30). As Omi points out, "You can be born one race and die another" (*Los Angeles Times* 4/15/95: A14). So which race should you love?

These prevarications and inconsistencies in U.S. racial classification are the result of the long and complicated legacy of black slavery and segregation, specifically of the "one-drop rule": that is, anyone who has even a single drop of black blood (whatever that means)—or a single black ancestor—is considered black, regardless of the degree of white ancestry (or "white blood") involved. The rule was instituted to make sure that the mixed-race offspring of black slaves and white masters would remain enslaved—and the result is a bizarre binary approach to race that imagines everything in black and white and rejects anything in-between, effectively denying the existence of the category of "mixed race" and of racial gradations altogether. As Orlando Patterson notes, "The U.S. approach to racial identity has been most unusual. In much of the rest of the world, people make [social and class] distinctions based on gradations of color" (quoted in *Newsweek* 2/13/95: 64).

In 1790, the young nation created its very first citizenship law, limiting naturalization only to "aliens being free white persons." Except for an amendment after the Civil War granting citizenship to black slaves, that law was basically in place until 1952—resulting in generations of nonwhites (such as Japanese and Indians) trying to prove that they were "white" enough to attain citizenship. Early on, the "one-drop rule" had not been so strict: for example, in Virginia during the nineteenth century, a person with one-fourth "Negro blood" (a "quadroon") still qualified as white; but in 1910 the state made into law what had become by then customary, defining "white" as having less than one-sixteenth "Negro ancestry." In 1924, under pressure from white supremacists, it became illegal for whites to marry anyone with "a single drop of Negro blood." Many other states (on both sides of the Mason-Dixon line) adopted similar miscegenation laws based on the one-drop rule, effectively prohibiting interracial mixing. It was not until 1967—with the Supreme Court decision in *Loving* v. *Virginia*—that such miscegenation laws were declared unconstitutional (though some remain on the books even today).

One legacy of such binary thinking is that, according to polls, three out of ten white Americans still oppose marriage between blacks and whites—but whites are more tolerant of whites marrying Latinos or Asians (*Los Angeles Times* 4/27/98: A12). These attitudes, however, are changing quickly among younger people, who are much more tolerant of racial mixing altogether. Indeed, the current celebration of multiracial and multiethnic heritage (see discussion below) could well be viewed as, at last, a nationwide rejection of the one-drop rule, of its binary approach to racial issues, and of the resultant traditional abhorrence of "miscegenation." Patterson, for one, views racial mixing as a possible solution to the binary dead end: "If your object is the eventual integration of the races, a mixed-race or middle group is something you'd want to see developing. . . . The middle group grows larger and larger, and the races eventually blend" (*Newsweek* 2/13/95: 65). Will it be possible, in the future, to "Love Your Race(s)"?

The Good, the Bad, and the Ugly/Beautiful: Mixed Races

In the longstanding, binary, and Manichean logic of white racism, white was good; black (actually, anything nonwhite, but especially black) was bad; and anything in between was ugly (and may as well have been labeled black). As a result, interracial relationships were considered "miscegenation" (and frequently banned by law), and any offspring from interracial relationships were called derogatory terms like *mutts, mongrels, half-breeds, hapas,* and so on. Bolstered by the pseudoscientific logic of scientific racism in the late nineteenth and early twentieth centuries, white Americans considered mixed-race individuals to be "unnatural," degenerate, confused, and conflicted. Cynthia Nakashima summarizes such notions: "that it is 'unnatural' to 'mix the races'; that multiracial people are physically, morally, and mentally weak; that multiracial people are tormented by their genetically divided selves; and that intermarriage 'lowers' the biologically superior white race; . . . that people of mixed race are socially and culturally marginal, doomed to a life of conflicting cultures and unfulfilled desire to be 'one or the other,' neither fitting in nor gaining acceptance in any group, thus leading lives of confused loneliness and despair" ("Invisible Monster" 165).

Such notions were applied not only to black-white offspring, but also to white-Asian mixed-race individuals. As Edward Byron Reuter, the leading expert on racial mixing in his time, wrote in 1918 (in *The Mulatto in the United States*): "Physically the Eurasians are slight and weak. Their personal appearance is subject to the greatest variations. In skin color, for example, they are often darker even than the Asiatic parent. They are naturally indolent and will enter into no employment requiring exertion or labor. This lack of energy is correlated with an incapacity for organization. They will not assume burdensome responsibilities, but they make passable clerks where only routine labor is required" (cited in Spickard, "What" 258).

If white U.S. society was historically unwilling to accept and welcome mixed-race Eurasian/Amerasian individuals, the individual Asian cultures in this country were equally inhospitable: up to the 1960s, most mixed-race Amerasians had to live their lives outside Asian American communities, which would simply not have them (Spickard, "What" 260). Even Edith Maude Eaton, now canonized as the pioneer Chinese American writer Sui Sin Far for writing sympathetic representations of Chinese Americans a century ago, was—as the daughter of a Chinese mother and a British father—allowed no place in the Chinese American community (Spickard, "Who" 14). Indeed, many Chinese in the United States were hostile not only to intermarriage with whites and with other non-Chinese peoples (such as Japanese and Filipinos) but even to mixing between different Chinese ethnicities (Cantonese, Hakka, Shanghai natives, Taiwanese, and so on). In both the Japanese American and the Chinese American communities, intermarriage was relatively infrequent, for not only did antimiscegenation laws forbid intermarriage with whites, but both groups were strongly prejudiced against each other and against other Asian peoples. In Asian American history, only Chinese-Hawaiian ("local") culture and Filipino American culture have had a history of broad tolerance for intermarriage (with much or most of their own populations eventually becoming "mixed").

Such interracial distinctions were lost on white Americans, who—with the longstanding logic of European "Orientalism"—perceived neither the distinctions between different Asian peoples nor the gradations of mixed-race individuals (whether Eurasian or inter-Asian): they were all considered "Orientals." This was a racist belief both reflected in and further encouraged by the categories instituted by the U.S. Census, which in the twentieth century initially classified all Asian peoples as "Orientals" and then later, in 1963, as "Asians and Pacific Islanders" (and has since included South Asians in the category of Asian Americans), lumping them all into a single monoracial category. Such an essentialist logic defines and classifies large and heterogeneous groups of individuals (from Manila to Manchuria, from Calcutta to Kyoto) as one and the same, validating racist ideas of essential differences. Meantime, those—such as mixed-race Eurasians—who didn't fit into the classifiable categories of the Census were left in a no man's land, marginalized by both groups as "inauthentic" and degenerate, and—through the logic of the one-drop rule—usually relegated to the lowest rung of the categories on the racial ladder. For example, if you were half-white and half-Chinese, you were Chinese, not white. This is what has become known, in multiracial academic discourse, as the "hypodescent" rule—in which a person's racial designation automatically "descends" to the lowest relevant rung on the racial ladder, rather than "ascending" to a higher rung.

This history of mistreatment and marginalization of mixed-race people is, however, undergoing a startling revolution. Love your mixed race? At least at the level of popular culture and popular perceptions, the mutt is no longer the Ugly but the Beautiful: America is learning to love the mutt. In an essay for *Newsweek*, Cose concludes with a triumphant prediction: "The color line is fraying all around us. The American future certainly will not be circumscribed by one long line with whites on one side and the 'darker' races on the other; there will be many lines, and many camps, and few will be totally segregated. Disparities will remain. But with the rudest remainders of racism washed away, it will be a lot easier to tell ourselves that we have finally overcome" ("Colors" 30). While I am, as will become clear, nowhere nearly as optimistic as Cose is, it is certainly true that attitudes toward the color line—especially in terms of interracial relationships and mixed-race individuals—have undergone a striking, startling, and salutary revolution. Between 1960 and 1992, as Cose points out (28), the number of interracially married American couples multiplied more than seven times. The rise has been especially remarkable for marriages between Asians and whites; in the United States today, children born to white-Japanese couples, for example, outnumber those born to fully Japanese couples—and the comparable figures for other Asian American groups are not far behind.

At U.S. universities, courses on multiracial identity are no longer a curricular oddity; and most campuses now have mixed-race student organizations. There are a number of popular magazines now specifically devoted to multiracial readers, issues, and lifestyles (including *Interrace*, *Interracial Voice*, *Mavin*, *Métisse*, and *New People*); Asian American magazines and newspapers—such as *A. Magazine*, *Asian Week*, and *Pacific Citizen*—regularly and repeatedly feature multiracial issues and stories. National news magazines such as *Time* and *Newsweek* have repeatedly trumpeted what *Newsweek* calls "the Age of Color," in which mixed-race individuals have been discovering that "suddenly it was cool to be mixed" (9/18/00: 41). As one biracial high school student from Oakland, California, is quoted as saying, "It's like everybody is mixed these days" (*Newsweek* 5/8/00: 70).

Indeed, in the early 1970s, only one out of every hundred children born in the United States was of mixed race; by 2000 the figure was nineteen out of every hundred. In very racially mixed states like California and Washington, the figure is now closer to one in ten (*Newsweek* 5/8/00: 70). Between 1970 and 1992, the number of interracial marriages quadrupled. Even before the 2000 Census, 2.2 percent of all U.S. marriages were interracial, about double the rate measured in 1980. Over 6 percent of African Americans marry someone from a different race, while fully 20 percent of Asian Americans marry interracially: the result, by 1997, was nearly two million interracial children under the age of eighteen (*Newsweek* 5/5/97: 59). In California, the most populous state and one in which whites are no longer a majority, about one in every ten marriages is a mixed-race union; among younger adults that figure surges even higher. Indeed, a 1994 *Los Angeles Times* poll conducted in California's Orange County found that 60 percent of young adults between the ages of eighteen and thirty-four had dated someone of another race (4/27/98: A14). No wonder that, among California's youth, being multiracial is chic, that "it's like everybody is mixed these days."

Our popular culture also reflects the degree to which the mutt has come out of the closet, with numerous cultural figures and popular icons now proudly announcing their multiracial or multiethnic identities: "Cablinasian" golfer Tiger Woods (Caucasian, black, native American, Thai, and Chinese); pop singer Mariah Carey (black Venezuelan and white); actors Keanu Reeves (Hawaiian, Chinese, white), Johnny Depp (Cherokee, white), and Dean Cain (Japanese, white); *Today Show* NBC newswoman Ann Curry (Japanese, white); and Secretary of State Colin Powell (Jamaican black, white). At the UC Berkeley campus, a multiracial student group calls itself Hapa, taking the derogatory Hawaiian slur for mixed race (literally, "half") and reclaiming that heritage with pride—in the same way that the Gay Pride movement has reclaimed the once-ugly word *queer*. Indeed, multiracial societies now abound, on both high school and college campuses (with support groups such as Prism at Harvard, Spectrum at Stanford, Hapa at Berkeley) as well as adult pride groups (such as Biracial Family Network in Chicago and I-Pride in San Francisco). At the level of popular culture and cultural chic, this really is "the Age of Color."

In view of both the exploding number of mixed-race Americans and the expanding consciousness and acceptance of mixed-race status, the U.S. Census Bureau and the Department of Justice, during the 1990s, considered and debated establishing a "mixed-race" category for the 2000 Census. Instead, it chose what Eric Liu describes as "a potentially more radical solution: allowing people to check as many boxes as they wish" (191). And there are indeed many boxes now to choose from: in the 1860 Census, just before the Civil War, there were only three Census categories (white, black, and "quadroon"); in 1990, there were five (white, black, American Indian and Alaskan Native, Asian and Pacific Islander, and Other); in 2000, there were sixty-three (including eleven subcategories under "Hispanic ethnicity" alone). People happily checked all the boxes that applied, revealing "that ever-increasing numbers of people are unwilling to identify themselves by a single ethno-racial category" (*New York Times* 7/29/01: AR28).

In actuality, the Census Bureau's decision to provide sixty-three listed designations was a hotly contested compromise between those who argued for keeping the status quo and those who argued for adding a single "multiracial" category. Multiracial advocacy groups had been pushing for the latter option, but the compromise decision was a bittersweet one for longstanding civil rights and ethnic advocacy groups—such as the NAACP, the National Urban League, the Japanese American Citizens League, and the National Council of La Raza—all of which argued that a separate multiracial category would be too large and amorphous to be meaningful. Noting that the categories in place had been created in 1977 so as to help government agencies enforce civil rights law, they argued that a multiracial option would lead to the under-representation of racial and ethnic groups such as African Americans, Latinos, and Asian Americans. They urged their members not to check more than one box, for fear of diluting their hard-won civil rights and political clout. As the *Los Angeles Times* (7/9/97: A13) reported in the midst of the debate:

> A multiracial category would undermine the Voting Rights Act, for example, by affecting the number and location of minority voting districts. The configuration of such districts is based on the number of people who identify themselves as members of a specific racial group; the law, as written, does not take into account mixed-race voters.
>
> Opponents also have expressed concern that a multiracial category could lead to reduced government and private financing of minority programs that are linked to Census figures. In addition, some fear it would cause mixed-race Americans to "disconnect" from the civil rights movement.

As Census Day 2000 approached, a flood of emails in Hawaii urged Native Hawaiians—many, perhaps most, of whom are multiracial—to identify themselves only as Native Hawaiians and not avail themselves of multiple options; the same plea was made by Native American advocacy groups: "We were pretty forward and upfront—just mark American Indian only," said Paula Starr, executive director of the Southern California Indian Center (*Salt Lake Tribune* 3/25/01: A3).

This was an especial concern for Asian American advocacy groups, since Asian Americans, as a whole, have been less eager to define themselves by a shared "Asian" race or ethnicity and were more likely to mark more than one race, thus potentially eroding a hard-earned pan-Asian voting bloc and splintering "Asian Americans" into numerous subgroups. As Glenn Magpantay, a lawyer with the Asian American Legal Defense and Education Fund, pointed out, "Racial and ethnic minorities may be diluted, diminished, and even disappear in certain contexts" (*Salt Lake Tribune* 3/25/01: A3). This comes at a time when Asian American organizations feel that they are on the verge of finally mobilizing a "pan-Asian movement" into a powerful political force that could unite the various Asian communities and help translate the formidable economic clout and the high levels of education of the Asian American communities into an organized political power. Asian American organizer Julie Lee points out that "Asians, more than any other immigrant group of its size, are poised to mature politically. We see professionals who had never voted before, highly educated people from Taiwan and engineers in the Silicon Valley, joining clubs and organizing their neighborhoods" (*Los Angeles Times* 7/12/98: A31).

The debate between Asian American civil rights groups and multiracial Asian Americans over the proposed single multiracial category was "intense and bitter" (Omi xi): "In the 1990s, both the Association of MultiEthnic Americans (AMEA) and Project RACE (Reclassify All Children Equally) actively lobbied for multiracial recognition. But this was met with resistance from Asian American/Pacific Islander organizations that feared such a policy would reduce the Asian/Pacific Islander count and erode civil rights protections. The National Coalition for an Accurate Count of Asians and Pacific Islanders (NAPALC) stated that 'adding a multiracial category would undermine the effectiveness of civil rights enforcement agencies because of the inconsistent counts and the uncertainties it introduces.'" The government's decision to offer sixty-three official racial categories was a compromise that was generally applauded by multiracial advocacy groups, since individuals could now check a combination of categories and would not be limited to monoracial designations.

The arguments in favor of monoracial designations had to do largely with issues of political clout by voting blocs such as African Americans, Asian Americans, and Chicanos. But I would suggest that the most radical, most threatening, and most unacknowledged threat of providing a single *multi-racial* category is that—assuming we could all for a moment actually agree on what "race" means—in actuality many of us, perhaps *most* of us, Americans of whatever racial/ethnic heritage, should in all honesty check such a category—in which case the dominant, majority racial/ethnic designation in the country would no longer be "white" but "multiracial." And we would almost all be in it. Love your race—if you can find it/them. After all, the very first mixed-race children in the country were born back in Colonial Jamestown. As Teresa Williams-Leon and Cynthia Nakashima remind us, "Our historical amnesia allows us to forget this nation's 'race-mixing' past with its complex tradition of hypodescent, one-drop rules, and 'passing.' Today, most of those who would be categorized as 'Latino' or 'African American' could also be considered 'racially mixed'—usually from many generations back. The same can be said for many Americans who are typically identified as 'European American,' 'Native American,' 'Pacific Islander,' or 'Asian American'" (11).

In *Racially Mixed People in America*, Maria Root notes that 30 to 70 percent of African Americans are estimated to be of multiracial ancestry—while Filipinos and Latinos are almost all multiracial, as are most Native Americans and native Hawaiians (see *A. Magazine* 3.1: 77). If we ignore the perverse logic of hypodescent and one-drop rules, most multigenerational Americans—white, black, or whatever—likely already have more than several drops of a different racial heritage (or two) in them. (Even foreign-born immigrants are frequently of mixed heritage.) Perhaps we should *all* check the multiracial box. This is especially true, as I will argue below, of Asian Americans.

What Is Asian American Identity?

Susan Koshy (472) usefully summarizes the origins of the concept of Asian Americanness from its inception in the student activism of the 1960s:

> The identity category "Asian American" was a product of the struggles of the 1960s but has been used to organize and interpret this set of immigrant experiences retrospectively and prospectively. The struggles of the 1960s also led to the establishment of the academic discipline of Asian American Studies. The term "Asian American" emerged in the context of civil rights, Third World, and anti–Vietnam war movements and was self-consciously adopted (in preference to "Oriental" or "Yellow") primarily on university campuses where the Asian American Movement enjoyed the broadest support. The opening up of higher education and the demographic

changes of the postwar years made possible, for the first time, the presence of Japanese, Filipino, and Chinese American students in significant numbers on some university campuses. From these beginnings, the term "Asian American" has passed into academic and bureaucratic, and thence into popular usage. . . . The Asian American movement was pivotal in creating a pan-Asian identity politics that represented their "unequal circumstances and histories as being related" [Lowe 71]. Asian American was a political subject position formulated to make visible a history of exclusion and discrimination against immigrants of Asian origin.

Two personal anecdotes, snapshots from my own past: First, 1969, I arrived in Cambridge, Massachusetts, to begin college at Harvard; I was eighteen, had gone to high school in North America, and spoke English fluently and without an accent. But I had grown up in various other countries (mostly in Taiwan, Mexico, Brazil, and Canada), was brought up Chinese, spoke Chinese, and had a Taiwanese passport (I was in the United States on both a diplomatic visa and a student visa); I did not feel fully American yet. One of my earliest memories of Harvard, however, was of being accosted by two Asian American student activists attempting to interpellate me into their cause. Although I understood that their cause was related to the black civil rights movement as well as the anti–Vietnam War protests, both of which had my sympathy and full support, this "Asian American" business struck me as positively weird. African Americans, I understood, had a long and shared history as a people in this country, a long legacy of slavery and mistreatment, and a rich and particular culture (of black music, literature, dialect, foods, and so on). But what was this "Asian American" thing? What did *that* mean? I myself felt sort of Chinese, not fully American, not particularly "Asian"—and certainly not Asian American, whatever that was. The other Asians I had met in the various cultures I grew up in—native Koreans, Japanese Brazilians, Mexican Filipinos, my grandmother's Thai friends, and so on—seemed no more related to me than a black or a white American. "Asian American" seemed to me a quite meaningless fabrication—and so those two intense young men were thoroughly unsuccessful in hailing me to their side.

Second, years later, having just completed my Ph.D. in English literature at Stanford University, I arrived in Los Angeles to begin my first full-time teaching job, at the University of Southern California. I had written a dissertation on James Joyce and was hired as a specialist in modern literature. So it was a real shock, on my arrival, to hear my new department chair say to me, "Good, now we have someone who can teach courses in Asian American literature." After my initial shock, I found myself incensed: I had worked very hard developing my credentials as a specialist in twentieth-century European modernism, just as scholars and students of Asian American studies and ethnic studies had worked equally hard in specializing in Asian American literature. It was an insult to both myself and them that someone should assume that just because I was clearly "Asian," I was qualified to do Asian American studies. (I had never in my student years taken a single course in Asian American literature.) This assumption was hardly a nod to authenticity but rather to tokenism and essentialism, even racism. And that it should come from an educated intellectual, an English professor like myself, was particularly distressing. In my anger, I immediately made clear, perhaps a bit too clear (I didn't in the heat of the moment consider how risky a thing it was for a new and untenured junior faculty member to stand up to his boss), that I had not been trained to teach Asian American literature—and that there were serious scholars who, unlike myself, had real expertise in that field.[3] This incident was, of course, an experience of essentialism and racialization *imposed* upon me by someone else. Although I was never again asked to teach Asian American literature, years later I would found, and become director of, the USC Asian American Studies Program. But this latter choice would be a *voluntary* affiliation, an individual *choice* to identify and affiliate; the distinction is an important one which I will return to later in this chapter.

This moment early in my career also drove home to me an important lesson and political reality. It was the reality of imposed racialization, borne out of the unacknowledged racism which I (like all Asian children in this country) had been experiencing in small ways and incidents throughout my childhood: the realization that many white Americans couldn't tell (and didn't much care to tell) if I was a nip, a gook, a chink, or what, sometimes taunting me with interchangeable racist slurs ("chin-chon-chinaman" and so on) and affecting grotesquely slanted eyes, repeatedly treating me (in spite of my flawless English) as a foreigner, an FOB (fresh off the boat). This is the political reality for Asians in the United States: to many white (and also black) Americans, we (assuming there is a "we" here) are all the same. It is but a small step, within such a logic, to assume that we all have the same racial essence/authenticity/authority (and thus we can all teach Asian American literature equally).

This lesson is also the racialized and politicized basis for Asian American identity, the motivation and rationale behind the Asian American movement and its identity politics. As an idea, "Asian American" is a purely political invention, a political expediency created in response to white racism and Orientalism, a very recent invention and term coined by the late UCLA historian Yuji Ichioka in the late 1960s. This "most basic rationale for pan-Asian solidarity" is, as Liu notes, "self-defense": "That is why so many Americans of various ethnic origins have chosen, over the last generation, to adopt a one-size-fits-all 'Asian American' identity. It is an affirming counterstatement to the narrative in which yellow people are either foreigners or footnotes. It is a bulwark against bigotry" (63). "The Asian American narrative," he points out, "is rooted deeply in threat" (69).

After all, if they see us as all the same and are going to (mis)treat us as if we were all the same, as threats to the American body politic, then we are going to join forces and organize into a larger group that cannot be pushed around so easily and so helplessly. Given such a rationale, it is also clear that the argument for Asian American solidarity is at its most persuasive at times of greatest anti-Asian discrimination and violence. The Wen Ho Lee affair, for example, did much to mobilize Asian American, especially Chinese American, political unity and voter registration. As Yen Le Espiritu wrote in 1992, "The [Vincent] Chin case makes it clear that, while political benefits certainly promote pan-Asian organization, it is anti-Asian violence that has drawn the largest pan-Asian support because it cross-cuts class, cultural, and generational divisions and necessarily leads to protective panethnicity. Thus, we can expect that, if racial hostilities against Asians escalate, pan-Asian organization will correspondingly increase" (*Asian American* 163–164). Espiritu's prediction was dead-on, for anti-Asian violence did escalate all through the 1990s, as did simultaneously the success of Asian American advocacy groups at pan-Asian political organization and voter registration. According to a 1997 NAPALC report, violent attacks against Asian Americans increased steadily between 1992 and 1996, with a record 534 cases reported nationwide in 1996 (Tuan 42); a subsequent report in late 2000 by a coalition of Asian American civil rights groups confirmed that this trend was continuing into the new century (*Newsweek* 11/6/00: 61). But the paradigmatic and motivating moment, the emblematic incident, of such violence—for many self-identifying Asian Americans—was still the 1982 killing in Detroit of Vincent Chin, in the midst of the economic slump in the U.S. auto industry and the growing popularity of Japanese cars (and the growth of Japan as a global economic power). As Espiritu points out, "In the Asian-American case, group members can suffer sanctions for no behavior of their own, but for the activities of others who resemble them" (*Asian American* 132). As Mia Tuan writes, "The killing of Vincent Chin, a 1.5 generation Chinese-American mistakenly accused of being a 'job-stealing Jap,' stands as the tragic embodiment of this disregard for ethnic and generational differences" (Tuan 43). For those unfamiliar with the story or with the acclaimed documentary film *(Who Killed Vincent Chin?)*, I provide Ron Takaki's summary of the incident: "On June 19, 1982, this twenty-seven-year-old Chinese-American went to a Detroit bar with three friends to celebrate his upcoming wedding. There, two white auto workers—Ronald Ebens and his stepson, Michael Nitz—taunted him, reportedly calling him 'Jap.' Ebens complained: 'It's because of you, motherfuckers, that we're out of work!' A brief scuffle ensued. Chin quickly left the bar, and was chased and hunted by Ebens and Nitz. They finally trapped Chin in front of a McDonald's restaurant where Nitz held their prey while Ebens bludgeoned him with a baseball bat" ("Who Killed Vincent Chin?" 23).

One could well comment on the various forms of hate and racism involved in this case of ethnic mistaken identity, not to speak of violence. But one thing that is clear is that not much has changed since the days of Fu Manchu or of the Yellow Peril or of Japanese internment: whether native-born Americans or recent immigrants, Asians in the United States are simply not considered "real" Americans. They simply don't qualify in the popular imagination as Americans, are forever branded as what Lisa Lowe calls (in *Immigrant Acts*) "the foreigner-within."

So, since we Asians are all the same, all perpetual foreigners—we have chosen to organize together for self-defense, for political expediency, and for political clout. Pakistanis, Tongans, Sikhs, Koreans, native Hawaiians, Filipinos, Chinese, Japanese, Vietnamese, whatever—come one, come all, however little you may have in common: we can all pretend to be in fact what they think we are, "the same." And what potential we have for real political muscle! From 1990 to 2000 the nation's Asian population soared more than 43 percent, to roughly eleven million, making us the fastest-growing (and most highly educated) minority group (*Newsweek* 11/6/00: 61); California alone has more than five million Asian Americans. Many, especially first-generation immigrants, are still reluctant to get involved politically, not to speak of identifying as Asian American; but many more are doing so in ever greater numbers, and Asian Americans are likely to be an increasingly powerful force on the political landscape in coming years.

Still, I keep going back to that initial reaction I had as an undergraduate at Harvard over thirty years ago—that, as an identity and affiliation, "Asian American" is inherently fabricated, inherently inauthentic, even—as Liu says—"contrived" (63). I wonder not only about the cultural vacuousness of such an artifice manufactured out of political expediency but also about the real and inherent dangers in such an identity construction. For the truth is that a pan-Asian identity was not our idea, but the idea of the nativist, racist attitude in the United States, an attitude that lumps us all together and treats us all as the same "yellow" horde. In the face of the white insistence on treating us as all the same, Asian Americans "eventually form[ed] an identity based in part upon such a demand. . . . Young Asian American activists rejected the stereotyped term 'Oriental' and coined their own term, 'Asian American'" (Espiritu, *Asian American* 162). But isn't there a real and present danger in subscribing to the same racist logic as those who oppress us? What is "Asian American" if not the flip side of "Oriental" and of Orientalist bigotry, only now worn with pride? The essentializing logic behind this homogenization of a clearly "heterogeneous entity" (Lowe 65) remains unchanged. And it is again the logic of racialization. As Liu suggests, what is worrisome is that we are being asked to imagine "Asian American identity" as some sort of racial or ethnic reality, more than a mere political coalition: "What troubles me is associating with a certain kind of person whose similarity to me is defined on the primary basis of pigmentation, hair color, eye shape, and so forth[,] . . . the very badge that was once the source of stigma. . . . For what is such pride, in this light, but shame turned upside down?" (78) How real is such an identity? Liu suggests that "what's missing from Asian American culture is culture" (79).

After all, it is hard to have a "culture" when Asian Americans are not really a "people" but a large and rather arbitrary grouping of numerous and heterogeneous peoples, nations, and ethnic groups. Liu writes further, "Thirty-some years ago, there were no 'Asian Americans.' Not a single one. There were Japanese Americans, Chinese Americans, Filipino Americans, and so on: a disparate lot who shared only yellow-to-brown skin tones and the experience of bigotry that their pigmentation provoked. Though known to their countrymen, collectively, as 'Orientals,' and assumed to share common traits and cultures, they didn't think of themselves at all as a collective. It really wasn't until the upheavals of the late 1960's that some of them began to" (67–68). Can one create a "people" with a shared cultural identity, in less than a generation, from a diverse set of peoples whose origins extend from East Asia and Southeast Asia to the Indian subcontinent, from the Philippines and Indonesia to Hawaii? Especially when so many of the Asians in the United States are foreign-born immigrants, still arriving every year in huge numbers? The label *Asian American,* indeed, includes more than thirty ethnicities and nations—many of them with a history of animosity and prejudice toward each other—and dozens of separate languages, from Tagalog to Mandarin to Urdu. I mean, does anyone really—deep down, in their guts—*feel* Asian American? The same way that one might *feel* Jewish or Chinese or even American? Being Asian American seems to me more like being a Democrat or a Republican, a voluntary affiliation that one does not emotionally confuse with a naturalized essence: indeed, perhaps this is a *good* thing about such an identity, because the sheer artificiality of Asian Americanness may help remind us that it is, as all identity constructions in fact are, a social construction and a strategic essentialism: we are less likely to confuse it with essence or nature and to then apply the usual corrosive politics and racism of authenticity and exclusion. I will have more to say on this key point later.

Who *feels* Asian American? Is there such a "people"? Can a shared cultural identity exist in such a short period of invention? For older generations of Asian Americans, and for recent immigrants newly arrived from Asian countries, such a feeling of a shared culture is certainly not a reality. However, as Espiritu and others have pointed out, "Native-born, American-educated Asians are much more receptive to pan-Asian ethnicity than their immigrant parents are. These second- and third-generation Asian Americans often consider themselves to have more in common culturally with other American-born Asians than they do with foreign-born compatriots" (*Asian American* 167). *Pace* Liu, the "culture" and the "people" that he points out (correctly) as missing are also clearly, and remarkably quickly, in the process of coming into being—especially in native-born generations of Asian Americans. This is an identity still very much in process, a still embryonic creation that is clearly maturing into adulthood startlingly quickly: the story of Asian Americanness is a Bildungsroman that is still being written, not fully drafted yet. And we can all still contribute to this rough draft in progress.

I return to the notion of an identity-in-process toward the end of this chapter. For the purposes of the current discussion, however, I will now lay out what I see as the relationship between Asian American identity and mixed-race status. Even though "Asian American" is itself clearly *not* a race, not an ethnicity, not a "people," and certainly not a real "culture"—I would argue that, as a functional (albeit patently artificial) category, "Asian American" is an inherently—and functionally—"mixed-race" identity and category. I would argue this for several reasons. First, ideologically speaking, in the United States Asian (or yellow or Oriental) has long been positioned somewhere between black and white, an in-between category; thus, it is—figuratively speaking—a "mixed" or middle category. More on this point in a moment.

Second, the lumping of so many ethnicities and peoples together into one convenient label results in a virtually "mixed" category, since the scope of "Asian American" intrinsically entails multi-ethnic and multiracial desig-nations—Chinese, Koreans, Indians, Samoans, Pakistanis, Filipinos, native Hawaiians, and so on. Since 1970 a huge wave of new immigrants has come to this country from Asia: whereas in previous decades the Asian American population had consisted mainly of Chinese, Japanese, and Filipino immi-grants, with only a smattering of other Asian populations, the 1990 Census revealed that there were now over a million and a half Chinese Americans; almost that many Filipinos; about eight hundred thousand Japanese Ameri-cans; about the same number of Asian Indians and of Koreans; six hundred thousand Vietnamese; two hundred thousand Hawaiians; and about a million other Asian and Pacific Islander Americans. Most of these new immigrants identify only with their specific ethnic or national culture (Chinese, Korean, and so on) and consider themselves ethnically and racially distinct. "Theirs are monoracialist world views" (Spickard, "Who" 19). To lump together more than a score of "monoracialist world views" into a single identity designa-tion necessarily renders such a designation—at least for the Asian peoples involved—a virtually multiracial (certainly multi-ethnic) category, in func-tion and perception if not in racial actuality.

Third, I am arguing that "Asian American" is a "mixed-race" designa-tion, however, not only for ideological or figurative reasons, such as in the two points above. Rather, it is also, and at the same time, a *literally* mixed-race or miscegenated category (again, assuming at least the discursive exist-ence of what we popularly think of as "races"). To begin with, racial mixing involving Asians in the United States—in spite of the longstanding laws against miscegenation—is hardly new and goes back a long way,. As Omi (x) points out, "From the initial arrival and settlement of Asian immigrants on these shores, multiraciality has been a reality"—and mixed-race Asian American communities have proliferated, from the Chinese-Irish families in New York to the Punjabi-Mexican families in California.[4] Since around 1920, there has been a large Filipino migration to the United States. Unlike the Chi-nese and Japanese immigrant communities, the Filipino community witnessed a lot of intermarriage (mostly with white Americans, but also with Mexican Americans and Native Americans), so that by now almost all second- or third-generation Filipino Americans are mixed-race progeny. Consequently, in Fili-pino American communities, unlike in most other Asian groups (especially the longstanding Japanese and Chinese American communities), there has been a broad and longstanding acceptance of intermarriage and multiraciality.

Indeed, for three particular contemporary Asian groups in the United States—South Asians, Filipinos, and Chinese in Hawaii—a collective identity is based largely on a mixed-race reality (Spickard, "Who" 17). Furthermore, since World War II, U.S. involvement in military conflicts in Asia has also resulted in many Asian "war brides" (especially from Japan, Korea, and Vietnam). Finally, since the early 1970s the rate of interracial marriage by Asians has simply skyrocketed. As Omi concludes, "The current interest in multiraciality among Asian Americans, therefore, has long and deep roots; such histories are thus not marginal to a broader Asian American historical narrative, but rather central to it" (xi).

Fourth, what is most striking is precisely this trend of interracial marriage by Asian groups since the early 1970s. To begin with, this period saw a biracial baby boom in the entire country, with the number of births of mixed-race children more than tripling—from 1 percent of all births in 1968 to 3.4 percent in 1989. But this boom was fueled particularly by Asian-white intermarriage. The 1980 U.S. Census reported a total of 1.2 million interracial marriages, which amounted to 2 percent of the nation's 53.5 million marriages, with two million children (under the age of eighteen)—the largest proportion of which were in Asian-white households (most often Asian mothers and white fathers) (*A. Magazine* 3.1: 21, 24). The result is "a proliferation of racially mixed Asian Americans" (*Los Angeles Times* 7/12/98: A30). In the Japanese American community alone, mixed-race births easily outnumber monoracial births by almost 40 percent: for every 100 births to two Japanese parents, 139 births took place to a Japanese and a non-Japanese parent (*A. Magazine* 3.1: 21). Of the 1.5 million interracial marriages counted in the 1990 Census, 31 percent had an Asian spouse, 22 percent had a Native American or Native Alaskan spouse, and only 14 percent had an African American spouse. Nearly *half* of all interracial children in interracial households surveyed in the 1990 Census (466,590 out of 1,037,420) were in families listing one "Asian" parent and one "White" parent. Since Asians make up just 3 percent of the U.S. population, these statistics are rather staggering—and suggest the *deeply* interracial nature of Asian America (Williams-Leon and Nakashima 6).

Indeed, these statistics are even more eye-opening when focused on the younger generations of Asian Americans, especially those born in the United States. The 1990 Census reported that 55 percent of Asian American women and 50 percent of Asian American men between the ages of twenty-five and thirty-four were married to non-Asians.[5] Among Asian Americans under the age of twenty-five, the percentages for women and men rise to 66 and 54 respectively (Liu 188). Which is to say that well over half of all young Asian Americans marry someone of a different race (usually white). Indeed, according to the 1990 Census, among native-born Chinese Americans, 48.2 percent of women and 44.5 percent of men married interracially; and among native-born Korean Americans, a staggering 73.3 percent of women and 69.7 percent of men married interracially (Kibria, *Becoming* 169)!

"In the 21st century, a typical Japanese American will be of mixed race, predicts Greg Mayeda, president of the Hapa Issues Forum, a Bay Area–based organization of racially mixed Americans" (*Los Angeles Times* 7/12/98: A31). Indeed, Census figures such as those quoted above suggest that this prediction might well turn out to be true of the Asian American population in general. This leads to a number of very interesting and speculative questions. Tuan wonders whether, in the long run, "rather than assimilating into the white majority, biracial and multiracial people may form a distinct racial category" (35). And Liu asks, "What will 'Asian American' mean when a majority of the next generation is of mixed parentage? Will membership in the race depend more on heredity or on heritage? Chromosomes or culture? Will it be a matter of voluntary affiliation, a question of choice? Or will the 'one-drop rule' that makes American blacks black make anyone with an Asian ancestor Asian? Who will pass for white—and who will want to?" (188) I will come back to these crucial questions in the concluding section of this chapter. For now, we might note that the nature of this widespread racial or ethnic mixing within the Asian American population is rather selective: when they are not marrying interethnically (see discussion below), Asian Americans are mostly marrying white. This has significant connotations for our understanding of Asian American collective desire—racial, political, and sexual. And it suggests that both the self-perception of Asian Americans and the general national perception of Asian Americans involve the potential of ascending toward whiteness.

Fifth, while most attention on Asian American intermarriage has focused on white-Asian marriages, another set of figures is equally startling, with equally large implications for the future of Asian American identity: the rates of interethnic marriage—that is, marriages between different Asian ethnic groups (for example, Chinese-Japanese, Korean-Chinese, Japanese-Indian), intra-Asian marriages. The fact is that Asian American interethnic marriages now outnumber interracial marriages between whites and Asians (Tuan 35; *Newsweek* 9/18/00: 62). Between 1980 and 1990, interethnic marriages involving Chinese Americans grew from 22.2 to 32.7 percent of all intermarriages among Chinese Americans, and from 8.7 percent to 23.1 percent of intermarriages among Korean Americans (Kibria, *Becoming* 170). These are compelling and important figures—for they suggest the nature and future of an Asian American panethnicity and perhaps even the construction and acceptance of a distinct Asian American "race" or ethnicity.

These figures are all the more remarkable in view of the traditional prejudices and bigotries *between* Asian populations. The Chinese and Japanese have a long history of mutual hatred and animosity, capped in the twentieth century by the Japanese occupation of China and World War II; the same is true between Koreans and Japanese. (When, as a student, I began dating a Japanese American woman, my Chinese mother—steeled by her bitter wartime experiences in China during the 1930s and 1940s—refused to speak to me.) The Japanese and the Chinese have both looked down on other Asian groups, such as Koreans and Filipinos, as racially and culturally inferior. For example, in the Japanese internment camps in the United States during World War II, "Japanese American women who had been partners with Filipino men before the war were ostracized. They had to live and eat separately from other inmates, were talked about by other Japanese American women, and were sexualized by Japanese American men as fair game" (Spickard, "Who" 15). For traditional native Asian groups, intra-Asian coupling *was* miscegenation.

Fully two-thirds of Asians in the contemporary United States are foreign-born (Tuan 38; *Los Angeles Times* 7/12/98: A30): for many such Asians (not born and raised in the United States), marrying an Asian outside their own Asian ethnicity is seen as interracial coupling and carries the same negative stigmas. But as Tuan points out, "Ethnic divisions that once stood firm are clearly blurring among the later generations; marriages between different Asian ethnic groups . . . that would have been socially frowned upon only a generation ago are now commonplace" (166). The remarkable number of interethnic marriages among Asians today, however, comes not from first-generation immigrants, but from native-born, second- or third-generation Asian Americans—precisely the population that is much more likely to self-identify as "Asian American" (rather than as Chinese, Japanese, Korean, and so on). It is they—the younger, U.S.-born Asians—who are forming a pan-ethnic, mixed-ethnic, identity—something approaching a "race." As demographers Larry Shinagawa and Gin Pang write in "Asian-American Panethnicity and Intermarriage" (144), "Race, increasingly more so than ethnicity, shapes the experiences and the development of identity among Asian Americans." Tuan predicts that "as distinct cultural patterns continue to be watered down and replaced by a more generalized Asian American culture, individuals are less likely to focus on ethnic differences and instead, recognize the similarities linking their experiences"—similarities, ironically, "grounded in their common experience of being viewed and treated as a distinct racial group in the United States." Nevertheless, "the resulting identity has taken on a life and meaning of its own as those members have taken to constructing a cultural base reflecting their common experiences" (167).

It is for all the above reasons that I contend that, both functionally (ideologically, politically, figuratively) and to a large degree also literally, "Asian American" can and should be considered a "mixed-race" identity designation. Indeed, the section which follows explores this "mixed" nature of Asian American identity in terms of its ideological position and long history as an in-between category, a racial mixing of sorts—between white and black, between "good" and "bad."

Good Subjects, Bad Subjects: White, Black, and Yellow

In his now-classic essay "Ideology and Ideological State Apparatuses," Marxist theorist Louis Althusser discusses how a dominant discourse hails and interpellates its subjects into subscribing to its ideology. He calls "good subjects" those who respond (and are thus successfully interpellated)—that is, those who adhere to the dominant ideology, usually without being aware that they are doing so. "Bad subjects," however, reject this dominant ideology and "on occasion provoke the intervention of one of the detachments of the (repressive) State apparatus" (the police, for example). In *Race and Resistance: Literature and Politics in Asian America*, Viet Thanh Nguyen invokes Althusser's terms and argues persuasively that the "bad subject" is "the dominant form of the Asian American body politic"—at least "in the imagination of Asian American intellectuals," who tend to "posit model minority discourse and the discourse of the bad subject as a binary." "If model minority discourse tends to idealize the model minority," notes Nguyen, "the discourse of the bad subject responds by tending to idealize the bad subject" (144).

To put it more crudely, and in racial terms, there is the good, the bad, and the ugly (or the in-between): white is good, black is bad, and yellow is mixed and could go either away. Yellow has always been defined, in the United States, in terms of the black-white axis and polarity and has functioned discursively within those terms, often used as a wedge against blacks. Yellow has always been somewhere between "black" and "white" (as discursive positions, as bottom and top rungs, on the racial ladder of dominant ideology): once inherently (through the logic of the one-drop rule) always tending toward blackness and incapable of rising to "whiteness" and a superior station in the dominant ideology, yellow/Oriental/Asian has been reconceived by the dominant ideology as "the model minority"—that is, as "almost white" (but not quite).

As Gary Okihiro has asked, "Is Yellow Black or White?" Or as Tuan (163) asks, "Are Asian ethnics 'forever foreigners' or 'honorary whites'?"[6] Okihiro writes, "Implicit within the question is a construct of American society that defines race relations as bipolar—between black and white—and that locates Asians (and American Indians and Latinos) somewhere along the divide between black and white. Asians, thus, are 'near whites' or 'just like blacks'" (33)—depending on your viewpoint. To view race in such bipolar terms is, of course, severely problematic.[7] But such has been the history of attitudes toward "yellow" Asians or "Orientals" in the United States. And it has been a long and varied history, storm-tossed between the poles of black and white.

For example, it was a Chinese man who established the important U.S. principle of citizenship by birthright: in the wake of the anti-Chinese sentiment that resulted in the Chinese Exclusion Act in 1882, a Congressional act that not only closed the door on Chinese immigration but forbade legal Chinese American residents from becoming citizens, American-born Wong Kim Ark was denied reentry into the country because he was Chinese. Wong sued, and his appeals reached the Supreme Court, which in 1898 ruled that anyone born in the United States is automatically a citizen by birth. But when, twenty years later, Bhagat Singh Thind, an Indian-born immigrant living in Oregon, challenged a law barring Asians from becoming naturalized citizens by arguing that Indians were after all of Aryan stock (and thus not legally Asians), the Supreme Court disagreed, concluding that Indians were Asians and thus *not* white. In 1914, a Japanese native named Takao Ozawa applied for naturalization after twenty-eight years of residence and extensive "Americanization" in the United States; Asians, he claimed, had not been specifically excluded under the nation's naturalization laws, and so he should qualify as a "free white person." Eight years later, the case reached the U.S. Supreme Court, which turned down Ozawa's application, rejecting his claim to "white person" status.

Even as early as Reconstruction, right after the Civil War and black emancipation, the introduction of Asian migrant workers to the South was already being used by dominant white culture as a wedge, a "model minority" if you will, by which to punish African Americans (as "bad subjects"). For example, in 1869 the *Vicksburg Times* wrote that "emancipation has spoiled the negro, and carried him away from fields of agriculture"; but "our colored friends who have left the farm for politics and plunder, should go down to the *Great Republic* today and look at the new laborer who is destined to crowd the negro from the American farm" (Okihiro 45). As Powell Clayton, the governor of Arkansas at the time, acknowledged, "Undoubtedly the underlying motive for this effort to bring in Chinese laborers was to punish the negro for having abandoned the control of his old master, and to regulate the conditions of his employment and the scale of wages to be paid him" (by hiring people willing to work for even lower wages; see Okihiro 45). As Okihiro (54) concludes, the U.S. capitalist system repeatedly and "deliberately pitted African against Asian workers, whereby Asians were used to discipline African workers and to depress their wages," resulting in "mutual ethnocentrism and prejudice" among two oppressed minority groups. This pattern continues, as exemplified in the black-Korean violence that surfaced in the 1992 Los Angeles riots.

But if Asians could be used to put down blacks, they were also not to imagine that they might ascend to a superior racial position. Indeed, antimiscegenation laws—begun as early as 1691 in Virginia—seeking to ban racial mixing from creating "hybrid races" and contaminating the white race, were aimed at Asians as well as at blacks. At the 1878 California constitutional convention, John F. Miller deplored children born to Chinese and white parents as "a hybrid of the most despicable, a mongrel of the most detestable that has ever afflicted the earth"; two years later California passed its own antimiscegenation law, forbidding marriages between whites and nonwhites, whether "negro, mulatto, or Mongolian" (see Okihiro 51).

The racial history and status of the Chinese in the United States is especially mixed (in every sense). Before the 1870 Census, the Chinese in Louisiana were counted as whites for lack of a separate category (besides white and black). But in 1927, the U.S. Supreme Court, in response to a challenge to Mississippi's Jim Crow schools by the Chinese in Mississippi, cited its landmark 1896 decision *Plessy* v. *Ferguson* (the "separate but equal" doctrine) and upheld Mississippi's law that the Chinese were not white—and thus were "colored" and could be legally kept out of white schools. Okihiro enumerates further (53):

> The Chinese, however, occupied an ambiguous position racially, as reflected in Louisiana's census. In 1860, Chinese were classified as whites; in 1870, they were listed as Chinese; in 1880, children of Chinese men and non-Chinese women were classed as Chinese; but

in 1900, all of those children were reclassified as blacks or whites and only those born in China or with two Chinese parents were listed as Chinese. In Mississippi, according to sociologist James W. Loewen [in his book *Mississippi Chinese*], the Chinese were initially assigned a "near-Negro position" with no more legal rights or political power, but neither whites nor blacks "quite thought of them *as* Negroes," and they later served in some respects "as middlemen between white and black."

The contemporary Asian American movement had its origins in the black-power and civil rights movements of the sixties and in the solidarity (and inspiration) Asian American students felt with (and derived from) their African American counterparts. In that sense, "Asian American" as a contemporary political identity originated by considering itself as "black," as a "minority discourse" (rather than as a "model minority discourse"), as a recalcitrant "bad subject" protesting against dominant white ideology. As Okihiro writes about this generation of Asian American activists, "Many of us, Asian and Pacific Americans, several generations native-born, came of age during America's imperialist war in Vietnam and the African American freedom struggle of the 1960s. Many of us found our identity by reading Franz Fanon and Malcolm X, Cheikh Anta Diop and W.E.B. Du Bois, Leopold Senghor and Langston Hughes" (60). The current Asian American activist movement, fueled by Asian American studies as an academic discipline on college campuses and led by Asian American intellectuals who similarly came to their identity consciousness in the sixties, has inherited—as Nguyen points out—the mantle of the "bad subject" and aligns itself with "bad subject" recalcitrance, in opposition to the dominant white discourse about Asians as the "model minority." Nguyen notes that, as a result, the liberal Asian American intellectual movement runs the risk now of not being representative of, and of losing touch with, the more moderate or conservative Asian American population at large—who may, in large measure, view a "model-minority" or "honorary-white" status as a good thing, "who may indeed see themselves as a model minority from the perspective of the dominant class—in other words, accepting the positive attributes of the model minority while rejecting the ideological critique" (Nguyen 147). Liu writes further, "One thing Professional Asian Americans are quick to point out is that they are not honorary whites. Fair enough. . . . But something Professional Asian Americans sometimes overlook is that they are not honorary blacks either" (73).

Nguyen (146–147) succinctly summarizes what he calls "the model minority thesis" as functioning thus:

> In the model minority thesis, the model minority works as a buffer between whites and blacks, who are separated by not only racial difference but a related class antagonism as well. . . . The structure of domination that favors whites and is controlled by them positions Asian Americans as a minority that can succeed without government or social assistance, through sheer hard work and perseverance based upon a system of social values that prioritizes family, education, and sacrifice. These social values that all Asian Americans reputedly share . . . also prioritize obedience and hierarchy, which means that Asian Americans are reluctant to blame others for any lack in their social position and are willing to accept their social position with gratitude. Asian Americans are therefore a model minority because they demonstrate to other minorities what can be achieved through self-reliance rather than government assistance, self-sacrifice rather than self-interest, and quiet restraint rather than vocal complaint in the face of perceived or actual injustice.

As a result, Nguyen points out (147), "ideologically, the model minority becomes a scapegoat, drawing the ire of other minorities for the systemic inequities that they experience" (as happened with Korean American small-business owners in Los Angeles). A *Newsweek* story on anti-Asian hate crimes reported, "The same stereotype that often fuels anti-Asian bias—that of the ultrasuccessful minority prospering faster than other ethnic groups—also often prevents attacks from being recognized as hate motivated"—and often prevents Asians from being considered victimized minorities. After a violent hate crime occurred against a Korean American student at the SUNY Binghamton university campus, the students in the Asian Student Union on campus reached out to black and Latino students to help protest the attack—and were shocked by the response. As Rizalene Zabala, a Filipino American and the president of the Asian Student Union, said, "[They] simply didn't see us as minorities. They think if you're Asian you're automatically interning at Merrill Lynch and that you're never touched by racism" (*Newsweek* 11/6/00: 61). Which is to say that the black and Latino students regarded Asians—in spite of the Asian American student movement's longstanding solidarity with their causes—as basically and virtually "white."

Indeed, the social place of many Asian Americans would seem to justify such a stereotyped estimation, especially in terms of economic and educational success. While they make up only 4 percent of the overall population, Asian Americans have the highest median income of all racial groups, including whites, and a higher percentage of Asian Americans earn advanced degrees than any other group.[8] At elite universities, Asian American students are spectacularly over-represented: for example, one in four undergraduates at Stanford and Wellesley are Asian American; one in five at Harvard, Northwestern, and the University of Pennsylvania. In the University of California system, Asian Americans make up 41 percent of the undergraduate student body at Berkeley, 40 percent at UCLA, 43 percent at Riverside, and a staggering 58 percent at Irvine. The result of all this educational and economic success on the part of Asians is an insistent animosity and resentment by other minority groups on the wrong end of the "model-minority" card being played by the dominant white culture. As Peter Kwong, head of Asian American Studies at Hunter College (New York City), says about the "model-minority" stereotype, "That label is clearly part of a hostile discourse between whites and blacks. Whites are basically saying to blacks, 'We're not racist, and the reason you're not as successful is because you're not working as hard as Asians'" (*Newsweek* 6/22/98: 68).

If "yellow"—as a "model minority"—is poised between black and white and is viewed and treated as potentially and honorarily white, what happens in the very interesting case of mixed-race Asian Americans? Are the dynamics the same? Are they considered honorary whites or honorary blacks? Does the one-drop rule still apply? Indeed, we discover that in such cases the one-drop rule varies, depending on the particular "mix" that goes into the "mixed-race" composition. Let's begin by looking at the case of black-Asian mixed-race identity. One instructive case study is that of the world's best golfer, Tiger Woods, who refers to himself as "Cablinasian," a term he coined as a boy to combine his Caucasian, black, Indian (Native American), and Asian roots. He has repeatedly stated that he embraces all sides of his family and lineage; "to be called [just] any one of them, he said, was to deny a part of him" (*Newsweek* 5/5/97: 59). Yet, in spite of his insistence on acknowledging his mixed and diverse lineage, he was recognized (and marketed) by U.S. culture as golf's great black hope. This in spite of the fact that he is more Asian than anything else: his father, Earl, is half African American, one quarter Native American, one quarter Chinese; while his mother, Klutida, is half Thai, one quarter Chinese, and one quarter Dutch. Which is to say that, in strict mathematical proportions, Woods is one quarter Thai, one quarter Chinese, one quarter African American, one eighth white, and one eighth Native American (see Liu 189, Omi xiii, and *Newsweek* 5/5/

97: 60). In other words, he is half Asian, and only a quarter black; Woods himself has said that "I am 90 percent Oriental, more Thai than anything" (*Asian Week*, 1997; quoted in Omi ix). As Omi asks, "Why isn't this superb golfer touted as the first Asian American to achieve a Grand Slam by winning the Masters, the U.S. Open, and the British Open golf tournaments?"(ix). It is true that, eventually, the media—at Woods's insistence—began marketing him a bit more around his mixed-race status ("I am Tiger Woods"), as an icon of multicoloration (for Nike, Benneton, Calvin Klein) more than as an Asian or Asian American. But the fact that his one-quarter African American heritage still does, in the eyes of most Americans, trump and obliterate his much greater (one-half) Asian heritage suggests the continuing power and hold on Americans' thinking of the one-drop, hypodescent rule—in which a person's race "descends" to the lowest possible rung on the racial ladder (here, black), rather than "ascending" to a higher possible rung (here, Asian or even white, since strictly speaking Woods is more white than black). As Angelo Ragaza, editor of *A.*, a magazine for Asian Americans, noted, "A lot of young Asian-Americans feel resentful that the media neglects his Asian heritage" (*Newsweek* 5/5/97: 60). Interestingly, once the media did begin responding positively to Woods's objection to being labeled only "black," it was the African American community which was most resistant to labeling Tiger Woods's identity as mixed-race, as Asian-black rather than as African American (Nakashima, "Servants" 47)—thus illustrating Patterson's comment that "the real paradox here is that the one-drop rule succeeded all too well, so much so that its most devoted adherents today are African Americans, in spite of its devastating role in their own history of exclusion" (16).

Similarly, few people are aware that Secretary of State Colin Powell is multiracial; that law professor Lani Guinier, the subject of a bitter confirmation controversy when nominated by President Bill Clinton in 1993 as assistant attorney general, is the daughter of a white, Jewish mother and a black, West Indian father (*Newsweek* 4/20/98: 71); that Ward Connerly, controversial University of California regent and author of California's 1996 Proposition 209 (against affirmative action), is African American, Irish, French Canadian, and Native American (and more Irish than anything). By the hypodescent one-drop rule, they are all black, sinking to the lowest rung on the ladder of whiteness (rather than rising to the status of Jew or Irish). As pop singer Mariah Carey—herself the daughter of an Irish mother and an African American and Venezuelan father—has pointed out (in the November 1998 issue of *Vibe*), the one-drop rule defines biracial people with African blood as "black," while multiracial Asians are deemed more "socially acceptable" and are "permitted" the luxury of a "racially mixed" status (see Williams-Leon and Nakashima 3).

Within Asian American groups, this inherited hypodescent logic results in a replication of the U.S. racial hierarchy: while multiracial Asian American individuals have had traditionally a hard time finding full acceptance in Asian American communities, these communities are most intolerant of multiracials who are part-African in heritage. As playwright Velina Hasu Houston (Japanese and African American) and sociologist Teresa Williams-Leon (Japanese and Caucasian) have noted, interracial mixing in Asian communities is "considered even more frightening if its multiracial composition includes African ancestry" (see Espiritu, "Possibilities" 28). Spickard has similarly written that it is rare for "Asian communities [to be] willing to treat mixed people of African American parentage as insiders" (quoted in Espiritu, "Possibilities" 28). As Espiritu has noted, "Legally and socially, multiracial people of African American descent have been forced by white Americans to identify only as black and have been raised almost invariably in the black community" (Espiritu, "Possibilities" 28).

The reality for black-Asian mixed-race individuals in the United States is very different from that for white-Asian individuals. For example, the *New York Times Magazine* (7/16/00: 31) interviewed a number of mixed-race New Yorkers, including Alisa Simmons, a young woman, daughter of a black father and a Korean mother, whose looks allow her to pass equally as black or as Asian: "When people look at me, they tend to fill in the blank with what they're comfortable with and often assume I'm Asian. So I hear things and see things that maybe I wasn't supposed to see or hear. I know what it feels like to be black in America and I know what it feels like to be Asian. Sometimes I'll wear my hair in little knots and put on some ratty jeans. Then, people perceive me as black. I'll walk into a store and I'm followed. But if I walk into the same store with my hair straight, people are more than happy to give me service because they assume I'm Asian." Asian cultures have been traditionally intolerant of black people; as sociologist Christine Hall, herself of mixed Japanese and African American heritage, notes, "The kids who are half-white got along much better than kids who are half black" (*A. Magazine* 3.1: 76). But African/Asian Americans are caught in a biracial Catch–22, often also having to prove to the black community that they are black enough. Song Richardson, a young Korean/African American, recalled an incident at Harvard in which fellow black students held a meeting about her and another friend who is half black and half white: "It was a meeting about why we were not acknowledging the fact that we were black and pretending to be someone else. It was very bizarre for me; it made me not want to hang out with them either. Even now, I feel like I have to make an extra effort to be with African Americans just to prove that I'm black" (*A. Magazine* 3.1: 77). Arguably, the very lowest rung on the hypodescent ladder belongs to mixed-race individuals who are part-black—for they are shunned by all groups and embraced by none.

Now let's turn to the case of "white Asians"—that is, Asian Americans who are, by virtue of the "model-minority thesis," considered "honorary whites" (and who, as I have pointed out, by virtue of high rates of intermarriage with whites are increasingly and literally part-white). Over the past century, the United States has changed many of its racial conceptions and misconceptions, eventually accepting and even embracing groups it had previously labeled as "undesirable" races: Poles, Romanians, Italians, Irish, Jews. As Cose notes, "They were all, in essence, made white. The question today is whether that process will extend to those whose ancestors, for the most part, were not European" ("What's White" 65). Cose observes rather optimistically that "white Asians" are professionally much in demand these days and that, for many Americans, Asian Americans are, for practical purposes, white: "This is not to say that Takao Ozawa would be better able today than in 1922 to convince a court that he is Aryan; but he almost certainly could persuade most Americans to treat him like a white person, which essentially amounts to the same thing. America's cult of whiteness, after all, was never just about skin color, hair texture, and other physical traits. It was about where the line was drawn between those who could be admitted into the mainstream and those who could not."

As Liu puts it, "Like so many other Asian Americans of the second generation, I find myself now the bearer of a strange new status: white, by acclamation. . . . *Some are born white, others achieve whiteness, still others have whiteness thrust upon them.* This, supposedly, is what it means to assimilate" (34–35). However, throughout this history of assimilation, in which the Irish, Jews, Romanians, and so forth, have each in turn "achieved whiteness," "the vocabulary of 'assimilation,'" as Liu points out, "has remained fixed all this time: fixed in whiteness, which is still our metonym for power" (35). One easy way U.S. culture has long been able to deal with cultural practices is to racialize them, as other, as different. But as Liu notes about the veiled racialism behind the "model-minority" theory (158), "Hard work and sacrifice? Deferral of gratification? Devotion to education? Today, anyone will tell you, these are 'Asian values.' But remember, only a few generations ago they were 'Jewish values.' And once upon a time, of course, they were

'Protestant values.'" And, Liu reminds us, sometime in the fifties and six-ties, "the Jews became white"—and, "today, many Asian Americans seem to be in a similar position" (162). Will Asian Americans similarly become white, ascend beyond "honorary whites" to actual whiteness? Or will they remain "forever foreigners," as their history in the United States heretofore has suggested?

Tuan notes that those who argue that Asians "may be undergoing 'whit-ening' processes similar to those experienced by southern, central, and east-ern European immigrants earlier in the [twentieth] century" are bolstered by demographic data "that paint an optimistic picture of their economic and so-cial standing." For example, the 1990 U.S. Census revealed that, in Califor-nia, the percentage of native-born Chinese and Japanese Americans who earned college degrees was significantly higher than that for native-born white Americans; this is also true of postgraduate degrees (Tuan 31). Similarly, an analysis by the Associated Press of data from the 2000 U.S. Census reveals a continued high rate of segregation of black communities in many cities ("As soon as black people move in, white people move out")—in direct contrast with white acceptance of Asians, for neighborhoods with mixed populations of whites and Asians are many and thriving: "Whites seem to have less of a tolerance for living with blacks than they do with Asians," says Roderick Harrison with the Joint Center for Political and Economic Studies (*Salt Lake Tribune* 12/3/01: A14).

Thus it is tempting to imagine Asians as being on the verge—like the Irish, Jews, Italians, and Romanians before them (all of whom had also been racialized and "simianized")—of becoming "white." Among those who think so are columnists Cose, as previously noted, and George Will. Will, citing Michael Barone's *The New Americans: How the Melting Pot Can Work Again*, reminds us that "the Irish were called 'lowbrowed' and 'simian'" and that "Italians were referred to as 'swarthy' with 'low foreheads,' a 'between' race—'whites, degoes, negroes.'" He suggests that the same thing may be happening with Asians in the United States, with special similarities to the history of the Jews: "Many East Asians in the last third of the 20th century were like Eastern Europeans in the last third of the 19th century—a distinct minority[,] . . . and their commercial acumen was resented. Many Asians, like Jews, are 'people of the book' (the Mandarin and Talmudic traditions) and are ascending America's surest ladder of social mobility, the system of higher education" (64) .

Indeed, the comparison with Jews, and with Jewish assimilation/ascent into whiteness, seems ubiquitous these days. As Liu notes, "Over the last few years, Asian Americans have come to be known as the New Jews. . . . Somewhere in that half-lit region between stereotype and sociology, the notion has taken hold that Asian Americans are 'out-Jewing the Jews'" (145). As Asian Americans become increasingly and conspicuously over-represented at the best U.S. colleges and universities, we find even Jewish intellectuals like Princeton historian Stanley Katz saying, "Some, maybe most of the very best students, are Asians. These kids strike me as the Jews of the end of the century"; Lawrence W. Levine, acclaimed historian at George Mason University, further compares stereotypes and mistreatment of Asian Americans to the similar prejudices that in previous decades had led to Jewish exclusion quotas at some Ivy League colleges: "There are a lot of similarities. They said Jews worked too hard and weren't fair competitors"—a complaint voiced frequently these days about Asian American students. Another historian, David Hollinger at UC Berkeley, notes that Asian American students frequently "come into my office eager to talk about the expansion of NATO, school vouchers, the future of the Democratic Party. They're engaging the same kinds of questions as earlier generations of Jewish and black intellectuals—public questions rather than pre-professional or technical ones." Novelist/poet Ishamel Reed, who teaches creative writing at UC Berkeley, says, "There was a time when my class was mostly white. Now, some of the best writers are Asian Americans" (quotations from *Los Angeles Times* 7/14/98: A14). Have indeed Asian Americans become the new whites, the new Jews?

Liu, referring to a series of ads in the *New York Times* run by the American Jewish Committee on "What Being Jewish Means to Me," suggests that "being Jewish today means, in no small measure, having the ability to run ads in the *New York Times* about what being Jewish today means. The public introspection of very public figures . . . is at once an announcement of having made it and an assertion that Jewishness did not prevent them from making it." He then asks rhetorically if we can imagine a series in the *Times* called "What Being Chinese Means to Me"—for "Chinese Americans do not imagine themselves a single entity whose voice should fit seamlessly into the daily digest of elite opinion" (Liu 148). In *Forever Foreigners or Honorary Whites*? Tuan is even more skeptical, pointing out that "Asian ethnics are not free to be symbolically ethnic to the extent that white ethnics [like Jews or Italians] are" (156)—that is, that while white ethnics have the luxury to choose whether they wish to identify ethnically in public, Asians do not have that choice; rather, "they must deal with others' expectations and an imposed racialized ethnic identity" (157). (As Liu writes, "The Sons of Italy, Daughters of Ireland, and so forth: whites can wear or remove their ancestry like a pendant. I do not feel so free" [132].) Tuan points to cases like the MSNBC gaffe (in 1998) during the women's Olympic figure-skating championships, in which the station ran a story under the headline "American Beats Kwan," even though Michelle Kwan is a native-born citizen and no less American than her rival Tara Lipinski. "By normalizing Tara Lipinski as the American and 'othering' Michelle Kwan, MSNBC . . . simply reflected what many others believe to be true, that Americans look like Tara while foreigners look like Michelle" (157). No matter how many generations our families have been in this country, Tuan implies, we Asian Americans are seen as "forever foreigners" much more so than as "honorary whites."

But the question of ascension to whiteness is also a question about the long-range prospect. Will there be a time when ads will run in the *New York Times* on "What Being Chinese (or Asian) American Means to Me"? Will U.S. history eventually be repeated and "white" again redefined—as it had been earlier to include Jews, Romanians, Italians, and Irish as white ethnics—to include Asian Americans? An instructive debate on this matter took place in print between two academic intellectuals, Asian American historian Ronald Takaki and neoconservative political scientist Nathan Glazer. Glazer argued, in a piece first published in 1975, that if the Irish—who had long been racialized by English and U.S. culture as "white negroes"—were able eventually to overcome such prejudice and to assimilate into the white mainstream, much as the Chinese seem to him to have done by the seventies, without having to depend on public welfare and government assistance, then so should blacks. Takaki takes issue with Glazer, whose argument depended on assuming Chinese, Irish, and blacks to be ethnically equivalent groups, by pointing to the racial difference that divides the white Irish from Chinese and blacks, who are not white, and to the fact that the mainstreaming of the Irish was possible because of the opportunities afforded by their whiteness (Glazer; and Takaki, "Reflections"). Nguyen, however, argues:

> Takaki's argument about the subordinate nature of ethnicity under race is fundamental for Asian American intellectuals, but it is based upon a tautology: the Irish can become white because they look white, and the Chinese cannot become white because they do not look white. Yet historical evidence demonstrates that in the nineteenth century the Irish *did not look white*, at least to other European Americans who had already claimed the mantle of whiteness. If the Irish can become white, when they were seen by others as black, or at least nonwhite, then what is to prevent any other non-white group

from doing the same? The situation of the Irish demonstrates that race is not inherently visible through physical characteristics such as skin color, hair texture, and eye and nose shape, but that race is something that we learn to see. (169–70)

What will happen in the future is of course impossible to predict with certainty. Asians are intermarrying in huge numbers with whites and are professionally and economically immensely successful and seem to be achieving whiteness. But developments like the Kwan gaffe; the 1996 "Chinagate" fundraising scandal and affair under the Clinton Administration (involving John Huang and the Democratic National Committee), which repeatedly found Chinese Americans homogeneously represented in the media as all foreigners at heart whose "real" allegiances are still to China, no matter how many generations they have been here (replicating the attitude toward Japanese Americans that resulted in the Japanese internment camps during World War II); and the Wen Ho Lee affair, involving alleged espionage at the Los Alamos laboratories—all suggest how hard it will be for the United States to shed its perception of Asians as forever "not white, not quite" (to borrow from Homi Bhabha). Conversely, whereas African Americans too continue to be racialized as other, no one ever questions that they are legitimate "Americans." Tuan writes:

> I am skeptical that within a few generations Asian-Americans would *automatically* be absorbed into the mainstream. Generations of highly acculturated Asian ethnics who speak without an accent have lived in this country, and yet most white Americans have not heard of or ever really seen them. They are America's invisible citizenry, the accountants who do our taxes, engineers who safeguard our infrastructure, and pharmacists who fill our prescriptions. Nevertheless, over the years they have continued to be treated and seen as other. . . . Whites [and one should add blacks, too] continue to feel a sense of "proprietary claim" to being the "real" Americans. (159, 161)

"For the problem, really," Liu suggests, "is not that the Asians who come here feel divided about America; it is that America feels divided about the Asians who come here" (127).

Yet these things are hard to predict: there is a lot of statistical and demographic evidence suggesting that Asians and whites are hardly separable or distinguishable anymore; that the acceptance of mixed-race individuals (like Keanu Reeves) as white signals that hypodescence may—as with Jews—

no longer apply to Asians in the future. But all it ever takes, it seems to me, is one or two highly visible events or issues to throw the nation right back into "yellow-peril" fever and exclusionary nativism: such as Pearl Harbor, which led to Japanese American internment; such as the 1980s' demonization of the Japanese during Japan's economic boom, which led to Vincent Chin's brutal murder and the continued, current growth in anti-Asian hate crimes; such as the Johnny Huang and Wen Ho Lee affairs; and so on. Both the demonization of the Japanese and the simultaneous stereotyping of Asian Americans as the "model minority" originated with the fear (and hatred) of those overachieving Asians who were buying up our houses and factories and filling the best places in our schools and colleges. What will happen if China really does become the next global superpower, both economically and politically, as it is on the verge of doing, competing with the United States for foreign markets and international political influence? Would my Ph.D. and professional status be any defense then against the ensuing wave of rising anti-Chinese nativism?

Indeed, what will be the long-term effects of September 11th on attitudes toward U.S. citizens, both foreign-born and native-born—especially those of South Asian and Southeast Asian descent, many of whom (Pakistanis, Malaysians, etc.) are Muslims and the rest of whom are frequently mistaken for Muslims? Will such Orientals (for we are back to European "Orientalism," in which everything east of the Mediterranean was considered "Oriental" and dangerous) now be further tarred as "forever terrorists"? As always the "bad subject," rejecting U.S. ideology? If so, we will have turned 180 degrees from the "model-minority thesis," which conceives of Chinese stockbrokers and South Asian computer programmers as the ideal "good subjects." I am haunted by Corky Lee's color photograph of a Sikh American candlelight vigil held in New York City's Central Park on September 15, 2001: four days after the September 11th terrorist attacks, these multigenerational Sikhs—draped in American flags, as if the red-white-and-blue could make us forget about their brown faces, their beards, their exotic shawls and turbans—gathered ostensibly (and I am sure genuinely) to express their grief and solidarity with other New Yorkers over their shared loss as Americans and New Yorkers. But the uncertain and troubled looks on their faces also hint at the real message motivating this assembly: please try to see us as Americans too; please do not punish us for being brown and other; know that being Sikh does not make us un-American, does not make us terrorists. The desperation I see in those faces, and in the almost pageant-like performance of patriotism, reflects their hard-nosed awareness of U.S. nativism and the dynamics

Sikh candlelight vigil in Central Park on September 15, 2001. *Photo by Corky Lee.* © *Corky Lee, 2001.*

of whiteness, and of the racial prejudice which every nonwhite person in the United States is made to feel almost daily in little ways. And their fear has not been unfounded: the evidence of the way foreigners, especially those who may look Muslim or brown, have been treated since then has not been reassuring, and conjures up memories of the Japanese internment and of the Chinese Exclusion Act. Will September 11th turn South Asian and other "brown" Asian Americans—and possibly by implication all Asians—into the essential and unreclaimable "bad subject" again? If so, we need no longer worry about the "model-minority thesis" of the Asian "good subject."

The Identity Laboratory

I conclude this chapter by assessing what I see as both the potential pitfalls—and, more important, the unique potential and promise—in the ongoing construction of an Asian American identity. In "Cultural Identity and Diaspora," Stuart Hall writes that a cultural identity is "a matter of 'becoming' as well as of 'being.' It belongs to the future as much as to the past. It is not something which already exists, transcending place, time, history and culture. Cultural identities come from somewhere, have histories. But, like everything which is historical, they undergo constant transformation. Far from being eternally fixed in some essentialized past, they are subject to the continuous 'play' of history, culture and power" (225). With parallel logic, Lowe—citing Hall's argument—suggests that "rather than considering 'Asian American identity' as a fixed, established 'given,' perhaps we can consider instead 'Asian American cultural practices' that produce identity." "Such processes," she goes on to say, "are never complete and are always constituted in relation to historical and material differences" (Lowe 64). This could not be more true than with Asian American identity, a nascent identity still very much in the making.

As previously noted, the notion of an Asian American identity itself is only one generation old; previous generations of Chinese, Japanese, Filipinos, Koreans, Hawaiians, and so on, felt a sense of ethnic pride and community, but would have regarded a panethnic Asian American culture as not only an absurd myth but something rigorously to be avoided. But, miraculously, such a cultural identity is, even as we breathe, being formed and shaped in U.S. high school and college campuses across the country. Visiting high schools in Southern California from time to time during my twenty years as a professor at the University of Southern California, I witnessed increasingly that, at lunch or recess, Japanese American, Filipino American, Korean American, Chinese American, Samoan American, and South Asian students tend to all cluster at the same pan-Asian lunch table—much as African American students and Chicano students cluster at their own, ethnically distinct tables. This would have been unthinkable in previous generations, in which Japanese, Chinese, Koreans, and so forth, viewed each other with a distrust and animosity that bred ethnic intolerance. As Liu writes,

> Asian American activists, intellectuals, artists, and students have worked, with increasing success, to transform their label into a lifestyle and to create, by every means available, a truly pan-ethnic identity for their ten million members. They have begun to build a nation. . . . There is something fantastic about all this, and I mean that in every way. That the children of Chinese and Japanese immigrants, or Korean and Japanese, or Indian and Pakistani, should so heedlessly disregard the animosities of their ancestors; that they should prove it possible to reinvent themselves as one community; that they should catalog their collective contributions to society so very sincerely: what can you say, really, but "Only in America"? (69, 71)

We are witnessing, as Liu puts it, "the invention of a race" (71).

Intermarriage statistics support this: not only do about 50 percent of

Asians in the United States intermarry, but, of these, according to Shinagawa and Pang, interethnic marriages—that is, marriages between different Asian ethnic groups—now outnumber marriages between whites and Asians, as we have seen. This is a highly significant piece of data, for it suggests the growing choice of a common, panethnic identity—even a common racial identity—among the various Asian American groups, as formerly distinct ethnic divisions are now blurring with later generations. As Shinagawa and Pang suggest about their findings, "Race, increasingly more so than ethnicity, shapes the experiences and the development of identity among Asian Americans" (144). "The resulting identity," Tuan notes, "has taken on a life and meaning of its own as those members have taken to constructing a cultural base reflecting their common experiences" (167).

Koshy points out that, unlike African American, Native American, or Chicano literatures, Asian American literature "inhabits the highly unstable temporality of the 'about-to-be,' its meanings continuously reinvented" and that "the very newness of the field . . . [has] deferred questions about its founding premises"; one could generalize this point to not just literature, but culture and identity. She correctly points out that such newness leads to as-yet unresolved problems and indecidabilities in the very conception, meanings, and premises of Asian Americanness (467–468). But I view this unresolvedness—and such newness—as advantages, for we have here that rare case, that rare event, in one's own lifetime: a functioning laboratory in which a group identity is still very much in the process of being formed, not yet finished and hardened and "naturalized" into a petrified "essence." How this identity will be understood and defined is still very much in flux. Sure, all identities are constantly (as Hall notes) in transition and changing, but that is hardly how most public discourses surrounding such individual identities (whether Irishness, Englishness, Jewishness, Indianness, and so on) imagine them. Unlike these other identities, "Asian American" has not yet been reified in the popular imagination into some authentic and natural category. Indeed, we thus can still shape and affect its yet-to-be-determined qualities and future; there is, as there is not with identities that have been imagined for centuries, at least the possibility still of avoiding the same ethnocentric pitfalls and racist essentialisms that have plagued the imagined authenticity of these much older identity categories. As Mohandas Gandhi argued, "It is good to swim in the waters of tradition, but to sink in them is suicide" (cited in Prashad 113). Asian American identity has not yet been saddled with a weighty tradition that will drag it to the water's bottom.

Mind you, there are already danger signals that such hardenings of "tradition" and authenticity may be coming down the pike. As Lowe has importantly pointed out:

> The articulation of an "Asian American identity" as an organizing tool has provided a concept of political unity that enables diverse Asian groups to understand unequal circumstances and histories as being related. The building of "Asian American culture" is crucial to this effort, for it empowers the diverse Asian-origin community vis-a-vis the institutions and apparatuses that exclude and marginalize it. Yet to the extent that Asian American culture fixes Asian American identity and suppresses differences—of national origin, generation, gender, sexuality, class—it risks particular dangers: not only does it underestimate the differences and hybridities among Asians, but it may also inadvertently support the racist discourse that constructs Asians as a homogeneous group, that implies Asians are "all alike" and conform to "types." (71)

Indeed, what worries Lowe as "the most exclusive construction of Asian American identity—one that presumes masculinity, American birth, and the speaking of English" (72)—parallels the pattern of the exclusivist constructions of a nationalist identity/essence in so many national cultures, with their similar glorification of masculinity, the soil, language, and religion as signifiers of authenticity—the danger of what Lowe elsewhere has referred to as "the risk [for Asian American identity] of a cultural politics that relies upon the construction of sameness and the exclusion of difference" (quoted in Espiritu, "Possibilities" 32)—which is to say the very rhetoric and dynamics of authenticity we have been investigating in this study, the languages of essentialism and racism. Nguyen warns that Asian American leaders need to be flexible in their creation of a discourse about Asian America: "Asian American intellectuals, who have prided themselves on their alignment with America's bad subject, must contend with those who are not 'hailed' by the discourse of Asian America as the bad subject, who do not respond to the call that they are Asian American, or at least do not respond in the way desired" (166). Whereas the "identity" in "Asian American identity" is still not fully formed and is still in process, it is not too early to ask, as does R. Radhakrishnan, "Will the ideology of Asian-America be single or plural? Will it be capitalist, nationalist, hybrid, hyphenated, Marxist, post-Marxist, ethnic or postethnic, gendered, sexualized? . . . 'Which Asian-America?'" (253)

Indeed, there are already manifestations, danger signals if you will, of a nascent rhetoric of authenticity and exclusion. One such danger area is in attitudes toward mixed-race Asian Americans. From the example (cited earlier) of pioneer Asian American writer Edith Eaton (Sui Sin Far), to the Japanese American community in the 1930s "thrust[ing] out of their midst most mixed people" (Spickard, "What" 257), to mixed-race students today at college campuses who find themselves not welcomed by their Asian American student organizations because they don't "look" sufficiently Asian (see, for example, Spickard, "What" 257), the attitude of Asian communities in the United States toward mixed-race Asians has frequently been inhospitable. As Stephen Murphy-Shigematsu explains, "It has been difficult to include biracial Asian Americans in Asian American communities"—for they are "often seen as threatening to Asian American communities and individuals. There is a feeling that openly discussing this topic amounts to sanctioning interracial marriage and endorsing the death of Asian American ethnic groups" (quoted in Spickard, "What" 261). As Asian American political organizations grow and as Asian American studies becomes a common curricular subject in U.S. colleges and universities, "many mainstream Asian American groups still do not know quite what to do with multiracial Asians" (Spickard, "What" 262)—or how to incorporate them into Asian American studies curricula. An instructive example of the invisibility of multiracials was the protest in 1990–1991 of the hit musical *Miss Saigon,* in which Asian American activist groups argued bitterly that an Asian actor, rather than the white actor chosen, should have been given the lead role of the Eurasian pimp. In the midst of this ballyhoo, no one bothered to suggest the possibility of a mixed-race Eurasian actor.

Another danger zone was the agenda of "real" Asian American literature as elaborated during the 1970s by Frank Chin, whose Asian American anthology (*Aiiieeeee!*) articulated an Asian American authenticity, as Koshy puts it, "in purist and separatist terms"—distinguishing between what Chin called "real" Asian Americans, who are "American born and raised" and first-generation immigrants from Asian countries who kowtow to the stereotype of the passive and subservient Oriental. As Koshy puts it, "The authentic Asian American is here defined as a prototypical No-No Boy: a political subject who says no to Asia, no to America, and is decidedly male" (476). Chin's articulations and his subsequent debate with Maxine Hong Kingston have been controversial and formative, within Asian American activist and academic circles, in the discussion of who is a real or authentic Asian American.

Indeed, some groups have always been more central to the project than others. The native-born were more central than first-generation immigrants, for the latter were more closely tied to their Asian cultures while the former were the founders of the very notion of an Asian American identity. Chinese and Japanese Americans have for decades stood at the center of an Asian American identity, with Filipinos on the margins; by the 1990s, Koreans had also become central to Asian American discourse, with a number of more recent groups now also on the margins, including Southeast Asians, South Asians, and Pacific Islanders (Spickard, "Who" 21). David Palumbo-Liu (396) notes that the dynamics of centrality and marginality operate also within the fields of literary and cultural production, that the "recent explosion in the production and marketing of Asian American literature betrays a particular ideological strategy" which involves "foreground[ing] the rise of certain Asians (primarily among second and third generation Chinese and Japanese Americans) while ignoring the continuing struggles of others"—as exemplified by "the current popularity of certain *Chinese* American texts" (by Chinese American writers like Amy Tan, Gish Jen, and David Wong Louie). As Lowe writes, "The essentializing of Asian American identity also reproduces oppositions that subsume other nondominant groups in the same way that Asians and other groups are marginalized by the dominant culture: to the degree that the discourse generalizes Asian American identity as male, women are rendered invisible; or to the extent that Chinese are presumed to be exemplary of all Asians, the importance of other Asian groups is ignored" (71).

One group very much on the outer margins of Asian American identity and of the academic field of Asian American studies is South Asians. As Nazli Kibria, herself a South Asian scholar of Asian American studies, notes, South Asian Americans in Asian American studies programs and conferences feel "a powerful sense of marginality," for they "remain largely at the margins rather than the center of scholarship and writing on Asian America"; underlying this marginalization is the issue of "who is a real Asian American": says Kibria, "South Asian claims to legitimate 'Asian American-ness' are suspect because of perceived racial difference" ("Not Asian" 252–253). Indeed, within South Asian American culture itself—as with other Asian American communities—we also see subdiscourses of authenticity and exclusion seeping in: for example, New York City now hosts two South Asian–pride parades in August of each year, an India Day Parade as well as a Pakistan Day parade—but in the India Day parade of 1994, while Miss Universe (Sushmita Sen) and the Hindu Right (Bharatiya Janata Party) float were exciting the crowds, "the organizers had forbidden the South Asian Lesbian and Gay Association (SALGA) from participating" (Prashad 117).

Finally, as Nguyen points out, "the discourse of the bad subject" behind the formation and development of Asian American identity, as both an academic and a political ideology, has experienced a "gradual slide from a politically necessary strategic essentialism to a co-opted and commodified essentialism as the dominant, if not sole, form of Asian American identity, which in the end limits the degree of opposition to pluralism and capitalism that the discourse of the bad subject wishes to promote" (150)—in the process rejecting (and restricting) the development of multiple and diverse versions of Asian Americanness. After all, many Asian Americans think of the model-minority stereotype (the discourse of the "good subject") as a good thing and want to assimilate into dominant ideology and rise to whiteness, even vote Republican, and so on. As Nguyen reminds us, "The subject who refuses to be hailed by dominant ideology can also refuse to be hailed by resistant ideology. It is that refusal that signals the limits of the discourse of the bad subject and the limits of Asian America" (157).[9]

But can we avoid a continuing slide into such essentialisms and into the rhetoric and dynamics of exclusionary authenticity? It is important to remember that Asian American identity is still in a very formative stage, still very malleable and quite unshaped, not yet hardened into a reified and ossified "nature." It is still in constant flux and formation, and we still have the opportunity to mold both its shape and its contours/margins. Lowe (82) reminds us:

> The grouping "Asian American" is not a natural or static category; it is a socially constructed unity, a situationally specific position, assumed for political reasons. It is "strategic" in Gayatri Chakravorty Spivak's sense of a "strategic use of a positive essentialism in a scrupulously visible political interest." The concept of "strategic essentialism" suggests that it is possible to utilize specific signifiers of racialized ethnic identity, such as "Asian American," for the purpose of contesting and disrupting the discourses that exclude Asian Americans, while simultaneously revealing the internal contradictions and slippages of "Asian American" so as to insure that such essentialisms will not be reproduced and proliferated by the very apparatuses we seek to disempower.

Indeed, I am more optimistic that such essentialisms can be avoided (and not "naturalized") in the case of Asian American identity than in the case of other, longstanding identity formations that have hardened into a long history, rhetoric, and practice of authenticity, purity, and exclusion—precisely *because* Asian American identity is so patently and obviously a strategic/political fabrication, a coalition which various ethnic and national groups have entered into *voluntarily* for strategic purposes, rather than because they deeply believe in a shared and essential racial or national destiny. What will this identity mean as it becomes increasingly "mixed" ethnically and racially? Again, as Liu asks, "Will membership in the race depend more on heredity or on heritage? Chromosomes or culture? Will it be a matter of voluntary affiliation, a question of choice?" (188) Benedict Anderson has convincingly suggested that part of the power of the "imagined community" of "nation" is that "dying for one's country, which usually one does not choose, assumes a moral grandeur which dying for the Labour Party, the American Medical Association, or perhaps even Amnesty International can not rival, for these are all bodies one can join or leave at easy will" (144). I suggest that an Asian American identity should be treated as somewhere in between the presumed essentialness and naturalness of a nation or race, on the one hand, and a purely voluntary affiliation like Amnesty International, on the other; that we should aspire to the nongrandiosity of voluntary affiliations like Amnesty International or the Labour Party. Indeed, it would be very salutary for us to understand that identities are not essences but rather more like one's choice to subscribe to Amnesty International for a strategic and political utility—with the *strategic* nature of the enterprise always in the foreground—lest one should begin to emphasize the "essentialism" over the "strategic."

As I have argued earlier in the chapter, Asian Americanness is *so* obviously and patently a fabrication, a nonessential identity of very recent and strategic origins, that the sheer inauthenticity (even absurdity) of the conceptual category can perhaps be thus turned to useful advantage—as a way voluntarily and consciously to *perform inauthenticity*. After all, "Asian American" is itself an "interpellation" in the Althusserian sense: Chinese Americans and Samoan Americans and Pakistani Americans are all hailed by Asian American discourse to join a shared identity formation, although they may feel little or nothing in common with each other. Indeed, "Asian America" is as heterogeneous and thus as vacuous an identity designation as can be imagined. And it is likely to continue being so in the foreseeable future, for even as native-born (second, third, etc.) generations of Asian Americans construct a more homogeneous shared culture together, still fully two-thirds of Asians in the United States currently are foreign-born, with large waves of new immigrants arriving each year; thus, the instabilities and frictions between distinct native Asian cultures and a fabricated, panethnic Asian American culture/ identity (as a voluntary affiliation) will continue to be a glaringly unavoidable feature of the Asian American landscape.

So, if the category is so clearly inauthentic, so clearly *not* a national or cultural or racial "essence" with a corresponding "moral grandeur," so clearly a strategic fabrication constructed for political and ideological purposes, then we can perhaps treat it as a performative category that we can continue to shape and mold to particular purposes, always in process and transition—rather than ever buying into a reified and essential, "natural" identity, with all the toxic dynamics of authenticity that come along with such an identity. (After all, such essentialized authenticity is also the result of Orientalist racism, of our being *involuntarily* lumped together as "all looking alike.") Radhakrishnan suggests that we should "espous[e] a Gramscian model of the intellectual as leader/persuader/activist" and that "Asian-American intellectuals, scholars, and teachers should take up the responsibility of creating, molding, and bringing into being a certain kind of bloc known as Asian-America" (253–254). Similarly, Koshy writes that "it then becomes our responsibility to articulate the inner contradictions of the term [Asian American] and to enunciate its representational inconsistencies and dilemmas. . . . Asian American Studies is uniquely positioned to intervene in current theoretical discussions on ethnicity, representation, and writing not despite, but because of, the contested and contestatory nature of its formation" (491).

In other words, what I am suggesting is that Asian American identity is so patently inauthentic that its great advantage is that it will not let us forget its own fabrication as a form of "strategic essentialism," its origin as a strategic use of inauthenticity: in this way, it can allow for a practice of *performing inauthenticity* as a conscious strategy by which to remind ourselves of the importance of a shared, coalitional identity and, at the same time, of the voluntary, nonauthentic nature of all such identities: as a reminder that *all* essentialisms are strategic and not innate; and in the hope that Asian American identity can avoid many of the pitfalls of authenticity and essentialist racism that plague other, older forms of group identity which have grown to imagine themselves as an originary race or a natural essence from which others must be excluded. Rather, Asian American identity can perform inauthenticity as a constant reminder that, as with membership in Amnesty International or in a health and fitness gym, we are *voluntarily choosing* to belong to a group with the absurd but useful (and in practice increasingly real) claim that Sikhs, Filipinos, Samoans, and Koreans in the United States all share the same hyphenated identity. We can do so for the purposes, at once, of making useful political alliances; of taking and reclaiming pride in our heritages; of creating a shared future and increasingly viable mixed identity; and finally of reminding ourselves that all identities are inauthentic at base, that we are all Hapas, all messy mixes that defy any attempts at defining an authentic purity.

CHAPTER 7

Coda

LIVING CULTURES

⌣·

T his study has explored the contemporary anxiety over cultural authenticity and identity by taking up several specific case studies—academia, Irishness, international adoption, Jewishness, Asian American identity—of the ways particular cultures construct authenticities and authentic identities to combat feelings of vacated or inauthentic identities in our contemporary world. Each of these case studies is, of course, very specific and different from each of the others—and so the argumentative meat, if you will, the real substance, of this study lies in the specific analyses provided within each chapter; furthermore, there are countless topics one could have also chosen to include in a study of authenticity and identity. As a result, it would be foolhardy and indeed ludicrous to imagine that I could in good conscience, in a concluding chapter, make neat, satisfying, and totalizing generalizations, summaries, and conclusions about this larger topic—authenticity and identity—which binds these individual chapters together. Nevertheless, there are certain threads and connections we can usefully make note of among these particular case studies and chapters. And we can then further make some observations and speculations about these threads.

One central thread is the anxiety of "losing the subject" in our contemporary world: the anxiety of a bleaching out of specific cultural, racial, ethnic, and national identities that seemingly threaten to render one nondistinctive and thus inauthentic. As Vijay Prashad writes about this anxiety among South Asians ("desis") in the United States today: "It is easy to empathize with the longing for some cultural resources in the United States. To be lost at sea in the midst of a relentless corporate ethic and a passionate consumer society is not comfortable for our souls; people seek some sort of shelter. Always afraid of being mass produced, individuals want to make some sort of statement of distinction, some cultural statement" (118). This is, he notes, part of a general angst: "Migrants fear the loss of their culture, just as much as the young whites fear (falsely) that they have never had a culture at all. Just as white Americans don the robes of the East or reinvent their ethnicities of Europe, just as blacks seek connections with Africa in name, religion, and food, just as Latinos find links with Latin America, so too do desis seek some icon in their homeland for solace" (118–119). As a result, he points out, we have seen "the formation of numerous organizations and stores in the cities, especially in the Indian ghettos" to tend to such cultural anxiety: "such spaces," he notes, "offer their services as the channels of the 'authentic culture'" for these desis seeking "authentic cultural lives" (119).

Similarly, we have seen how Irish Americans—and, indeed, the Irish themselves—have embraced an "authentic" Irish past and culture, in an ethnocentric haze of nostalgia and stereotype, to assert their cultural authenticity and difference. "Holocaust Jewishness" and Israeli identification also serve, for many U.S. Jews, as versions of such constructed authenticities. One very visible sign of this urge to find an authentic cultural self is the ubiquity and popularity in the United States today of what I have been referring to as the "heritage industry"—whether in the form of Irish "retribalization centers" on university campuses teaching Gaelic and Irish step dancing; Indian or Pakistani pride parades and festivals; classes in Norwegian and in Viking nautical skills; Chinese language and calligraphy classes (and screenings of *Mulan*) for adopted Chinese kids and their parents; and so on. Everyone wants an authentic culture and identity to claim as one's own genuine self—and thus there are many willing consumers for those who would peddle "authentic cultures."

Another central thread connecting these chapters is the rhetoric and mechanics of authenticity, a process of searching for an originary past upon which to base a cultural authenticity, a process which—as we have seen—repeatedly leads to ethnocentric practices of excluding others who don't fit the constructed criteria and whom one can thus label as "inauthentic." I am reminded of the French philosopher Ernest Renan's definition of a nation as "a group of people united by a mistaken view about the past and a hatred of their neighbors" (quoted in Bronner 6).

Our study of Irishness—which asked "What is Irishness?" and "What is the 'Irish spirit'?" and thus, by extension, "What is *any* national or cultural identity?"—provides the pattern for such mechanics. The Irish national project of self-definition in the past century has been an attempt to combat the longstanding and pejorative labels of a racist and imperialistic English discourse of Irishness—by means of a retrospective and nostalgic construction of an originary and authenticating essence, a supposedly authentic Irish/ Gaelic difference: in response to the anxiety of a loss of self-representation and subjectivity and in order to prove that the Irish are indeed a very particular and distinct people, the Irish thus defined themselves and their national identity in terms of their supposedly specific "otherness" and difference—thus in fact mirroring an English construction of Irish identity as ineluctably "other" and different. The quest for authenticity, in a nationalist politics, frequently takes this familiar form of a national nostalgia for origins, a yearning for a premodern and uncontaminated past that somehow authorizes and defines the authenticity and essence of the cultural present— in an attempt to define an Irish uniqueness and authenticity as a static otherness already frozen in the past. Both the English imperial discourse of Irish otherness and the "narrow-gauge" nationalist construction of a distinct and unique Gaelic otherness collude in a process of "imperialist nostalgia."

The practical result, frequently, of such a national rhetoric of authenticity is not only recycled national or ethnic stereotypes but also a nativist, exclusionary urge that results in both discursive and actual practices of "ethnic cleansing." These are discursive processes that attempt to deny the messy hybridity and current realities of actual cultures and of (not purely tribal) populations—reflected, in the case of the Irish, in a fear of the cosmopolitan, the global, and the hybrid. After all, how well can the essential centrality of the Irish Catholic peasant—as a discourse of authenticity—hold up in a contemporary Ireland that is increasingly nonagrarian and urban, that has grown into an international economic powerhouse nicknamed "the Celtic Tiger," and that is a major presence in the cultural realms of international music, film, literature, and dance?

Such a mechanics and rhetoric of authenticity are also reflected, for example, within academic discourse—with its obsession over authentic and inauthentic voices, with the concern over who can authentically speak for a fetishized position of subaltern otherness. The effects of such a rhetoric of authenticity range from tokenism (for example, particular subaltern critics— like Gayatri Spivak—and particular postcolonial texts—like Chinua Achebe's *Things Fall Apart*—being widely accepted as representative and typical) to essentialism and even racism (for example, that brown Indians can be properly deemed "postcolonial" but white Irish cannot). Hovering in the background, however, is always the very real danger of appropriation, in which the understandable urge to seek one's own cultural identity and subjectivity can result in the culture's more dominant voices (e.g., Irish Americans, Jewish

Americans, Italian Americans—for "we are all ethnic") appropriating the contested positions granted, in academic culture, to minority racial and ethnic voices, to voices of radical "otherness."

Such mechanics are also reflected, within the United States today, in the concern on the part of white adoptive parents over losing the authentic cultural heritage of their adopted children—resulting in attempts at retrieval and preservation that, in many ways, parallel the dynamics and problems of attempts by nationalist movements to preserve a lost and originary national culture. In the case of international adoption, this quest for an authentic heritage often takes the form of a "roots mania"—in which well-meaning white parents attend cultural festivals with their adopted children and send them to "culture camps" so that they can immerse themselves in their "cultural heritage"—a "heritage" too often made up of stereotyped, Orientalized, and nostalgic notions and images that are somehow imagined to be the child's "real" identity—as opposed to the actual lived experience of the child growing up in contemporary U.S. culture.

Or, for example, in the case of Jewish American culture, the continued reification of Yiddishness as "Jewish culture" represents not the real presence of a lively and ongoing living culture and way of life, a set of daily practices, but rather—within these mechanics of authenticity—a sentimental construct bathed in nostalgia and resulting in Borscht Belt stereotypes that are, in themselves, as essentialist and racist as some of the negative stereotypes behind anti-Semitism. In view of the elusively complex but obsessive debate over authentic Jewishness ("Who is a Jew? What is Jewishness?"), diasporic Jews feel challenged by feelings of inauthenticity and a need to authenticate one's identity—and the easiest thing to do is to fall back on the stereotypes of an authentic identity, the stereotyped marks of an essential Jewish difference. Whereas for contemporary Jews many of these stereotypes are of an anti-Semitic nature which they have no trouble rejecting, one of the traits of an essential Jewishness is a quality embraced—and a status envied—both by anti-Semites and by Jews themselves: the status of victim, of the perpetual scapegoat, within a cult of victimhood that is problematic as an essential identity (just as the stereotypes of "lovable losers" and of heroic failure are troubling for an Irish identity). The diasporic investment in victimhood as a naturalized Jewish essential identity allows both the Holocaust and the embattled state of Israel to serve as therapeutic tonics to a diasporic Jewish authenticity.

Indeed, the mechanics of authenticity are always in danger of constructing, and then "naturalizing," new authenticities as part of an essential, hallowed identity—whether it is the Holocaust as originary moment, the suffering Jew, the necessarily impoverished and backward Irish peasant, the rigid and limited positions available to subaltern voices in the U.S. academy, or the Asian American as either (take your pick) model-minority "good subject" or as necessarily subversive "bad subject."

Some speculations and observations. It is one thing when, as I have been suggesting, members of First World cultures feel themselves to have vacated, inauthentic, or whitebread identities and then try to fill that vacuum by seeking an authentic self amid a haze of nostalgic essentialisms; this has been a main thread connecting the specific case studies in this book. But where there is also intense interest in specific identities other than those one could claim as one's own, there may be—I have also been suggesting—something else going on. In such situations, the "roots mania" (when it isn't one's own roots at stake) may also function, in terms of "cultural work," as a sop to conscience. Just as England in the 1970s and 1980s witnessed a wave of popular cultural productions concerning India as the crown jewel of the former British Empire, in a phenomenon frequently referred to as "Raj nostalgia" (e.g., films like *A Passage to India, Heat and Dust, The Jewel in the Crown*, and revived interest in the novels they were based on)—so also in the United States we have contemporary versions of such "imperialist nostalgia." After all, not only did white U.S. culture nearly exterminate Native American populations altogether, but "Indian schools" nearly wiped out tribal languages, religions, and cultures. Similarly, for example, urban schools in the nineteenth and twentieth centuries were responsible for the elimination of Yiddish as a living language in this country, in a project of assimilating others and erasing their particular other cultures. So that the broad cultural interest today in Native American culture (artifacts, clothing, beads, rituals, sweat lodges, closeness to nature, and so on) or in Yiddish culture (Tony Kushner, klezmer music, and so on) may function unconsciously as a sop to conscience: Yes, we took you away from your people and your land and we erased your culture and your language—but look how intensely interested we really are in that culture. As I have argued, a construction or reification of an authentic identity based on nostalgia is most possible and likely when the particular culture being authenticated has been largely and already eradicated. Similarly, we see an intense interest in contemporary Germany, on the part of German youths, in Jewishness and in the Yiddish culture that their parents and grandparents helped exterminate.

In both academia and in U.S. culture at large, we see such a discursive and cultural process manifest in our intense interest in ethnic, postcolonial, and multicultural voices and authenticity, a feel-good multiculturalism with little risk. In the case of our interest in colonial and postcolonial histories, literary culture in the United States can decry the despotic legacies of European imperialism while occluding its own troubled—and continuing—history of colonialism and neocolonialism. As suggested by the "post" in "postcolonial," these are issues from past history that an American can safely take sides on now because they seem to carry no risk to one's *present* culture; rather, they are the miserable legacies of those brutish European imperialists. Especially in academia, contemporary postcolonial and ethnic studies provide scholars in the Western academy the luxury of having it both ways: to speak for and on behalf of the subaltern other (and to be on the side of the oppressed), even to advance one's career through such study, without having to change our comfortable scholarly and professional practices in any significant way.

Within U.S. culture at large, such a cultural process manifests itself in phenomena such as those I have referred to as "Irish chic" and "Jewish envy." In the particular case of "Irish chic" in U.S. culture today, as I have argued, what is still popularly recognized as a distinct and "authentic" ethnic/cultural identity—Irishness—can thus function as a legitimate way to deal with ethnicity, and even class and race, without actually having to stray from the comfortably familiar (i.e., whiteness). Irishness may be both popular and comfortable today precisely because it remains an identifiable (and presumably authentic) ethnicity that is nonetheless unthreatening and familiar. In popular culture, as in academia, one can have the ideological justification of doing ethnic studies or "performing ethnicity" simply by doing Irish studies—while actually still working within the familiar and with whiteness, and without having to venture into the more uncomfortable realms of racial and Third World difference.

In the particular case of international, transracial adoption, this phenomenon—i.e., therapeutic identification to sop one's conscience—is manifest in the response of white adoptive parents who cling to their children's racial, ethnic, and national identities as if they were their own. Traditionally, culture is passed from parents (and the community) down to children; here, we see an anxious attempt by white parents to have children pass a culture and heritage *up* to them. One wonders: Who is trying to get repaired here? Whose needs are being met? Whose identity is really at stake here? Whose anxiety is at issue, whose concern over authenticity, whose guilt? After all, as with Native American cultures, it is the white parents who have sundered the adopted child from his or her native heritage, culture, and people. One wonders, then—in the parents' attempts to honestly deal with the challenge of raising a child so visibly different from themselves—if what is really at stake here is, once again, the unacknowledged and uncomfortable realms of racial difference.

*T*his quest for an authentic identity, in all its manifestations, also involves what to me is a truly disturbing implication—having to do with popular assumptions of what constitutes "culture" and "identity." Is a cultural identity something fluid, messy, ongoing, always in process, always still being created? Or is it something identifiable as authentic and thus nameable, categorizable, frozen, essentialist, and rigid? Both the anxiety that one's own identity may be inauthentic and the urge to fill such inauthenticity via a "heritage industry" or a "roots mania" are premised on the assumption of the invisibility or nonexistence of one's own culture. The disturbing implication is that to so many people—Irish Americans seeking to "catch the Irish spirit," white parents trying to provide their adopted children with an authentic culture, Jewish parents who feel they have no Jewishness to transmit to their children, and so on—their own culture is either invisible or lost. Renato Rosaldo has made the point that members of the dominant majority are invisible to themselves: it is always *other* people who have cultures, while the self seems transparent. No wonder we have the whitebread blues. We seem to forget that our own lived and complex daily experiences, however they may elude authentic classification or nostalgic simplification, do constitute themselves into a very particular, real, and living culture that we are creating and shaping and transmitting to our children. Indeed, what we may see as our dull, transparent whitebread culture may itself be conjured up nostalgically by later generations as an authentic culture they will wish they could have had instead of their own dull present lives: this has, indeed, already begun to happen with the fifties and sixties in U.S. culture, reified and authenticated now as genuine cultural periods of their own. Rather, we tend to romanticize and idealize culture and community: we expect them to be monovocal, beautifully coherent, satisfying, harmonious, and static. What culture—in spite of all the tour guides and travel books—has ever really been that way?

Both Irish and Irish American cultures find themselves looking backward toward an authentic cultural identity based on the nostalgic icon of the Irish Catholic, Republican peasant. In the Jewish world, the loss of what has long been considered genuine Jewish culture—that is, *Yiddishkeit,* the traditional Jewish culture of Central and Eastern Europe—results in a desire for a "real," concrete, specific cultural Jewish difference—as if the various versions of contemporary Jewish life being lived in different places did not themselves constitute "culture."

This same presumed invisibility of one's own actual "culture" is often applied to the notion of one's personal and cultural "identity." As I asked in the adoption chapter: If you didn't know you were adopted and didn't think you were adopted, then would your life—as you had lived it—-be any less genuine or authentic? Does the past or the heritage you didn't know about change the solidity or reality of the life you did actually experience? How important, then, is such an unlived past or heritage to your own authenticity and identity? The basic question here is: What is it, after all, that composes our genuine, authentic personal identity? Is it our lived experience, the sum total of how we each have (individually and collectively) lived? Or is it our cultural, ethnic, or racial heritage, an inherited past but not one that has been necessarily lived or experienced? I am not suggesting that this has to be an either/or choice: rather, to admit to a heritage and a past that strengthens and enriches one's present life, that adds to one's ongoing identity formation based on a complex compilation of ongoing influences and experiences, grants the past a role in informing and enriching one's identity, while still acknowledging that one's "identity" is based largely on lived experiences, and influences. For a child adopted as a baby, the cultural "heritage" of one's birth mother can only be a dead past detached from one's actual lived experience (and presumably from the actual lived experience of the adoptive parents); and the immersion in such a past culture, like that of a nationalist search for origins and like nationalist "revivals," can be but an act of "reviving" what is already lost (more than actual "preservation"), an exercise in cultural nostalgia and sentimental Orientalisms.

Thus, whether we are talking about the "Irish spirit," or authentic Jewishness, or authentic Chineseness, I would want to remind us of a more supple and flexible notion of "cultural identity"—again, in Stuart Hall's definition: "Far from being grounded in a mere 'recovery' of the past, which is waiting to be found, and which once found, will secure our sense of ourselves into eternity, identities are the names we give to the different ways we are positioned by, and position ourselves within, the narratives of the past" ("Cultural Identity and Cinematographic Representation" 70). In a different essay ("Cultural Identity and Diaspora"), Hall elaborates further that a cultural identity is "a matter of 'becoming' as well as of 'being.' It belongs to the future as much as to the past. It is not something which already exists, transcending place, time, history and culture. Cultural identities come from somewhere, have histories. But, like everything which is historical, they undergo constant transformation. Far from being eternally fixed in some essentialized past, they are subject to the continuous 'play' of history, culture and power" (225). Such a definition allows for the ongoing discursive processes by which identities are formed in response to real-world situations, political contingencies, and cultural specificities (both local and global)—and by which they are constantly changing and being created.

Such a flexible notion of cultural identity reshapes our very notions of identity and authenticity, illuminating the reality that we *create*—not merely inherit or "retrieve"—culture. This is a powerful and empowering understanding, for it allows us to imagine and recognize ourselves as active agents participating in the making and shaping of our cultures. For example, Adam Pertman, the author of *Adoption Nation*, tells the *Los Angeles Times* that he believes that transracial adoption—precisely because it is so visible—is having a profound effect on, and changing, how we even conceive of families in American culture: "Do you think kids in L.A. grow up thinking kids look just like Mommy and Daddy? Of course not, because they have a little Chinese girl in their class who has two white mommies. We are raising a generation who will not have the same notions of family that we do. And it's because of this trans-racial stuff" (8/04/02: E3). Nor will they have the same notions of "American" (as "white") identity. Which is to say that our very notion of "American" cultural authenticity is being reshaped; and it is we who are doing so.

Similarly, I am a Chinese native who teaches English and Irish literature: this small reality helps (in a small way) to dismantle preconceived notions not only of Irish authenticity but also of Chineseness. When I first began my career as a university professor in 1979, I was virtually the only English professor I knew who was Asian; most Asian Americans in academia were scientists, and most Asian American college students expected to major in the sciences. But because there has been an increasing number of role models of Asians in the humanities, at universities across the country now many Asian American students are majoring in the humanities and see no contradiction or problem with the idea of a Chinese American or a Sikh immigrant discussing Milton or Beckett. It is *we* who are making such changes.

Similarly, the Jewishness that I see my wife and her cohort of Jewish feminist scholars and theologians constructing and transmitting is a very real, living *active*-ity, something that shapes and changes and constructs culture. Their realities—lesbian rabbis, Chinese American kids (like my son) *davening* in Hebrew in *shul,* and so on—are resulting in a reshaped U.S. Jewish culture that has now even witnessed Asian American rabbis and lesbian rabbis leading active congregations. As Rachel Adler, Jewish feminist theologian and author of *Engendering Judaism,* and a good friend, wrote to me and my wife, Maeera, "I'm thinking here of Maeera and our friends. The Jewishness we are transmitting is a living thing. We reshape it as we transmit it. Our children see us rethinking, reacting to what affects us as Jews and as American Jews, learning a kind of fluidity and cultural authority that belongs to transmitters. . . . I'm thinking of an early Zionist song from the long ago days of our innocence. It went: 'We have come to the land to build and to be rebuilt'" (personal correspondence, July 2002). We rebuild both the land and the culture—and in the process rebuild ourselves.

Contemporary Asian American culture and identity are especially interesting in terms of such ongoing cultural rebuilding—for in reality they are being built now for the very first time. The previous generation of Chinese, Japanese, Filipinos, Koreans, Hawaiians, and so on, felt a sense of ethnic pride and community but would have regarded a panethnic Asian American culture as an absurd myth and something to be avoided. Nevertheless, a generation later, such a cultural identity is being formed and shaped in U.S. high school and college campuses across the country. Such newness provides us with that rare event in one's living experience: a cultural laboratory in which an unformed group identity is still in the process of being formed, not yet finished and hardened and "naturalized" into a frozen "essence." How this identity will be understood and defined is still very much under formation and negotiation. Unlike much older identity formations—whether Irishness, Englishness, Jewishness, Chineseness, and so on—"Asian Americanness" has not yet been constructed in the popular imagination into some authentic and natural category. Thus, we can still shape and affect its qualities and future— and perhaps, just perhaps, we can avoid some of the familiar ethnocentric pitfalls and racist essentialisms that have plagued the imagined authenticities of much older identity categories.

Indeed, as I argued in the previous chapter, Asian Americanness is so obviously and patently a fabrication, a nonessential identity of very recent and strategic origins, entered into by its adherents *voluntarily* (rather than "naturally") for the purposes of strategic coalition building, that the sheer inauthenticity of the category can perhaps be turned to useful advantage: voluntarily and consciously *to perform inauthenticity*, a conscious strategy by which to remind ourselves not only of the importance of a shared group identity but, equally important, of the voluntary, nonauthentic, messy, hybrid, "mixed" and impure nature of all such identities—rather than to imagine, once again, a shared identity as an originary race or natural essence from which all "inauthentic" others must be excluded.

NOTES

Chapter 2 *Who Can Speak as Other?*

1. The ways we read Joyce are changing so quickly that, in a graduate seminar on Joyce that I taught recently, the students—armed with works by Colin MacCabe, Cheryl Herr, Seamus Deane, Emer Nolan, Enda Duffy, James Fairhall, Tom Hofheinz, myself, and others—said they didn't understand how anyone could have ever imagined Joyce to be an apolitical writer.

2. See, for example, Kevin Barry's attack on David Lloyd, Luke Gibbons, Terry Eagleton, and myself for our postcolonial approaches to Irish literature—as reported in the *Irish Times* 7/27/95: 8 ("Challenging Critique Stirs Up Joyceans").

3. As Reizbaum writes further, "The predicament of women's writing in Scotland and Ireland provides an analogy, then, with the fate of Scottish and Irish literature on the whole, which has been trapped by its cultural identity, excluded from the canon from without because of it, or included at the expense of or through a distortion of it" (176).

4. In Chapter 5, I discuss the very interesting case of Binjamin Wilkomirski, a Swiss author who claims (and perhaps believes) that he was a Holocaust survivor and who wrote an award-winning book about his childhood experiences at Auschwitz—but who also turns out to be a "cultural impersonator."

5. Eagleton continues: "erstwhile dominant groups who, having fallen upon hard political times, present themselves as victimized minorities should not be surprised if they evoke the odd exasperated reaction from others" (*Heathcliff* 272).

6. I recall discussing with a colleague an effort by some right-wing groups in the United States to start a national holiday called "Caucasian Day," to compete with Martin Luther King Jr.'s Birthday, Chinese New Year's, etc. She bristled: "Come on, who needs a Caucasian Day? *Every* day is Caucasian Day!"

7. This forum, organized by Sander Gilman, occurred on December 27, 1995. The presentations were: (1) "How Ethnic Am I?" by Sabine Goelz; (2) "The Jewish Science: Ethnicity and the Knowledge of Psychoanalysis" by Daniel Boyarin; (3) "Crypto-Ethnicity" by Linda Hutcheon; and (4) "Demotic Metropolitans and

Vernacular Cosmopolitans" by Homi Bhabha. See also Gilman's discussion of this point and of my comments in his introduction to the January 1998 special issue of *PMLA* on ethnicity (113 [1998]: 19–27) and my response in *PMLA* 115 (1998): 449–450.

8. As Sabina Sawhney notes, the Vicar and Virago Affair lays bare the comfortable system "of patronage and tokenism" that so aggravates Spivak and Gunew: "On the one hand, Rahila Khan assumes the ideal persona to assuage white-liberal guilt and, on the other, she placidly inhabits the margin, presumably providing a colorful border for the dominant white subject"; this process transforms her into an anthropological case study, an "artifact who . . . is presumed to have an un-mediated relation with her ethnicity and whose information can then be appro-priated for the benefit, improvement, and entertainment of the members of the dominant culture" (212).

9. All citations to James Joyce's *Ulysses* follow the standard practice in academic Joyce studies, noting chapter and line numbers from the 1986 Vintage Books text edited by Hans Walter Gabler et al.

CHAPTER 3   *Inventing Irishness*

1. The 9/12/98 issue of *TV Guide* (page 11) notes that "Irish culture has swept the dance world ('Riverdance') and the book industry (*Angela's Ashes*), so why should TV be any different?" Quoting a TV executive's opinion that "Irish fami-lies make for good drama," the feature cites the new shows *Turks* (a drama set in Chicago about a family of Irish cops) and *To Have and to Hold* (more fami-lies of Irish cops, but in Boston, featuring—among others—Irish actress Fionnula Flanagan), both on CBS; Fox's sitcom *Costello* (about a foulmouthed Boston-Irish barmaid named Sue Costello); and NBC's drama *Trinity*. That same week, *Newsweek* (9/14/98: 70) previewed the fall television season with the storyline "A season of testosterone, ambiguous gayness and way too many Irish people"—similarly citing "Riverdance," *Angela's Ashes*, and the same group of new tele-vision programs.

2. On this last point, see also my closing arguments in Chapter 2.

3. The previous two paragraphs are adapted from my book *Joyce, Race, and Em-pire*, ch. 6.

4. Since the composition of this chapter, Hayden has authored a new book on the Irish, titled *Irish on the Inside: In Search of the Soul of Irish America*, in which he continues talking about "a distinct Irish soul."

5. I'm indebted here to Suman Gupta's article "'What Colour's Jew Joyce . . .': Race in the Context of Joyce's Irishness and Bloom's Jewishness."

6. Corkery thus summarily dismissed both Yeats and Joyce (the latter for being too vulgar and impure) as anti-Irish; no Ascendancy or Anglo-Irish writer, accord-ing to Corkery, could write authentic Irish literature because "[John Millington] Synge's class have always been reared on an alien porridge" (*Synge* 240).

7. W. J. McCormack has commented on a debate between Declan Kiberd and Kevin Barry regarding the intellectual histories of Protestant culture and of Catholic culture, a distinction (based on such blanket terms as *Catholic* and *Protestant*,

which assume essential differences) whose very assumptions McCormack questions:

> When "protestant culture" and "Catholic culture" are set up by Kiberd and Barry, their phrases require more concise definition. For, if culture is used in its anthropological sense, then it would be required of them to show that Catholics and Protestants ploughed in different ways, ate different food, harnessed their horses differently, bought clothes at different times, and instilled different values in their children. . . . Undoubtedly, certain activities—the eating of fish, the consumption of alcohol, the use of Sunday—do distinguish Catholics from members of the reformed churches—but other factors including social class, prosperity and poverty, climate and geographical variety are at work. Some attention to the vast, supportive web of cultural practices held in common by Irish Catholics, protestants, and persons not coming under those headings, might be timely. (97)

8. See also Gibson's *Joyce's Revenge: History, Politics, and Aesthetics in "Ulysses."*
9. Part of this section was originally delivered as a paper at the International James Joyce Symposium in London, June 24–30, 2000. As I mentioned at the time, the debate concerning cosmopolitanism is one that should be of both import and interest to members of the International James Joyce Foundation in view of our implied concerns with both the universal/global (the International, the modernist, the "European") and the local/particular (James Joyce and Irish literature). As Bruce Robbins writes about globetrotting academics like ourselves, "In the interest of self-defense as well as self-knowledge, then, intellectuals seem called on to rethink their narratives of where *they* come from [are we ourselves "citizens of the world"?] and to propose some alternative account of their undeniable yet perpetually denied cosmopolitanism—an account that will help negotiate between the charge of elitism . . . and the charge of nomadic, touristic delectation of distant cultures" (100, my emphasis). Gathering annually in some of the world's metropolitan/imperial centers (such as London, Rome, Paris, Frankfurt, Zurich) to discuss, as elite cosmopolites and intellectual mandarins, the literatures and cultures of a previously colonial people long on the margins of global economies and polities, we should indeed take on such an issue as part of our conscious agenda.
10. Such an exclusivist claim is implied by the journal *boundary 2*'s slogan that "The global deforms and molests the local," in which a romanticized "local" is cast as the only sort of genuine culture, which artificial influences like globalism would necessarily deform.
11. See Leerssen 231 on the implications of this signature.
12. As Robbins notes, "The class privilege ascribed to the cosmopolitan would have to be invented if it did not exist, for it provides an ideal solution to nationalism's internal problems. By means of such an ascription, class division is exorcised, projected onto a group that seems both internal and external, indigenous and alien. This group can be racialized (the Jews) or sexualized (homosexuals), as it so often has been, but it can also serve its purpose without race or sexuality. These days, when it is generally believed that racial and sexual sensitivities are running

dangerously high, there is obviously some usefulness in a national scapegoat category—the cosmopolitan—that can avoid both" (71).

13. A much longer analysis of *Dubliners* and *A Portrait* in terms of cosmopolitan-
    ism is included in Cheng, "'Terrible Queer Creatures': Joyce, Cosmopolitanism,
    and the Inauthentic Irishman."

14. See also my *Joyce, Race, and Empire* 206–218 on the further ironies of "A Na-
    tion Once Again."

15. This was still true at the time I wrote this chapter. But in mid–2002 Mary
    Robinson resigned her position as head of the United Nations Commission for
    Human Rights.

CHAPTER 4   *International Adoption and Identity*

1. In *Adoption Nation: How the Adoption Revolution Is Transforming America,*
   Adam Pertman writes (5), "This is nothing less than a revolution. After a decade of incremental improvements and tinkering at the margins, adoption is re-
   shaping itself to the core. It is shedding its corrosive stigmas and rejecting its
   secretive past; states are revising their laws and agencies are rewriting their rules
   even as the Internet is rendering them obsolete, especially by making it simpler
   for adoptees and birth parents to find each other; single women, multiracial families, and gay men and women are flowing into the parenting mainstream; middle-
   aged couples are bringing a rainbow of children from abroad into their
   predominantly white communities; and social service agencies are making it far
   easier to find homes for thousands of children whose short lives have been squan-
   dered in the foster-care system."

2. As Ford Madox Ford's narrator asks in *The Good Soldier*, upon discovering that
   what he thought was a happy marriage had for all these years been rife with in-
   fidelity and sordidness, "If for nine years I have possessed a goodly apple that
   is rotten at the core and discover its rottenness only in nine years and six months
   less four days, isn't it true to say that for nine years I possessed a goodly
   apple?" (7)

3. As the *Los Angeles Times* reported in August 2002, "Between 1995 and 2001,
   the number of immigrant visas issued to orphans coming to the United States
   more than doubled, from 8,987 to 19,237. More than half of these adoptions are
   from countries where non-Caucasians are the dominant racial group, while people
   adopting are overwhelmingly Caucasian" (8/4/02: E3).

4. I myself prefer Stuart Hall's definition of "cultural identity": "Far from being
   grounded in a mere 'recovery' of the past, which is waiting to be found, and which
   once found, will secure our sense of ourselves into eternity, identities are the
   names we give to the different ways we are positioned by, and position ourselves
   within, the narratives of the past" ("Cultural Identity and Cinematographic Representation" 70).

5. Indeed, should Californian parents who adopt a baby from Alabama start practicing Southern cuisine?

CHAPTER 5 *The Inauthentic Jew*

1. See, for example, Wirth-Nesher and also Whitfield, *In Search*.
2. See, for example, *Etz Hayim* 201 n. 25.
3. Reform Judaism also accepts patrilineal descent.
4. "For example, at a recent forum, a clean-cut Israeli-Arab academic, Michael Karayanni mentioned that all vacancies had miraculously disappeared when he tried to find an apartment near his university outside Tel Aviv. Another professor, a Jewish man who labels himself a leftist, exploded at the insinuation that this might constitute racism. 'But that's a security issue!' he said. In other words, Israeli Jews consider themselves justified in seeing every Arab, even an Israeli Arab, as a potential terrorist" (Sontag 51). The latter attitude has, in the wake of September 11, 2001, unfortunately, also been taken up by white citizens of the United States toward Arab American citizens.
5. As Maude McLeod, the oldest member of New York's black Hebrew community, noted in 1999 (at the age of ninety-five), "I did not join the Hebrew faith— I *returned*. I simply was on the wrong road and found my way back. That's my experience. In the Bible Jeremiah says he is black. Solomon says he is black. And David was and Samuel was and Jacob was. That's where I come from" (*New York Times Magazine* 9/26/99: 116).
6. See also the videotape "Lost Tribes of Israel" and the book by Parfitt.
7. The degree to which this is true is contested; see, for example, Biale.
8. Two new surveys were released in October 2002, just as I finished writing this chapter—and they created an instant controversy: one by the California-based Institute for Jewish and Community Research, finding a current U.S. Jewish population of 6.7 million; and the second by the United Jewish Communities, listing the U.S. Jewish population at only 5.2 million. Claims of inaccuracy and undercounting were immediately leveled at the latter survey, even by members of the survey's own advisory committee, noting that the figure is way too low, and that the survey—among other problems—did not account for "nondisclosure" (the unwillingness by some Jewish respondents to identify themselves to survey callers as Jewish), which has been tested to be about 13 percent. *Forward* 10/11/02: 1, 9, 11; and 10/4/02: 11.
9. The times are, however, changing quickly: Angela Warnick Buchdahl of the Westchester (N.Y.) Reform Temple is now the first Asian American to be ordained as a rabbi. *Forward* 10/4/02: 15.
10. As Kim Chernin writes, "Arafat is not Hitler. The Palestinian terrorists are not the SS. We are no longer the victims. The world has changed, but Jewish identity has not kept up with it. If we lived in the present, we would have to acknowledge that the Jewish people of the twenty-first century are no longer the world's foremost endangered species. We would have to recognize that we, as a people, are ourselves capable of victimization" (16).
11. See also, for example, Ezrahi on this issue.
12. Leon Wieseltier suggests that since "we [U.S. Jews] do not any longer possess a natural knowledge" of Jewish victimization and suffering, "in order to acquire such a knowledge, we rely more and more upon commemorations—so much so

that we are transforming the Jewish culture of the United States into a largely commemorative culture" (22).

13. The springtime Lag b'Omer festival, celebrated by Tunisian Jews on Djerba Island at the ancient Ghriba Synagogue, honors a Jewish author of the kabbala—and attracts Jews from around the world. One of the local Tunisian Jews observes that the attraction of the festival to Jews worldwide "to me makes more sense than visiting Warsaw or a concentration camp—because here, you see the living, not the dead" *(New York Times* 4/15/02:A3).

14. I thank David Schulman for this line.

15. This section is much indebted to Finkielkraut's *The Imaginary Jew* and quotes at length from this work.

16. Of course, the legacy of this culturally inherited trauma is, for post-Holocaust Jews, sometimes not so uncomplicatedly simple—and can be at times both troubled and complex.

CHAPTER 6   *Asian American Identity*

1. Part of this paragraph is adapted from pages 16–17 of my *Joyce, Race, and Empire.*

2. See, for example, Noel Ignatiev's *How the Irish Became White,* L. Perry Curtis Jr.'s *Apes and Angels: The Irishman in Victorian Caricature,* Vincent Cheng's *Joyce, Race, and Empire,* Karen Brodkin's *How Jews Became White Folks . . . ,* Ian Haney-Lopez's *White by Law: The Legal Construction of Race,* and F. James Davis's *Who Is Black?*

3. Three or four years later, King-Kok Cheung, a young Miltonist, was hired across town at UCLA. Some years after that, and after we had become good friends, I learned that she had undergone exactly the same initial experience at UCLA that I did at USC. King-Kok, however, ended up agreeing to teach Asian American literature and indeed has subsequently made a successful career for herself as a leading Asian Americanist. Nevertheless, she still harbors resentment over the essentialist assumption.

4. This is a significant population with an interesting, though little-known, history. As Paul Spickard writes, "One group of a few hundred Punjabi men settled down in the Imperial Valley of California and married immigrant women from Mexico. . . . They and their mixed-race children formed almost the only Indian community in the United States in the years before there was an Asian America. They identified strongly with the Punjab, but there was little Indian content to their lives. The families spoke English and Spanish, and most were Catholic, although they did tend to eat a mixture of Mexican and South Asian dishes. Identificationally, the mixed people grew up with the label 'Hindu,' but as with the Hawaiian Chinese, this meant mixed—Punjabi-Mexican American" ("Who" 16).

5. In the past, the white-Asian intermarriage rate largely involved Asian women and white men: the 1980 Census had found nearly three times as many marriages between Asian women and white men as between Asian men and white women *(Newsweek* 2/21/00: 49). By 1990 this was clearly no longer the case.

6. Helen Zia recalls that, as little girls, her two closest friends—one an African American girl and the other a white girl—demanded of her, "Helen, you've got to decide if you are black or white" (4).

7. As Angelo Ancheta writes in *Race, Rights and the Asian American Experience* (13), "In essence a black-white model fails to recognize that the basic nature of discrimination can differ among racial and ethnic groups. Theories of racial inferiority have been applied, often with violent force, against Asian Americans, just as they have been applied against blacks and other racial minority groups. But the cause of anti-Asian subordination can be traced to other factors as well, including nativism, differences in language and culture, perceptions of Asians as economic competitors, international relations, and past military involvement in Asian countries. . . . All of these considerations point to the need for an analysis of race that is very different from the dominant black-white paradigm."

8. The high levels of education are a bit misleading, since they also reflect the self-selecting nature of the families (and individuals) who get accepted into the United States as legal immigrants; these are often foreign families in which education and achievement are already emphasized as particularly important values, more so than the average for the particular Asian (Chinese, Korean, etc.) populations from which they originate. In contrast, among immigrant families that are not admitted through this sort of self-selection—such as refugees from Cambodia and Laos or families of Vietnam "war brides"—the population on welfare is extremely high, with low levels of education (see *Los Angeles Times* 7/12/98: A31). Indeed, these are significant class differences and disparities *within* the Asian American population.

9. Nguyen cites as an illustration of these limits the controversial debate within academic Asian American studies over Lois Yamanaka's novels, especially *Blu's Hanging*; see Nguyen 157–166.

BIBLIOGRAPHY

Achebe, Chinua. *Things Fall Apart*. New York: Fawcett Crest, 1969.

Adler, Rachel. *Engendering Judaism*. Philadelphia: Jewish Publication Society, 1998.

Alcoff, Linda Martín. "The Problem of Speaking for Others." Roof and Wiegman 97–119.

Althusser, Louis. "Ideology and Ideological State Apparatuses." Trans. Ben Brewster. *Lenin and Philosophy and Other Essays*. New York: Monthly Review Press, 1971.

Ancheta, Angelo N. *Race, Rights and the Asian American Experience*. New Brunswick: Rutgers University Press, 1998.

Anderson, Benedict. *Imagined Communities: Reflections on the Origin and Spread of Nationalism*. Rev. ed. London: Verso, 1991.

Appadurai, Arjun. *Modernity at Large: Cultural Dimensions of Globalization*. Minneapolis: University of Minnesota Press, 1996.

Appiah, Kwame Anthony. "Cosmopolitan Patriots." *Critical Inquiry* 23.3 (1997): 617–639.

Arnold, Matthew. "On the Study of Celtic Literature." 1910. *English Literature and Irish Politics,* vol. 9 of *The Complete Prose Works of Matthew Arnold*. Ed. R. H. Super. Ann Arbor: University of Michigan Press, 1973.

Attridge, Derek. "Oppressive Silence: J. M. Coetzee's *Foe* and the Politics of the Canon." Lawrence 212–238.

Axtell, James. *The European and the Indian: Essays in the Ethnohistory of Colonial North America*. New York: Oxford University Press, 1981.

Banton, Michael. *Racial Theories*. Cambridge: Cambridge University Press, 1987.

Barone, Michael. *The New Americans: How the Melting Pot Can Work Again*. Washington: Regnery, 2001.

Bartov, Omer. "A Tale of Two Holocausts." *New York Times Book Review* 6 Aug. 2000: 8.

Baudrillard, Jean. *Simulacra and Simulation*. Trans. Sheila Faria Glaser. Ann Arbor: University of Michigan Press, 1994.

Bendix, Regina. *In Search of Authenticity: The Formation of Folklore Studies*. Madison: University of Wisconsin Press, 1997.

Benjamin, Walter. *Das Kunstwerk im Zeitalter seiner technischen Reproduzierbarkeit.* 1936. Frankfurt: Suhrkamp, 1963.

Berger, John. *Pig Earth.* London: Writers and Readers, 1979.

Bhabha, Homi. "Of Mimicry and Man: The Ambivalence of Colonial Discourse." *October* 28 (Spring 1984): 125–133.

Biale, David. *Power and Powerlessness in Jewish History.* New York: Schocken Books, 1986.

Boehmer, Elleke. *Colonial and Postcolonial Literature.* Oxford: Oxford University Press, 1995.

Boyarin, Jonathan. *Thinking in Jewish.* Chicago: University of Chicago Press, 1996.

Brennan, Timothy. *At Home in the World: Cosmopolitanism Now.* Cambridge: Harvard University Press, 1997.

Brodkin, Karen. *How Jews Became White Folks and What That Says about Race in America.* New Brunswick: Rutgers University Press, 1998.

Bronner, Ethan. "Israel: The Revised Edition." *New York Times Book Review* 14 Nov. 1999: 6.

Brown, Terence. *Ireland: A Social and Cultural History, 1922–79.* Glasgow: Fontana, 1981.

Budgen, Frank. *James Joyce and the Making of "Ulysses."* Bloomington: Indiana University Press, 1960.

Buruma, Ian. "Young Poles, New Jews: Poland's New Jewish Question." *New York Times Magazine* 3 Aug. 1997: 33–57.

Cairns, David, and Shaun Richards. *Writing Ireland: Colonialism, Nationalism, and Culture.* Manchester: Manchester University Press, 1988.

Calisher, Hortense. *Sunday Jews.* New York: Harcourt, 2002.

Callaghan, Dympna. "The Vicar and Virago: Feminism and the Problem of Identity." Roof and Wiegman 195–207.

Cheng, Vincent J. *Joyce, Race, and Empire.* Cambridge: Cambridge University Press, 1995.

———. "'Terrible Queer Creatures': Joyce, Cosmopolitanism, and the Inauthentic Irishman." *James Joyce and the Fabrication of an Irish Identity.* Ed. Michael Patrick Gillespie. European Joyce Studies 11. Amsterdam: Rodopi, 2001.

Chernin, Kim. "Seven Pillars of Jewish Denial." *Tikkun: A Bimonthly Jewish Critique of Politics, Culture and Society* 17.5 (2002): 15–20.

Cheung, King-Kok, ed. *An Interethnic Companion to Asian American Literature.* Cambridge: Cambridge University Press, 1997.

Chin, Frank, et al., eds. *Aiiieeeee! An Anthology of Asian-American Writers.* New York: Anchor Books, 1975.

Clifford, James. "Four Northwest Coast Museums: Travel Reflections." *Exhibiting Cultures: The Poetics and Politics of Museum Display.* Ed. Ivan Karp and Steven D. Lavine. Washington: Smithsonian Institution Press, 1991.

Connery, Donald S. *The Irish.* London, 1968.

Conrad, Joseph. *Heart of Darkness.* 1902. New York: Dover, 1990.

Corkery, Daniel. *The Hidden Ireland: A Study of Gaelic Munster in the Eighteenth Century.* Dublin: Gill, 1925.

———. *Synge and Anglo-Irish Literature.* London: Longmans, Green, 1931.

Cose, Ellis. "The Colors of Race." *Newsweek* 1 Jan. 2000: 28–30.

———. "What's White, Anyway?" *Newsweek* 18 Sept. 2000: 64–65.

Curtis, L. Perry, Jr. *Anglo-Saxons and Celts: A Study of Anti-Irish Prejudice in Victorian England.* Bridgeport: University of Bridgeport, 1968.

———. *Apes and Angels: The Irishman in Victorian Caricature.* Washington: Smithsonian Institution Press, 1971.

Davis, F. James. *Who Is Black? One Nation's Definition.* University Park: Pennsylvania State University Press, 1991.

Deane, Seamus. *Heroic Styles: The Tradition of an Idea.* Pamphlet 4. Derry: Field Day, 1984.

———. "Joyce the Irishman." *The Cambridge Companion to James Joyce.* Ed. Derek Attridge. Cambridge: Cambridge University Press, 1990.

———. *Strange Country: Modernity and Nationhood in Irish Writing since 1790.* Oxford: Clarendon, 1997.

Deleuze, Gilles, and Félix Guattari. *Kafka: Toward a Minor Literature.* Trans. Dana Polan. Minneapolis: University of Minnesota Press, 1986.

Duff, Charles. *James Joyce and the Plain Reader.* London: Desmond Harmsworth, 1932.

Duffy, Enda. *The Subaltern Ulysses.* Minneapolis: University of Minnesota Press, 1994.

Eagleton, Terry. "Form and Ideology in the Anglo-Irish Novel." *Bullan* 1.1 (1994): 17–26.

———. *Heathcliff and the Great Hunger: Studies in Irish Culture.* London: Verso, 1995.

———. "The Ideology of Irish Studies." *Bullan* 3.1 (1997): 5–14.

Ellmann, Richard. *James Joyce.* Rev. ed. Oxford: Oxford University Press, 1982.

Eskin, Blake. *A Life in Pieces: The Making and Unmaking of Binjamin Wilkomirski.* New York: Norton, 2002.

Espiritu, Yen Le. *Asian American Panethnicity: Bridging Institutions and Identities.* Philadelphia: Temple University Press, 1992.

———. "Possibilities of a Multiracial Asian America." Williams-Leon and Nakashima 25–34.

Etz Hayim: Torah and Commentary. New York: Rabbinical Assembly, 2001.

Ezrahi, Sidra DeKoven. "Racism and Ethics: Constructing Alternative History." *Humanity at the Limit: The Impact of the Holocaust Experience on Jews and Christians.* Ed. Michael A. Signer. Bloomington: Indiana University Press, 2000.

Fairhall, James. *James Joyce and the Question of History.* Cambridge: Cambridge University Press, 1993.

Finkielkraut, Alain. *The Imaginary Jew.* Trans. Kevin O'Neill and David Suchoff. Introd. David Suchoff. Lincoln: University of Nebraska Press, 1994.

Fitzgerald, F. Scott. *The Great Gatsby.* 1922. New York: Collier, 1992.

Ford, Ford Madox. *The Good Soldier.* 1915. New York: Vintage Books, 1951.

Forward, Toby. "Diary." *London Review of Books* 4 Feb. 1988: 21–22.

——— (as Rahila Khan). *Down the Road, Worlds Away.* London: Virago Press, 1987.

Foster, R. F. "Anglo-Irish Literature, Gaelic Nationalism and Irish Politics in the 1890's." *The Political Culture of Modern Britain: Studies in Memory of Stephen Koss.* Ed. J.M.W. Bean. London: Hamish Hamilton, 1987.

————. *Modern Ireland 1600–1972*. London: Penguin Books, 1988.

Gates, Henry Louis, Jr. "Authority, (White) Power and the (Black) Critic: It's All Greek to Me." *Cultural Critique* 7 (Fall 1987): 19–46.

Gibbons, Luke. *Transformations in Irish Culture*. Cork: Cork University Press, 1996.

Gibson, Andrew. "'History, All That': Revival Historiography and Literary Strategy in the 'Cyclops' Episode in *Ulysses.*" *Essays and Studies: History and the Novel*. Ed. Angus Easson. Burty St. Edmunds: D. S. Brewer, 1991.

————. *Joyce's Revenge: History, Politics, and Aesthetics in "Ulysses."* Oxford: Oxford University Press, 2002.

————. "'Strangers in My House, Bad Manners to Them!' England in 'Circe.'" *Reading Joyce's "Circe."* Ed. Andrew Gibson. European Joyce Studies. Amsterdam: Rodopi, 1994.

Gifford, Don, and Robert J. Seidman. *"Ulysses" Annotated: Notes for James Joyce's "Ulysses."* Rev. ed. Berkeley: University of California Press, 1988.

Glazer, Nathan. "The Emergence of an American Ethnic Patttern." 1975. *From Different Shores: Perspectives on Race and Ethnicity in America*. 2nd ed. Ed. Ronald Takaki. New York: Oxford University Press, 1994.

Gold, Michael. "Jewish Law and Adoption." *Reform Judaism* Summer 2001: 14.

Gopnik, Adam. "A Purim Story: The Funny Thing about Being Jewish." *New Yorker* 18 & 25 Feb. 2002: 124–131.

Gordis, Daniel. *Does the World Need the Jews? Rethinking Chosenness and American Jewish Identity*. New York: Scribner, 1997.

Gorman, Herbert S. *James Joyce: His First Forty Years*. New York: B. W. Huebsch, 1924.

Gourevitch, Philip. "The Memory Thief." *New Yorker* 14 June 1999: 48–68.

Gupta, Suman. "'What Colour's Jew Joyce . . .': Race in the Context of Joyce's Irishness and Bloom's Jewishness." *Bullan* 1.2 (1994): 59–72.

Hall, A. M. *Tales of Irish Life and Character*. Edinburgh: Foulis, 1910.

Hall, S. C., and A. M. Hall. *Ireland: Its Scenery, Character, etc.* 3 vols. London: How & Parson, 1841–1843.

Hall, Stuart. "Cultural Identity and Cinematographic Representation." *Frameworks* 36 (1989): 68–81.

————. "Cultural Identity and Diaspora." *Identity: Community, Culture, Difference*. Ed. Jonathan Rutherford. London: Lawrence and Wishart, 1990.

Haney-Lopez, Ian. *White by Law: The Legal Construction of Race*. New York: New York University Press, 1996.

Hayden, Tom, ed. *Irish Hunger: Personal Reflections on the Legacy of the Famine*. Boulder: Roberts Rinehart; Dublin: Wolfhound Press, 1997.

————. *Irish on the Inside: In Search of the Soul of Irish America*. London: Verso, 2001.

Hazony, Yoram. *The Jewish State: The Struggle for Israel's Soul*. New York: Basic Books, 2001.

Herr, Cheryl. "The Silence of the Hares: Peripherality in Ireland and in Joyce." *Joycean Cultures/Culturing Joyces*. Ed. Vincent J. Cheng, Kimberly J. Devlin, and Margot Norris. Newark: University of Delaware Press, 1998.

Hobsbawm, Eric, and Terence Ranger, eds. *The Invention of Tradition*. Cambridge: Cambridge University Press, 1983.

Hofheinz, Thomas C. *Joyce and the Invention of Irish History*. Cambridge: Cambridge University Press, 1995.

Hoksbergen, R.A.C. *Child Adoption: A Guidebook for Adoptive Parents and Their Advisers*. London: Jessica Kingsley, 1997.

Hurston, Zora Neale. *Their Eyes Were Watching God*. 1937. New York: Harper & Row, 1990.

Hyde, Douglas. "The Necessity for De-Anglicising Ireland." 1892. *Language, Lore and Lyrics, Essays and Lectures*. By Hyde. Ed. Breandan O Conaire. Dublin: Irish Academic Press, 1986.

Ignatiev, Noel. *How the Irish Became White*. Cambridge: Harvard University Press, 1995.

Jacoby, Susan. *Half-Jew: A Daughter's Search for Her Family's Buried Past*. New York: Scribner, 2000.

Jameson, Fredric. "Modernism and Imperialism." *Nationalism, Colonialism, and Literature*. By Terry Eagleton, Fredric Jameson, and Edward W. Said. Introd. Seamus Deane. Minneapolis: University of Minnesota Press, 1990.

Johnson, Clifton. *The Isle of the Shamrock*. London: Macmillan, 1901.

Johnston, Dillon. "Cross-Currencies in the Culture Market: Arnold, Yeats, Joyce." Waters 45–78.

Joyce, James. *The Critical Writings of James Joyce*. Ed. Ellsworth Mason and Richard Ellmann. New York: Viking Press, 1964.

———. *Dubliners: Text, Criticism, and Notes*. Ed. Robert Scholes and A. Walton Litz. New York: Viking Press, 1969.

———. *Finnegans Wake*. New York: Viking Press, 1939.

———. *A Portrait of the Artist as a Young Man*. 1916. New York: Viking Press, 1964.

———. *Ulysses*. 1922. Ed. Hans Walter Gabler et al. New York: Vintage Books, 1986.

Kaplan, Caren. "Deterritorializations: The Rewriting of Home and Exile in Western Feminist Discourse." *The Nature and Context of Minority Discourse*. Ed. Abdul JanMohamed and David Lloyd. Oxford: Oxford University Press, 1990.

Kiberd, Declan. *Inventing Ireland: The Literature of the Modern Nation*. Cambridge: Harvard University Press, 1995.

———. "The Periphery and the Center." Waters 5–22.

Kibria, Nazli. *Becoming Asian American: Second-Generation Chinese and Korean American Identities*. Baltimore: Johns Hopkins University Press, 2002.

———. "Not Asian, Black, or White? Reflections on South Asian American Racial Identity." Wu and Song 247–254.

Kingston, Maxine Hong. *The Woman Warrior*. New York: Knopf, 1976.

Knox, Robert, M.D. *The Races of Men: A Fragment*. 1850. Miami: Mnemosyne, 1969.

Koshy, Susan. "The Fiction of Asian American Literature." Wu and Song 467–495.

Krause, David. "Sweetening Ireland's Wrong." *Irish Literary Supplement* Spring 1998: 13–14.

Kureishi, Hanif. *The Black Album*. New York: Scribner, 1995.

Lakritz, Andrew. "Identification and Difference: Structures of Privilege in Cultural Criticism." Roof and Wiegman 3–29.

Law and Order. Episode on Jewish Adoption. Writ. Aaron Zellman. Dir. Stephen Wertimer. NBC.

Lawrence, Karen, ed. *Decolonizing Tradition: New Views of Twentieth-Century British Literary Canons*. Urbana: University of Illinois Press, 1992.

Lear, Jonathan. "The Man Who Never Was." *New York Times Book Review* 24 Feb. 2002: 22.

Leerssen, Joep. *Remembrance and Imagination: Patterns in the Historical and Literary Representation of Ireland in the Nineteenth Century*. Cork: Cork University Press, 1996.

Liu, Eric. *The Accidental Asian: Notes of a Native Speaker*. New York: Random House, 1998.

Lloyd, David. *Anomalous States: Irish Writing and the Post-colonial Moment*. Durham: Duke University Press, 1993.

———. "Counterparts: *Dubliners*, Masculinity and Temperance Nationalism." *Semicolonial Joyce*. Ed. Derek Attridge and Marjorie Howes. Cambridge: Cambridge University Press, 2000.

———. "Cultural Theory and Ireland." *Bullan* 3.1 (1997): 87–92.

"Lost Tribes of Israel." *Nova* #2706. PBS. 22 Feb. 2000.

Lowe, Lisa. *Immigrant Acts: On Asian American Cultural Politics*. Durham: Duke University Press, 1996.

MacCabe, Colin. "*Finnegans Wake* at Fifty." *Critical Quarterly* 31.4 (1989): 3–5.

———. *James Joyce and the Revolution of the Word*. New York: Barnes & Noble Books, 1979.

Margulis, Jennifer. "The Power of Dominant Discourse: Literacy, Murder, Child Labor, and Big Business; the Untold Story of Iqbal Masih." Unpublished paper.

Martinez, Ruben. "The Next Chapter." *New York Times Magazine* 16 July 2000: 11–12.

McBride, James. *The Color of Water: A Black Man's Tribute to His White Mother*. New York: Riverhead Books, 1996.

McCormack, W. J. "Convergent Criticism: *The Biographia Literaria* of Vivian Mercier and the State of Irish Literary History." *Bullan* 2.1 (1995): 79–100.

Mercier, Vivian. *The Irish Comic Tradition*. Oxford: Oxford University Press, 1962.

Miles, Jack. "A Sling and a Prayer." *New York Times Book Review* 18 June 2000: 11.

Miller, David. *On Nationality*. Oxford: Clarendon, 1995.

Mittelberg, D., and M. Waters. "The Process of Ethnogenesis among Haitian and Israeli Immigrants in the United States." *Ethnic and Racial Studies* 15.3 (1992): 412–435.

Moran, D. P. *The Philosophy of Irish Ireland*. Dublin: James Duffy, 1905.

Morris, Benny. *Righteous Victims: A History of the Zionist-Arab Conflict, 1881–1999*. New York: Knopf, 1999.

Musleah, Rahel. "The New World of Adoption." *Reform Judaism* Summer 2001: 12–58.

Nakashima, Cynthia L. "Servants of Culture: The Symbolic Role of Mixed-Race Asians in American Discourse." Williams-Leon and Nakashima 35–48.

———. "An Invisible Monster: The Creation and Denial of Mixed-Race People in America." *Racially Mixed People in America*. Ed. Maria P. P. Root. Beverly Hills: Sage, 1991.

Nguyen, Viet Thanh. *Race and Resistance: Literature and Politics in Asian America.* New York: Oxford University Press, 2002.

Nolan, Emer. *James Joyce and Nationalism.* London: Routledge, 1995.

Novick, Peter. *The Holocaust in American Life.* Boston: Houghton Mifflin, 1999.

Nussbaum, Martha. *Cultivating Humanity: A Classical Defense of Reform in Liberal Education.* Cambridge: Harvard University Press, 1997.

O'Brien, Conor Cruise. *Writers and Critics.* London: Chatto & Windus, 1965.

O'Grady, Standish. *History of Ireland.* 2 vols. London, 1878–1880.

Okihiro, Gary Y. *Margins and Mainstreams: Asians in American History and Culture.* Seattle: University of Washington Press, 1994.

Omi, Michael. Foreword. Williams-Leon and Nakashima ix–xiii.

Omi, Michael, and Howard Winant. *Racial Formation in the United States.* 2nd ed. New York: Routledge, 1994.

Page, Clarence. "Racial Classifications Matter because Americans Are Not Colorblind." Syndicated column, Chicago Tribune Service. *Salt Lake Tribune* 2 Aug. 2001: A19.

Palumbo-Liu, David. *Asian/American: Historical Crossings of a Racial Frontier.* Stanford: Stanford University Press, 1999.

Parfitt, Tudor. *Journey to the Vanished City: The Search for a Lost Tribe of Israel.* New York: Vintage Books, 2000.

Patterson, Orlando. "America's Worst Idea." Rev. of *The American Misadventure of Race,* by Scott L. Malcomson. *New York Times Book Review* 22 Oct. 2000: 15–16.

Pertman, Adam. *Adoption Nation: How the Adoption Revolution Is Transforming America.* New York: Basic Books, 2000.

Prakash, Gyan, ed. *After Colonialism: Imperial Histories and Postcolonial Displacements.* Princeton: Princeton University Press, 1995.

Prashad, Vijay. *The Karma of Brown Folk.* Minneapolis: University of Minnesota Press, 2000.

Pratt, Mary Louise. *Imperial Eyes: Travel Writing and Transculturation.* London: Routledge, 1992.

Rabinow, Paul. "Representations Are Social Facts: Modernity and Post-modernity in Anthropology." *Writing Culture: The Poetics and Politics of Ethnography.* Ed. James Clifford and George Marcus. Berkeley: University of California Press, 1986.

Radhakrishnan, R. "Conjunctural Identities, Academic Adjacencies." *Orientations: Mapping Studies in the Asian Diaspora.* Ed. Kandice Chuh and Karen Shimakawa. Durham: Duke University Press, 2001.

Reich, Walter. "Line Up for Israel." *New York Times Book Review* 18 June 2000: 13–14.

Reizbaum, Marilyn. "Canonical Double Cross: Scottish and Irish Women's Writing." Lawrence 165–190.

Renza, Louis A. *"A White Heron" and the Question of Minor Literature.* Madison: University of Wisconsin Press, 1984.

Richards, Barry. "Whose Identity Problem? The Dynamics of Projection in Transracial Adoption." *The Dynamics of Adoption.* Ed. Amal Treacher and Ilan Katz. London: Jessica Kingsley, 2000.

Robbins, Bruce. *Feeling Global: Internationalism in Distress*. New York: New York University Press, 1999.

Rolleston, T. W. "Shamrocks." *Academy* 9 July 1887: 19.

Roof, Judith, and Robyn Wiegman, eds. *Who Can Speak? Authority and Critical Identity*. Urbana: University of Illinois Press, 1995.

Root, Maria P. P., ed. *Racially Mixed People in America*. Beverly Hills: Sage, 1991.

Rosaldo, Renato. *Culture and Truth: The Remaking of Social Analysis*. Boston: Beacon Press, 1989.

Roth, Philip. *The Human Stain*. Boston: Houghton Mifflin, 2000.

Said, Edward W. "Empire of Sand." *Weekend Guardian*. 12/13 Jan. 1991: 4–5.

———. *Orientalism*. New York: Vintage Books, 1979.

———. "Secular Interpretation, the Geographical Element, and the Methodology of Imperialism." *After Colonialism: Imperial Histories and Postcolonial Displacements*. Ed. Gyan Prakash. Princeton: Princeton University Press, 1995.

Sakai, Naoki. "Modernity and Its Critique: The Problem of Universalism and Particularism." *Postmodernism and Japan*. Ed. Masao Miyoshi and H. D. Harootunian. Durham: Duke University Press, 1989.

Sawhney, Sabina. "The Joke and the Hoax: (Not) Speaking as the Other." Roof and Wiegman 208–220.

Schor, Esther. "The Sacred and the Secular." *New York Times Book Review* 31 Dec. 2000: 17.

Segev, Tom. *The Seventh Million: The Israelis and the Holocaust*. Trans. Haim Watzman. New York: Hill & Wang, 1993.

Shapiro, James. "Too New to Know." *New York Times Book Review* 13 Aug. 2000: 18.

Shinagawa, Larry H., and Gin Y. Pang. "Asian-American Panethnicity and Intermarriage." *Amerasia Journal* 22.2 (1996): 127–152.

Shlaim, Avi. *The Iron Wall: Israel and the Arab World since 1948*. New York: Norton, 2000.

Shreiber, Maeera Y. "Jewish Trouble and the Trouble with Poetry." Unpublished manuscript.

Simmons, William S. "Culture Theory in Contemporary Ethnohistory." *Ethnohistory* 35.1 (1988): 1–14.

Simon, Rita J., and Howard Altstein. *Adoption across Borders: Serving the Children in Transracial and Intercountry Adoptions*. Lanham: Rowman & Littlefield, 2000.

Sollors, Werner. *Beyond Ethnicity: Consent and Descent in American Culture*. New York: Oxford University Press, 1986.

Sontag, Deborah. "Israel's Next Palestinian Problem." *New York Times Magazine* 10 Sept. 2000: 48–53.

Spickard, Paul. "What Must I Be? Asian Americans and the Question of Multiethnic Identity." Wu and Song 255–269.

———. "Who Is an Asian? Who Is a Pacific Islander? Monoracialism, Multiracial People, and Asian American Communities." Williams-Leon and Nakashima 13–24.

Spivak, Gayatri Chakravorty. "Questions of Multi-culturalism." *The Post-colonial Critic*. Ed. Sarah Harsym. London: Routledge, 1990.

Steyn, Juliet. *The Jew: Assumptions of Identity*. London: Cassell, 1999.

Stratton, Jon. *Coming Out Jewish: Constructing Ambivalent Identities.* London: Routledge, 2000.

Suchoff, David. Introduction. *The Imaginary Jew.* By Alain Finkielkraut. Trans. Kevin O'Neill and David Suchoff. Lincoln: University of Nebraska Press, 1994.

Takaki, Ronald. "Reflections on Racial Patterns in America." *From Different Shores: Perspectives on Race and Ethnicity in America.* 2nd ed. Ed. Ronald Takaki. New York: Oxford University Press, 1994.

———. "Who Killed Vincent Chin?" *A Look beyond the Model Minority Image: Critical Issues in Asian America.* Ed. Grace Yun. New York: Minority Rights Group, 1989.

Taylor, Lawrence J. "'There Are Two Things That People Don't Like to Hear about Themselves': The Anthropology of Ireland and the Irish View of Anthropology." Waters 213–226.

Trinh T. Minh-ha. *Woman, Native, Other: Writing Postcoloniality and Feminism.* Bloomington: Indiana University Press, 1989.

Tuan, Mia. *Forever Foreigners or Honorary Whites? The Asian Ethnic Experience Today.* New Brunswick: Rutgers University Press, 1998.

Waters, John Paul, ed. *Ireland and Irish Cultural Studies.* Spec. issue of *South Atlantic Quarterly* 95.1 (1996).

Webb, Virginia-Lee. "Manipulated Images: European Photographs of Pacific Peoples." *Prehistories of the Future.* Ed. Elazar Barkan and Ronald Bush. Stanford: Stanford University Press, 1994.

Whitfield, Stephen J. *In Search of American Jewish Culture.* Hanover: Brandeis University Press, 1999.

———. "The Jewish Wars." *New York Times Book Review* 3 Sept. 2000: 22.

Wieseltier, Leon. "Hitler Is Dead." *New Republic* 27 May 2002: 19–22.

Wilkomirski, Binjamin. *Fragments: Memories of a Wartime Childhood, 1939–1948.* Trans. Carol Brown Janeway. London: Picador, 1997.

Will, George F. "We Have Been Here Before." *Newsweek* 11 June 2001: 64.

Williams, Raymond. *The Country and the City.* New York: Oxford University Press, 1973.

Williams-Leon, Teresa, and Cynthia L. Nakashima, eds. *The Sum of Our Parts: Mixed-Heritage Asian Americans.* Philadelphia: Temple University Press, 2001.

Wirth-Nesher, Hana, ed. *What Is Jewish Literature?* Philadelphia: Jewish Publication Society, 1994.

Wisse, Ruth R. *The Modern Jewish Canon: A Journey through Language and Culture.* New York: Free Press, 2000.

Wu, Jean Yu-wen Shen, and Min Song, eds. *Asian American Studies: A Reader.* New Brunswick: Rutgers University Press, 2000.

Yeates, Ray. "My Famine." Hayden, *Irish Hunger* 191–200.

Yeats, William Butler. *The Collected Plays of W. B. Yeats.* New York: Macmillan, 1935.

Young, James E. "Bad for the Jews." *New York Times Book Review* 7 Nov. 1999: 38.

Zia, Helen. *Asian American Dreams: The Emergence of an American People.* New York: Farrar, Straus & Giroux, 2000.

INDEX

ABOUT THE AUTHOR

Vincent J. Cheng, the son of two career diplomats, grew up in various countries—Taiwan, Mexico, Brazil, the United States, Canada, Swaziland—speaking different languages, taking on different cultures, negotiating new identities. He is the author of several books, including *Joyce, Race, and Empire* (1995), and many scholarly articles. Having taught for many years at the University of Southern California, Professor Cheng is currently the Shirley Sutton Thomas Professor of English at the University of Utah and the director of the Tanner Humanities Center. He lives in Salt Lake City with his wife, Maeera, and their son, Gabi; together they happily take on the challenges of constructing and negotiating an ever-changing authentic identity.